2713

D0975365

THE
LEADERSHIP
SECRETS
OF
BILLY
GRAHAM

THE LEADERSHIP SECRETS OF BILLY GRAHAM

HAROLD MYRA
MARSHALL SHELLEY

GRAND RAPIDS, MICHIGAN 49530 USA

ZONDERVAN™

The Leadership Secrets of Billy Graham
Copyright © 2005 by Christianity Today International

This title is also available as a Zondervan ebook product. Visit
www.zondervan.com/ebooks for more information.

This title is also available as a Zondervan audio product. Visit
www.zondervan.com/audiopages for more information.

Requests for information should be addressed to:

Zondervan, *Grand Rapids, Michigan 49530*

Library of Congress Cataloging-in-Publication Data

Myra, Harold Lawrence, 1939–
  The leadership secrets of Billy Graham / Harold Myra and Marshall Shelley.
    p. cm.
  Includes bibliographical references and index.
  ISBN-10: 0-310-25578-3
  ISBN-13: 978-0-310-25578-9
    1. Leadership. 2. Leadership—Religious aspects—Christianity. 3. Graham, Billy,
  1918– 4. Evangelists—United States—Biography.
  I. Shelley, Marshall. II. Title.
  HM1261.M97 2005
  658.4'092—dc22
                                                                              2005004700

Interior design by Sharon VanLoozenoord

Printed in the United States of America

05 06 07 08 09 10 11 12 /❖ DCI/ 10 9 8 7 6 5 4 3 2 1

THIS BOOK IS DEDICATED
TO THOSE READERS

who sense the pressing need in today's world

for inspired leadership

who rise to its high calling

and are willing to carry its weight

who are determined to deepen and expand

their capacities and effectiveness

CONTENTS

THE
LEADERSHIP
SECRETS
OF
BILLY
GRAHAM

INTRODUCTION

Why Billy's Leadership Mystified Yet Intrigued Us, Then Sparked Us to Explore His Experiences—And the Principles That Can Guide Us All

When you hear the name *Billy Graham*, do you think first of his leadership? Most of us do not. We recall his preaching to vast crowds in stadiums. We see the gracious television guest, appearing with hosts from Johnny Carson and David Frost to Larry King and Barbara Walters—always responding with gentle wisdom, explaining the gospel, but humbly admitting his own limitations. We remember his leading the nation in dramatic times of grief, or helping inaugurate presidents, but more as national pastor than leader.

Yet Billy begins his autobiography by saying, "My responsibilities as chief executive officer of the Billy Graham Evangelistic Association have always demanded a tremendous amount of time and decision making."

Huh? CEO? Corporate decision making? Don't business types do all that for Billy Graham?

It's hard to realize he has been CEO for more than fifty years. Generations have known him as a national icon, a father figure with both convictions and compassion.

He has been the close friend of U.S. presidents, and Congress awarded him the Congressional Gold Medal. But we don't think of him as a leader of leaders, a man who has led a movement significantly affecting history. Effective leaders in Asia, Europe, Latin America—all over the world—speak of Billy's having ignited their own leadership and modeled for them vital principles. How did he become this visionary chief executive with entrepreneurial force, engaging not only millions of individuals but at the same time helping build strong, burgeoning institutions?

Billy himself would say he was simply the instrument God chose to use. Yet his multiple leadership roles generate lots of questions. *Life* magazine named him one of the one hundred most important Americans of the twentieth century, but wasn't that because of his inspirational and pastoral role? How did executive leadership fit in? And how could he do both? During his long career, he was mercilessly attacked by many, yet he won over the vast majority of once-hostile critics even as his organization set new high standards for nonprofit leadership. How could one man wear so many hats and see such extraordinary results?

■ ■ ■

I first got an inkling of all this in the mid-1970s when the board of *Christianity Today* appointed me its president and CEO. Billy had founded the magazine nearly twenty years before. Harold Ockenga, scholar, pastor of Boston's historic Park Street Church, first president of Fuller Seminary and later Gordon-Conwell Seminary, was chairman, but he cheerfully acknowledged that *CT* was "Billy's magazine"—that he served as chair under Graham's guidance.

Until I joined *Christianity Today*, I had the typical impression of Billy: larger-than-life, remarkably effective, a chaplain for the nation, and a lodestar for believers.

I did not think of him as an entrepreneurial CEO. In fact, when that reality first surfaced, I was jarred.

Sherwood Wirt edited Billy's *Decision* magazine, and we served together on the board of the Evangelical Press Association. He happened to refer to Billy as "the boss."

I was taken aback. Billy, "the boss"? Wasn't he the beloved evangelist? To my ears the word seemed crass and inappropriate. Yet to "Woody," a brilliant Ph.D. who viewed Billy in the highest terms, the word came easily.

A few years later, when I joined *CT*, I began to understand that Billy was not only CEO of the Billy Graham Evangelistic Association but also powerfully influenced many institutions. He encouraged, counseled, prodded, and cast the broad vision. After observing Billy at one CT board meeting, I thought, *He not only does all the things we see on TV and read about in the press, but behind the scenes he's inspiring the leadership of an entire movement.* Youth organizations like Young Life, Campus Crusade, Youth for Christ, InterVarsity. Academic institutions like Wheaton College, Fuller and Gordon-Conwell Seminaries. Humanitarian outreaches like World Vision, World Relief, the Salvation Army. Media ministries like Transworld Radio and *Christianity Today*.

I later learned his founding of *Christianity Today* had been thoroughly hands on (see chapter 14). Billy's accomplishments have been an integration of executive and entrepreneurial leadership with roiling streams of spiritual vitality. What is usually ignored, yet is central to what has been achieved, is his entrepreneurial vision, his driving and inspirational force as chief executive, his continuous growth as a statesman.

This came into full focus when I read the chapter titled "Level Five Leadership" in Jim Collins's excellent book, *Good to Great*. Collins, with a team of researchers, studied a highly select group of companies that for years had experienced "extraordinary results"—companies that had outperformed stars like Intel, General Electric, and Coca Cola. His studies revealed something unexpected. "We were surprised," wrote Collins, "shocked, really, to discover the type of leadership required." He found the CEOs with "extraordinary results"—what *Good to Great* calls "Level Five Leaders"—were not ego-driven but "self-effacing." They blended "extreme personal humility" with "fierce resolve." Instead of being "I-Centric," they channeled their ego needs away from themselves and into the larger goal. When interviewed, these leaders talked about others' contributions. Collins reported that they would say things like, "I don't think I can take much credit. We were blessed with marvelous people."

Soon after studying *Good to Great*, I contacted Billy about writing a book to help convey the principles of his leadership. When I received a letter back from him, I blinked and then smiled as I read it:

"It seems to me that the Lord took several inexperienced young men and used them in ways they never dreamed," Billy wrote. "The ministry sort of took off and got away from all of us! We all seemed to be a part of a tremendous movement of the

Spirit of God, and so many of the new organizations seemed to interrelate, or began as we talked and prayed together on our travels. It was natural to encourage and help them along."

On reading that, I shook my head and said aloud, "Unbelievable! Just like all those Level Five leaders."

The tone of his letter, as usual, was self-effacing, giving credit to others. He even urged me to "choose someone with better leadership skills than I. . . ." Although Billy soon gave me his blessing to write this book, his initial reluctance and humble spirit strongly affirmed key factors that created the "extraordinary results" of his lifetime of service.

What had started in my mind, however, as a fairly straightforward task—draw from Billy's experiences his key leadership principles—became a complex journey of exploration and discovery. Although the Level Five parallel fit and shed significant light, it didn't solve other mysteries. Yes, Billy has been a highly effective CEO for a half century. However, how could you do that while in the headlines and counselor to presidents? How did he create media breakthroughs and globally expand beyond cultural limitations? What alchemy of Spirit and character made all this happen?

Although hundreds of books and thousands of articles have been written about Billy, his role as an executive leader has been largely unexplored. This book's discovery process, then, would plunge into four deep pools:

First, Billy's closest associates. What would they say created this phenomenon? These thoughtful, highly accomplished leaders had labored beside Billy for decades in the "sweaty arena." What was it like to have Billy Graham as a boss? Or, how did fellow CEOs of large enterprises view serving him as a board trustee? What was really going on behind the scenes?

Second, books, articles, original letters, and other resources in our *CT* files, the Billy Graham Center, and elsewhere. We knew Billy's autobiography and William Martin's comprehensive *Prophet with Honor* would be essential. How might these familiar materials help answer the questions?

Third, leadership books like Collins's *Good to Great* and the essential works of Peter Drucker, Warren Bennis, and others, matched with biographical studies of great leaders. My bookshelves were loaded with these, but was Billy really a practitioner of such skills? And how was he the same, and how different, from history's greats?

Fourth, the resources that challenged, energized, and sustained him. He drew from not only the Bible, which he constantly quoted, but also the rich traditions of Christian scholars and theologians from many streams. How did they inform his leadership?

Marshall Shelley, editor of *Leadership* journal, agreed to plow into this "massive opportunity" with me and coauthor the book. We and editorial resident Collin Hansen started selecting and sorting the plethora of resources and interviewing key players, hoping to bring the fuzzy picture of Billy's leadership somewhat into focus.

We had plenty of questions. For instance, how could Billy have such a reputation for humility yet be so much in the spotlight and receive all those awards? Why did the press seek him out so much? He has used throughout his career the principles we see in Drucker and Bennis and other writers, but he's probably read few, if any, of those books. Where did these skills come from? And how could he endure all the harsh criticism year after year, and the betrayal by Nixon, yet maintain his optimism? Furthermore, how did he create his unusual rapport with business types?

We hoped to sort out questions and puzzle pieces into a coherent and helpful guide. Leadership is a fascinating, delightful subject—and vital to each of us. This book is not intended to lionize Billy, yet it's unapologetically positive because of its purpose. We asked, How could this book not only inform but also refresh and help each of us lead? That's why we decided to do chapter wrap-up sections, drawing from all four of our research categories.

The mosaic that emerged was complex. We found a very human Billy Graham and were surprised by the mix of candor, awe, and love that resonated among those who served with him. We've not attempted a scholarly analysis of Billy's legacy; we've unabashedly probed for the positive to distill transferable principles.

■ ■ ■

Billy always insists on simply being called "Billy." He titled his autobiography *Just as I Am*, a perfect description of his humble spirit, taken from the hymn sung when he invites people to come forward and receive God's love. With humble audacity and "ferocious resolve," Billy has led with full, even painful, awareness of his own strengths and limitations.

Those of us called to some sort of leadership realize that "just as I am" describes each of us as we face demanding, complex challenges. In the refining furnace of leadership, we sense we must seek empowerment from above. And we know we simply must do the best we can with what we have and who we are.

Billy Graham did that. Whatever the challenges and hurdles, whatever the limitations, he steadily led by full commitment to his biblical values. His lifetime of vigorous leadership invites us to engage with the same spirit, to consider his examples, and to reach, as he did, into the rich resources of leadership literature that resonate with scriptural principles.

Harold Myra

PART ONE

COMING ALIVE

The giants all had one thing in common:
neither victory nor success,
but passion.
PHILIP YANCEY

How is it that among millions of young men of no particular distinction, one ignites and becomes a driving force? How is it that—like a rocket on a launch pad with flame barely visible—one person is slightly lifted, then slowly gains momentum, thrusts upward, engines burning steadily with increasing velocity?

The phenomenon of Billy Graham's humble beginnings and the ever-increasing velocity of his executive leadership intrigued us. What combination of genes, culture, experience, religion, and internal response created the alchemy?

This first section consists of just one extended chapter exploring those questions. How did his extraordinary leadership get started? How did it continue in force throughout his life?

Numerous scholars and commentators have ranked Billy with the "greats." We were intrigued to find, in seeking to identify common principles, parallels with other great leaders like Teddy Roosevelt, who was "ignited" by similar forces. To put Billy in context, we include those experiences too, which may illumine some of what happens in these extraordinary lives.

CHAPTER 1

Igniting!

> Absolute identity with one's cause is the first
> and great condition of successful leadership.
> **WOODROW WILSON**

Leadership is forged in the furnace.

The gracious, positive spirit of a Billy Graham—or the broad smile of a Dwight Eisenhower or the exuberance of a Teddy Roosevelt—does not reveal the complex, painful stories of how they rose to great challenges or sustained their intensity. Far from being a formula to learn, leadership is a set of life experiences melded by intense heat.

The heat and struggle create often unexpected results. Jim Collins, as he researched corporate leadership for his book *Good to Great*, was caught off-guard by his team's research findings. "The good-to-great leaders seem to have come from Mars," is how he described his reaction to what they discovered about the very best corporate leaders. "We were surprised, shocked really, to discover the type of leadership required," Collins wrote. What his team found was a paradoxical blend of humility and "ferocious resolve."

Those two characteristics don't easily meld. Only the furnace can extrude such seemingly opposite characteristics. Billy Graham's lifetime of leadership has, indeed, been paradoxical in blending extraordinary humility with fierce intensity of purpose. He fits Collins's descriptions of highly effective leaders, for out of that burning, paradoxical blend have come remarkable results.

It's not just his countless television and stadium appearances or his leading the nation in times of grief or new beginnings. It has been his leadership of his team and of other leaders and of a broad Christian movement that has continually built momentum and created such impact on nations, cultures, and on millions of individuals.

All this from a skinny farm kid from Charlotte, North Carolina? What ignited all this? Who could have come anywhere close to predicting it?

Not his grade school teachers! According to one, he would have to be taken outside in the hall before he would recite his lessons. "In the classroom, in front of the other students, he would hardly open his mouth. He was terribly shy and timid."

His fifth-grade teacher said, "I just couldn't get him to say a word in class. I remember once, he just sat there looking at me after I asked him a question, and I finally burst out in exasperation, 'Billy Frank, don't just sit there—say *something*. Please, just say *something*.' Not a sound. He just kept staring at me. And to tell you the truth, I just forgot about him after he passed on out of school. Then, I don't know how many years later, I saw him for the first time on one of his television crusades. I simply couldn't believe it. His whole personality was so completely changed. He had such certainty, and the way the words were just pouring out—I kept thinking, *somebody's putting the words in his mouth, he's just pantomiming it out.* I couldn't get over it. I kept thinking, *Is that actually Billy Frank Graham? What in the world happened to him?*"

As a teenager, Billy's work on his parents' dairy farm took a far backseat to girls and baseball. His wavy blond hair, sharp blue eyes, and ever-present smile attracted the girls, and his charismatic personality opened lots of doors. But a college classmate remembered not only the "magic and charm of his youthful nature" but also his "loose, careless way," and his very messy room. "We would have been absolutely staggered back then," he recalled, "that he'd be able one day to run such a large and complex organization."

What in the world *did* happen to Billy Frank Graham?

■ ■ ■

Immersion in the furnace of leadership formation began with a painful experience with a beautiful young woman.

Emily Cavanaugh was a dark-haired college classmate whom Billy had asked to marry him, even though they had known each other only one semester. Her reluctance to immediately answer worried Billy; yet after months of deliberation, Emily finally accepted his proposal.

But one evening at a class party she sat with him on a swing and told him she had to give back his ring. "I'm not sure we're right for each other. I just don't see any real purpose in your life yet." She was interested in an older student, Charles Massey. She saw in him what she didn't see in Billy—goals, plans, responsibility.

Billy was devastated. "All the stars have fallen out of my sky," he wrote to a friend.

For months afterward, through the spring and summer, Billy roamed the streets for hours at night, praying for direction. He felt "a tremendous burden." He was not simply grieving a romantic breakup but confronting reality. In fact, many realities. He didn't, in fact, have a sense of purpose. He had a vague sense that God was calling him to preach, yet he had an equal sense that he, like Moses, was not eloquent enough for the task.

Some see such realities and simply move on. But in a manner that was to typify his long life of service, Billy agonized over all the elements with full engagement of his mind and emotions. Over and over again throughout his life, Billy would face conflicting realities of many sorts, and he would lay them before God with extreme earnestness, spending many entire nights on his knees or flat on his face in prayer, seeking the right course of action.

After months of angst, one autumn evening Billy wandered through a golf course, finally kneeling on the eighteenth green. Eyes filled with tears, he gazed upward. "All right, Lord! If you want me, you've got me," Billy declared. "If I'm never to get Emily, I'm gonna follow you. No girl or anything else will come first in my life again. You can have all of me from now on. I'm gonna follow you at all cost."

■ ■ ■

Russian poet Boris Pasternak once said, "It is not revolutions and upheavals that clear the way to new and better days but . . . someone's soul, inspired and ablaze."

Billy's soul was, indeed, ablaze. Unsophisticated, he was painfully aware of his limitations. But he was full of passion to fulfill what he believed God was calling him to: spreading the gospel, "the Good News," as a message of liberation and love.

Yet as he focused and energetically began preaching and receiving ever more invitations to speak, he sensed increasingly that his eloquence could not persuade or transform. His deepening humility was anchored in fact. He knew he was not an outstanding speaker and that his personal charisma was not enough to fulfill the great call he felt weighing upon him. He had entered a life of helplessness—helpless to do this work that was far larger than his capacities.

As he found some success as an evangelist, he continually sought a greater connection and empowerment. During a mission to the British Isles, he met a young Welsh evangelist named Stephen Olford, who had the spiritual qualities Billy longed for. "He had a dynamic . . . an exhilaration about him I wanted to capture." After hearing Olford preach on being filled with the Holy Spirit, Billy approached him and said, "You've spoken of something that I don't have. I want the fullness of the Holy Spirit in my life too."

Olford agreed to set aside two days when Billy was scheduled to speak at Pontypridd, just eleven miles from the home of Olford's parents. The two would talk and pray during the day, pausing long enough for Billy to preach at night.

"This is serious business," Billy told him. "I have to learn what this is that the Lord has been teaching you."

In the small stone hotel, Olford led Billy step by step through the Bible verses on the Spirit's power, which had produced Olford's profound spiritual renewal a few months earlier. The effects of the mentoring, however, were not evident in that evening's service.

"Quite frankly," said Olford later, "his preaching was very ordinary. Neither his homiletics nor his theology nor his particular approach to Welsh people made much of an impact. The Welsh are masters of preaching, and they expect hard, long sermons with a couple of hours of solid exposition. Billy was giving brief little messages. They listened, but it wasn't their kind of preaching." The crowd was small, passive, and to Billy's invitation, unresponsive.

The next day Olford continued the instruction, telling Billy that he "must be broken" like the apostle Paul, letting God turn him inside out.

"I gave him my testimony of how God completely turned my life inside out—an experience of the Holy Spirit in his fullness and anointing," said Olford. "As I talked, and I can see him now, those marvelous eyes glistened with tears, and he said, 'Stephen, I see it. That's what I want. That's what I need in my life.'" Olford suggested they "pray this through," and both men knelt on the floor.

"I can still hear Billy pouring out his heart in a prayer of total dedication to the Lord," said Olford. "Finally, he said, 'My heart is so flooded with the Holy Spirit!' and we went from praying to praising. We were laughing and praising God, and Billy was walking back and forth across the room, crying out, 'I have it! I'm filled. This is a turning point in my life.' And he was a new man."

As Billy recalls the experience years later, "I was beginning to understand that Jesus himself was our victory, through the Holy Spirit's power."

That night, when Billy preached, "for reasons known to God alone, the place which was only moderately filled the night before was packed to the doors," said Olford. "As Billy rose to speak, he was a man absolutely anointed."

Members of the audience came forward to pray even before Billy gave an invitation. At the end of the sermon, practically the entire crowd rushed forward.

"My own heart was so moved by Billy's authority and strength that I could hardly drive home," Olford remembers. "When I came in the door, my father looked at my face and said, 'What on earth happened?' I sat down at the kitchen table and said, 'Dad, something has happened to Billy Graham. The world is going to hear from this man.'"

Indeed, in Pasternak's phrase, Billy's soul was "inspired and ablaze."

■ ■ ■

George Bennett and Allan Emery of Boston served for decades in key roles on Billy's board. Both were extremely successful—Emery in the wool business and Bennett in finance. Bennett had served as treasurer of Harvard University; Emery served as chair of the executive committee of Billy's organization and eventually as its president.

In Emery's home, overlooking Boston's bay, Emery points out the place where the British sailed in with a great fleet during the Revolutionary War. A history buff, he explains both the major events and how his immediate neighborhood fit into them. Bennett, who in his nineties still swims more than a mile, points out the spot on the distant shore at which he starts his annual spring swim across the bay. Both men are giants of accomplishment and have vivid memories of Billy's international leadership.

"So, with all this history in Boston and its vitality and intellectual horsepower," we asked, "how did the Bostonians react when Billy first came here?"

Emery smiled, a bit mischievously. "He came on the heels of his Los Angeles crusade in 1949, which was his first national attention. The Boston group looked down their noses at anyone fresh from L.A. and were calling him 'Hillbilly Billy.' Even Harold Ockenga, pastor of historic Park Street Church, was reluctant about him. Billy thought he might be invited to speak there, but Dr. Ockenga didn't think Billy was qualified; he didn't have a degree."

Emery grinned, "So when Billy spoke to a group of New England pastors prior to the Boston crusade, Ockenga had him speak, not from the pulpit but in one of the Sunday school rooms. Billy did so with no complaints. There was quite a response, much more than expected! That was my first association with Billy, and his profound humility came through and a sense of purpose, a sense of direction."

"What do you mean, 'profound humility'?"

"I was amazed at Billy. He had brought Grady and T. W. Wilson and Cliff Barrows with him to Park Street Church, and he wanted us to pray with him. He said, 'The one thing I want you to pray for is this: That I will not take credit for the successes of these things whatsoever, because if I do, my lips will turn to clay.'

"He never did take any credit. He never let anybody make him a big shot. It's humility I have never seen in anybody else."

"So Boston adjusted its thinking about 'Hillbilly Billy'?"

"Let me give you an example," said Emery. "Billy always saw the big picture. Cardinal Cushing—who was then an archbishop—wanted to meet with him, but many of our campaign board members were strongly against it."

"Back then, it was an era of a great gulf between Evangelicals and Catholics?"

"Yes, but Billy said, 'When I accepted the call to ministry, I told God I'd go anywhere he wanted me to go. I'd go to hell if he'd give me a safe conduct out.' So Billy went to meet with the archbishop! And that was one of the most amazing press conferences you can imagine. It was packed. After meeting with him, Cushing told the press, 'If I had six Billy Grahams, I wouldn't worry about the church in America.' At the end of the press conference, a reporter asked Cushing what message he had for his constituency. He simply said, 'Go hear Billy.'"

"And since those early days?"

Bennett responded, "Some here in Boston are suspicious of Christians, thinking they say one thing and do another. But in Billy they saw someone completely up front about everything; a man without guile. People would listen, and it made believers out of many who were doubters. Any school, including Harvard, found it hard not to say yes to Billy if there was an opportunity to have him on campus.

"As Allan said, he had a tremendous sense of humility, and does have. Yet he also has what a friend of mine calls 'command presence.' When Billy comes into a room, you know something's very unusual. His voice just makes you want to listen. Yet he understands it's a gift the Lord bestowed on him."

Bennett and Emery observed and experienced early in Billy's ministry his intensity and humility. They saw for the next half century that he never flinched from the furnace.

What furnace? As seen elsewhere in this book, Billy experienced plenty of intense heat throughout his ministry. He may have had enjoyable moments playing golf with presidents and staying overnight with them in the White House, yet he also had to deal with firestorms of criticism. Some of them were ferocious attacks on off-the-cuff statements printed under national and international headlines. He was jolted by the Watergate revelations of "the dark side" of his friend Richard Nixon, then felt the pain of having his private conversations with him, taped without his knowledge, made public.

The Bible tells us that everyone alive "is born to sorrow, as the sparks fly upward." Everyone experiences personal tragedies and inevitable grief, but leaders bear all these along with the weight of knowing how much their decisions, attitudes, and actions affect others. And to Billy Graham has always been added the weight of knowing he had been given enormous opportunity and, therefore, responsibility before his God.

Billy rose to the larger-than-life challenges. He never flinched from the furnace—but he let its intense heat extrude him into an extraordinary leader.

■ ■ ■

Leadership. Theodore Roosevelt's "arena" statement is perhaps the most famous quotation of all on the subject. Many a commencement address and inspirational speech have included the ringing words:

> It is not the critic who counts; not the man who points out how the strong man stumbles, or where the doer of deeds could have done them better. The credit belongs to the man who is actually in the arena, whose face is marred by dust and sweat and blood;

who strives valiantly; who errs, and comes short again and again because there is no effort without error and shortcoming; but who does actually strive to do the deeds; who knows the great enthusiasms, the great devotions; who spends himself in a worthy cause; who at the best knows in the end triumph of high achievement, and who at the worst, if he fails, at least fails while daring greatly, so that his place shall never be with those cold and timid souls who know neither victory nor defeat.

It would be instructive to consider Roosevelt himself at some length, for he was a remarkable example of just that spirit. Four presidents grace Mount Rushmore. Three, it could be said, were pressed into greatness by circumstance. Washington, Jefferson, and Lincoln led in times of national crisis. T.R., by sheer force of his personality and leadership, stepped into a series of great challenges and opportunities and shaped the nation for a new century. Charles Krauthammer has said that "the only great president we have had in good times is Theodore Roosevelt."

Many who hear of his prodigious enthusiasm and athletic energies, his determination to conquer fear and taste all of life, to be scrupulously honest and constantly lifting others—especially the downtrodden—have wondered where all that came from. What got all those engines firing? How did this man of great causes and purpose and drive become Theodore Roosevelt?

In ways more dramatic than the early experiences of Billy Graham, yet similar in spiritual heritage, Teddy was a product of the furnace of personal suffering and disappointment.

As a boy, he was quite the opposite of the dramatic president with the "bully pulpit." He was thin like Billy Graham, but no athlete! Asthmatic, fearful, he was often horribly sick. Like Billy, no one expected great things from him; in fact, considering his frailties, they simply hoped for his survival.

Yet in a remarkable process, this fearful boy "remade himself" and was ignited into the powerful and inspirational world figure that went on to win the Nobel Peace Prize and a large place in history.

What forces came together to make this leader? The factors in his transformation start with the president's father.

The senior Theodore Roosevelt was to New York what George Bennett and Allan Emery are to Boston. Wealthy, but fully engaged in charitable works, he was deeply concerned for the unfortunate. As one of the most prominent men in the city, he worked face-to-face with homeless children, helped to establish hospitals and museums, served on boards, and gave of both his time and money. He was a staunch Christian believer. David McCullough, in *Mornings on Horseback*, his essential book on young Roosevelt, writes:

> The older Theodore's pious and adoring sister-in-law called him Greatheart. The name had come to her on a Sunday morning as she watched him walk to church with his children—the warrior Puritan, Greatheart, from *The Pilgrim's Progress*, stout Greatheart, guide and protector of wayfaring innocents, fearless leader in life's purposeful journey.

He loved children, and he loved his frail, sickly little "Teedie." When the boy's asthma attacks would come in the night, he would walk the floor with him in his arms or bundle him for a carriage ride in the night air. He took all his children on adventurous trips, and his little namesake adored him.

He also challenged the fearful boy to "make his body," acknowledging that the workouts would be "hard drudgery," but he believed his son could do it.

Although Teedie rose to the challenge with weights, pulleys, and punching bags—hour after hour, month after month—his persistent effort produced little. He was still a thin, frail boy at the beginnings of adolescence. "I was nervous and timid," T.R. wrote in his autobiography:

> Yet . . . I felt a great admiration for men who were fearless and who could hold their own in the world, and I let this desire take no more definite shape than daydreams. Then an incident happened that did me real good. Having an attack of asthma, I was sent off to Moosehead Lake. On the stagecoach ride thither I encountered a couple of other boys who were about my own age, but very much more competent and also much more mischievous. They found that I was a foreordained and predestined victim, and industriously proceeded to make life miserable for me.

He determined from then on to "train myself painfully and laboriously, not merely as regards my body but as regards my soul and spirit." His determination ultimately paid off, so that as a student at Harvard—now Teddy—he became a lightweight boxer. He embraced physical action all his life, conquering his fears, explaining: "By acting as if I was not afraid, I gradually ceased to be afraid."

But lying ahead was an even greater crisis than his dealing with the dichotomy of his dreams versus his weak and sickly body.

When Teddy was midway through college, the future president's father, whom he now considered his "best and most intimate friend," became sick with cancer of the stomach. For three months he suffered, and when he was nearing death, crowds gathered outside their home, including orphans and homeless children who loved him. When his father's agony ended in his untimely death, his family was devastated. Young Theodore considered it a "hideous dream." For months he anguished over the loss, remembering the Sunday when he had "kissed the dear, dead face."

In the margin of his Bible he wrote, beside Psalm 69, "I am weary of my crying: my throat is dry: my eyes fail while I wait for my God." He remembered his father's walking with him in his arms when he was an asthmatic child. "Sometimes, when I fully realize my loss, I feel as if I should go mad."

Yet the younger Theodore, despite the depths of his grief, did not go mad. With two more years left at Harvard, he went back to his studies, athletics—and the pursuit of a young woman with whom he had fallen deeply in love and whom he determined to marry. "She won't have me, but I'm going to have *her*!" he told a friend. He eagerly, passionately focused his last two college years on winning Alice Lee.

Unlike Billy's experience with Emily Cavanaugh, Theodore was successful, and he was deliriously happy when she accepted his proposal. He wrote in his diary, "I do not think ever a man loved a woman more. . . ."

The remarkable passage of "making" himself physically and emotionally in adolescence, then emerging from the depths of grief over his father with a determination to emulate him, resulted in his entering politics. Armed with the elder Theodore's values and a driving sense of purpose, he fearlessly plunged into this new world.

Yet only three years after his marriage began, everything fell apart.

As Theodore boldly made speeches against corruption, Alice was nearing childbirth. She delivered a healthy baby girl and all seemed well. But then Theodore, that same day, received a disturbing telegram and rushed home, where he found in one room his beloved and devoted mother was dying, and in another his wife, Alice, mortally ill.

The two women died within hours of each other, Alice in Theodore's arms.

Again, "strange and terrible fate" had plunged him into deepest grief. "The light has gone out of my life," he wrote in his diary.

The story of his yet-again remaking himself, plunging back into politics, and then leaving the East for the raw life of the frontier, was another terrible, extruding furnace. Roosevelt felt he had nothing to live for. He embraced the strenuous rugged life, branding and driving cattle, flattening a drunken cowboy who threatened him with a gun in each hand, pursuing three thieves and capturing them himself. He exulted in the Wild West. Eloquently describing riding horseback to the top of a plateau, he wrote this famous line: "Black care rarely sits behind a rider whose pace is fast enough."

Roosevelt carried much "black care," and he rode fast, even frenetically, as he tried to outdistance it. But he was also remaking himself. Three years after leaving the East, he came back, husky, solid, "clear bone, muscle, and grit," according to a friend.

The black care would always be with him. But it is what Roosevelt chose to do about that care that made him emerge as such an extraordinary leader. He led robustly with both awareness of life's tragedies as well as its human potential. For inspiration, he often remembered his father's example; between small portraits of Lincoln and Grant, he hung above his desk a large oil portrait of his father.

■ ■ ■

Roosevelt's man in the arena, "face marred by dust and sweat and blood, spending himself in a worthy cause, daring greatly"—how is such a leader formed?

The summation above of TR's formative years is one of many sketches we could have included to show the process of leaders being formed in the furnace.

"Extrusion" is the word used to describe the process of forcing a material through a die. The metal that eventually emerges has been extruded, reshaped into a useful form.

The extrusion process for Billy Graham started early and lasted a lifetime. As a young man, he wrestled with God as not only loving Father but also "consuming fire." During those sleepless pacings in Florida and impassioned yearnings in Wales, he felt the weight of compelling claims and eternal consequences. To understand the passion of Billy Graham, one must recognize his distinct crucible was not of multiple deaths of loved ones or similar grief but, at the very core, the intensity of the Call. It was the crucible that continued to refine, purify, and empower him all his life.

■ ■ ■

Before its theater release, Mel Gibson took his film on Christ's passion to West Virginia, where Billy and his team were meeting, to show it privately to Billy. Sitting with his close associates, the evangelist watched the vivid enactment of Christ's crucifixion. Deeply moved, he wept.

In a sense, it was the core of what he had lived all his life.

"*The Passion of the Christ*," he said after viewing the film, "is a lifetime of sermons in one movie." Billy's own lifetime of sermons and leadership has been always in the context of what he understood Jesus to have endured to bring others peace and hope, and what he himself must endure to communicate that message.

Sherwood Wirt, longtime editor of Billy's *Decision* magazine, observed, "All attempts to explain Billy Graham fail unless they begin at the cross."

What did he mean by that? Billy read often in the Bible the words of Jesus to his disciples, "Whoever desires to come after me, let him deny himself, and take up his cross, and follow me. For whoever desires to save his life will lose it, but whoever loses his life for my sake and the gospel's will save it." Billy denied himself in countless ways and took up his cross—and followed Jesus.

Mel Gibson's film depicts the depths of Jesus' physical agony. The Bible describes also his mental anguish, saying that the night before his crucifixion he was "overwhelmed with sorrow to the point of death," and "offered up prayers and petitions with loud cries and tears." On the cross, Jesus felt abandoned by his heavenly Father, crying out, "My God, my God, why have you forsaken me?"

The cross represents a furnace of a different sort. This understanding of Jesus, who reached out in love to children and the poor but died in agony to save mankind while blessing his persecutors, fills a follower with intensity and awe. When one believes that one's actions are not random and meaningless, and even more important, that one's actions influence eternal realities far larger than what happens in one's brief life, it humbles and sobers the soul.

For Billy, it also created a laser focus. Christians believe that the salvation of a single soul is of supreme value; all else fades beside this greatest consideration—that each person will live forever, either separated from God, or blessedly and joyfully in community with him. Billy knew the Bible stated Jesus had suffered the horrors of the cross "for the joy that was set before him." He too was fueled by that proffered joy.

■ ■ ■

What a strange alchemy great leadership is! A potent combustible pressured into a person's life—like high octane fuel: once dark decay drawn from the deeps but suddenly in new form, ignited and powerful.

The furnace that forges leadership burns steadily, and this is particularly true among those charged with very large responsibility. Billy was a friend and counselor to many American presidents during times of crisis. All these chief executives experienced extreme personal testing. One can read in each of their lives, from Eisenhower through George W. Bush, growth through immersion in the crucible.

For instance, Ronald Reagan biographer Peggy Noonan uses just that word to describe the period when the future president, as a young actor, experienced a string of calamities, including near-death in a hospital, the fading of his acting career, and the loss of his marriage. Jane Wyman's filing for divorce devastated him. And yet this is the man whose legacy is his optimism, the man who stirred the morale of a nation with his upbeat charm.

"These days were the crucible," writes Noonan, "the essential experience of his adulthood, the great educator, the time that formed him and that he referred back to all of his life."

In the same way that Theodore Roosevelt modeled his life after his evangelical father, who had lived with such vigor and love, Ronald Reagan modeled his after his evangelical mother, "a little tornado of goodness," to use Noonan's phrase. The great test came when, returning from service in World War II, his career opportunities wilted, and he eventually found himself in a different war. As president of the Screen Actors Guild during the McCarthy blacklist battles, he firmly opposed the brutal tactics of the Communists, yet stood firm against the unfair accusations. He was caught in the middle, but the experiences toughened him, taught him, enabled him to take in stride unfair accusations and avalanches of press criticism. It also made him more intently a man of prayer.

During his presidency, Reagan reached out to Billy, who was going through what was perhaps the evangelist's greatest strategic crisis. In 1982 it seemed the media and all America had turned against him for agreeing to travel to the Soviet Union, and seemingly being used by the U.S.S.R. for propaganda purposes. President Reagan took Billy aside. "You know what's been in the press," he said. "I believe that God works in mysterious ways. I'll be praying for you every mile of the way."

History now depicts both Reagan and Billy as heroes in those struggles in the early 1980s with the Soviets. But at the time, both had to meet those tests with the endurance of the tested leader.

Out of the crucibles, positive leadership. Paradox. Leadership requires awareness of one's own emotions and depths; awareness of multiple forces shaping perceptions and drives; awareness of the dark and the light and the large consequences of one's acts.

■ ■ ■

Woodrow Wilson's quote, which heads this chapter—"Absolute identity with one's cause is the first and great condition of successful leadership"—is personified in Billy Graham, and all of his leadership principles flow from that identity. A Scottish minister once said this about Billy: "My first impression of the man at close quarters was not of his good looks but of his goodness; not of his extraordinary range of commitments but of his own 'committedness.' To be with him even for a short time is to get a sense of a single-minded man; it shames one and shakes one."

The peaks of Billy's achievements and those of the presidents he befriended tower above us, and we realize, too often, our own resolve melts away in the furnace. How can we as ordinary leaders deal with the heat we feel and rise to challenges greater than our capacities? How can we experience the ignited life that communicates hope and emits light? How can we emerge from our own struggles and cauldrons with clarity, power, and commitment?

Most of us feel we muddle along rather than rise to greatness. *Fast Company* magazine describes those who love what they do and are "lit by passion" as highly productive and successful. Yet in seeking the call—the sense of fit and meaning that fuels that passion—the writer's research indicates "Most of us don't get epiphanies. We only get a whisper." He found that almost all of the people he interviewed "found their calling after great difficulty . . . it's up to you to do the work of discovery."

The principles of Billy's remarkable amalgam of humility and intense resolve are gifts any leader can seek. One can neither read

Good to Great and countless other leadership books, nor face the often overwhelming demands of leadership, and not understand why Billy was wrestling so mightily. We see the necessity of the burning purpose in a leader and the humility to balance it out. The leader who wants to grow throughout his lifetime, as Billy has, realizes it's a lifelong quest.

POINTS TO PONDER

BILLY GRAHAM:

Art and education may refine the taste, but they cannot purify
the heart and regenerate the individual.

His [Christ's] words were simple yet profound. And they shook
people, provoking either happy acceptance or violent rejection.
People were never the same after listening to Him. . . .
The people who followed Him were unique in their generation. They
turned the world upside down because their hearts had been turned
right side up. The world has never been the same.

THE BIBLE:

As the deer pants for streams of water,
so my soul pants for you, O God.

PSALM 42:1

PART
TWO

GETTING STARTED

When you discover your mission, you will feel its demand. It will fill you with enthusiasm and a burning desire to get to work on it.

W. CLEMENT STONE

While still in his twenties, Billy Graham became nationally known. With his team he laid the foundations for decades of international ministry. What set him apart from so many other young men of the period?

Among many factors, we've selected four, which in those critical early years lifted his trajectory and kept him from stumbling.

His careful forming of his core team resulted in the phenomenon of their serving together all their lives.

United, the team determined they would not be tripped up by the many temptations of men on the road, and they built in commitments to make their intentions stick.

Instinctively, Billy lasered in on the mission, despite countless other opportunities.

As a young man, Billy had to decide how he would handle all the harsh criticism hitting him from both left and right.

■ ■ ■

We look at these dynamics in his life, then in each chapter explore how today we might apply these principles in our own leadership challenges.

CHAPTER 2

Forming the Team

> I'd rather interview fifty people and not
> hire anyone than hire the wrong person.
> **JEFF BEZOS**

Extraordinary!

That's a word one hears often when leaders and scholars are asked to describe Billy's bringing together his early team, then effectively leading it and keeping it dynamic for more than half a century. Dallas businessman Bill Mead, the first chairman of Billy's executive committee, said when asked how so much had been accomplished, "He had perpetuity of his team! He knew how to get things done."

The odds against such perpetuity are long. Leadership literature indicates that "teams at the top" of an organization encounter far greater challenges than those of other teams. The team leading an organization must confront failures and adapt to successes, handle its own personnel disputes within the team, adjust strategy to brutal new realities, adapt to growth, resistance, and reversals—an endless list of dynamics that disrupt trust and bruise egos. Highly effective teams are tough to form and tougher to continually lead.

How could Billy's original team stay together as the BGEA (Billy Graham Evangelistic Association) ministry burgeoned, related organizations were founded, and the pace accelerated? How did the core leadership evolve and adjust, yet in chemistry and commitments stay the same?

The questions are especially intriguing in light of the era in which the team was formed. In recent years the words *team* and *participatory management* are givens. But when Billy was getting started, hierarchy was the traditional structure. After all, this was the period when Peter Drucker did his study of General Motors, which disappointed its leaders because he revealed how people were not being empowered. Drucker went on over the decades to write brilliantly about leading others, but at the time of Billy's forming his team, the wealth of today's significant insights about participative leadership was largely undiscovered.

In fact, Warren Bennis and Burt Nanus recently updated their classic book, *Leaders*, and stated that even two decades ago, important aspects of leadership were being "overlooked or undervalued," among them, empowerment, building trust, and shaping values. The corporate, academic, and denominational worlds, heavily hierarchical in Billy's early years, often looked at those in Billy's movement as youthful upstarts.

"It seems to me that the Lord took several inexperienced young men and used them in ways they never dreamed," Billy responded when first contacted about the concept of this book. His instinct was to immediately defer credit to God and to the team. "The ministry sort of took off and got away from all of us! We all seemed to be a part of a tremendous movement of the Spirit of God, and so many of the new organizations seemed to interrelate, or began as we talked and prayed together in our travels."

All that is true; Billy and his colleagues were part of a remarkable phenomenon. Late during World War II and after, thousands of Youth for Christ rallies sprang up almost spontaneously across the country. YFC's first full-time employee, Billy traveled incessantly, speaking and engaging with pastors, YFC directors, and other leaders of the emerging evangelical movement.

YFC was a sprawling, sink-or-swim *movement*, indeed, with top leaders in its Chicago "headquarters" but directors in various cities carrying considerable clout. The quality of local programs depended on who was in charge. In some cities YFC roared ahead as it evangelized young people with the support of a broad range of local churches; in others it limped along.

Leadership counted. Aspiring young leaders with fire in the belly could fail—or succeed beyond expectations. Energetic entrepreneurship drove the movement forward, but the nature of its passion made the results far different from corporate expansion. Its leaders believed they were dependent on the Holy Spirit, who could do the only truly valuable work. That meant prayer, and that meant a powerful bonding dynamic. Hundreds of leaders would pray together long into the night, kneeling on auditorium floors. They would confess sinful attitudes to each other and ask for God's cleansing and empowerment. Together they pored over the Bible to understand and implement their theology. Whenever a major challenge or event occurred, the key players met for serious prayer. Out of that brash, driven, try-anything culture came a spirit of *teamwork*.

Before his own team evolved, Billy spent years in those evangelical trenches, in both America and Europe, deepening his convictions, refining his strategies, and sensing who could be ministry soul mates. From the time of his conversion in Charlotte, Billy had been close to the Wilson brothers, Grady and T.W., and at various times held meetings with them. In Chicago he recruited George Beverly Shea to be his soloist. These men, with Cliff Barrows, became his core team.

Cliff Barrows was arguably the most crucial teammate Billy ever recruited. He was a skilled and charismatic emcee and musician, leading the program in giant gatherings, a creative force in leading new initiatives, a candid counselor, and a man who knew how to both follow and lead.

In the summer of 1945, shortly before a meeting in Asheville, North Carolina, was to begin, Graham learned that the scheduled song leader had left for Chicago. Cliff and Billie Barrows were on their honeymoon in the area, but they agreed to fill in. The talented couple more than filled the bill: Cliff song-leading and singing a solo; Billie playing the piano and joining Cliff in a duet. It was the beginning of a lifetime partnership.

In the fall of the next year, Graham invited the couple to join him and others for six months of ministry in England. Cliff, with his musical talents and excellent preaching ability, had a growing ministry of his own, but he accepted the invitation.

It is said people bond when they live through crises or face large challenges together. Those cold six months in an England impoverished by the war challenged the Americans in many ways. Opposition from clergy, an exhausting schedule, lack of adequate money—these young men, still in their twenties, were amazed, stretched, deepened, enriched—together. The chemistry was right, and they were profoundly influenced by the breadth and depth of the churchmen they worked with: Anglicans, Plymouth Brethren, Methodists, Baptists, Presbyterians of various folds. Grady Wilson said the trip "changed Billy's life. It was the beginning of the team of Cliff Barrows and Billy Graham."

By the fall of 1947, Graham was ministering in a campaign in Charlotte with his core team: Cliff Barrows, Grady Wilson, and George Beverly Shea. It was Barrows who most matched up to Billy in striking good looks, spiritual intensity, leadership, and platform charisma. Later, Barrows and his wife, Billie, were wrestling with the decision about their own trajectory. Billy had invited them to join him full time.

William Martin explains the difficulty that presented:

> For Cliff Barrows, becoming the second member of the Graham/Barrows Campaign team meant the subordination of his own ministry to Graham's. Such a subordination was not easy. When he and Billie were not traveling with Graham in Europe, they were enjoying considerable success with their own revivals, mostly on the West Coast. Cliff was a gifted preacher, and he and Billie combined talent, enthusiasm, transparent sincerity, and a remarkable lack of egotism into a highly winsome package. They clearly had the option to remain in a leading role with YFC or to establish their own independent evangelistic ministry, or to get off the road and serve as a pastor.

When we talked to Cliff, we found that even after sixty years, he vividly recalled the difficulties he then faced: "I struggled with that decision for a couple of years, because I wanted to pursue preaching." The financial uncertainties of relying on the "love offerings" given to traveling evangelists was also a deterrent.

But eventually, after praying and weighing all the factors, "the Lord told me, 'Do the music for Billy and whatever has to be done, and I'll take care of the preaching opportunities,'" remembers Cliff. "When we made that decision, the peace of God came into my mind and heart. I went to him in Philadelphia on an early morning and said, 'Bill, you know the struggle we've had about whether we join your team, and the Lord has given us peace in our hearts. As long as you want us to, I'll be content to be your song leader, carry your bag, go anywhere, do anything you want me to do.'"

Cliff recalls that Graham said, "May we serve together until the Lord returns, or until one of us is called home to heaven."

Cliff's decision marked the beginning of a remarkable team, two men who recognized that their strengths were complementary rather than competitive. Together they could accomplish more than either could alone.

It has often been said that a person who would lead must first learn to follow. Cliff Barrows pushed aside his own early dreams seeking a greater good, and he did so enthusiastically. Dallas businessman Fred Smith, who early in Billy's career led the singing in some of his meetings, told us about a music minister who was fired because he kept expanding his worship music, encroaching more and more on sermon time. In contrast, "Cliff Barrows, even in the smallest meetings," Fred said, "started right on time. He has a sense of broadcast and telecast; he knows how ingredients fit into a total program. For years I've watched Cliff during Billy's sermons. He's the most intense listener in the whole stadium."

Cliff, in saying to Billy, "I'll carry your bag, go anywhere," committed himself unreservedly. Yet team roles are not always comfortable. Once, someone taunted Grady Wilson, "Grady, how does it feel to be a caddy for Billy?" Surely Grady felt some sting at such moments, but he knew being part of an effective team requires different roles at different times. *Count It All Joy*, the title of his autobiography, is the phrase that captures his spirit. These men of high capacity saw the larger picture, and when Billy Graham spoke of his dreams, the dreams were theirs as well. Strong team members have strong egos, and playing second fiddle can feel unnatural. But team players know the greatest glory is the entire team's victory.

It helped that Billy's team knew beyond the shadow of a doubt that he was not in it for his own glory. They sensed his humility, and they also understood the price he paid for playing his role on the team day after day, year after year. At times Grady would have to step in for Billy at the last minute to preach or hold a press conference. Knowing how the press could spin anything, and how the slightest misstep could wound Billy's ministry, Grady felt the pressure. Once, after standing in for him, he told Billy, "I never realized what you go through night after night, standing before large crowds in these great auditoriums and stadiums. I'm a nervous and physical wreck after each time I've had to substitute for you."

Billy had many opportunities to meet with the powerful and to walk with royalty. But leadership always comes with a price. A team understands that each player contributes, each has burdens to bear and challenges to confront, and each must follow.

Dwight Eisenhower knew how to follow George C. Marshall and President Franklin Roosevelt; in contrast, Douglas MacArthur found it very difficult to follow anyone, and eventually President Truman had to fire him. Even U.S. presidents must relate up as well as down in that they must listen to the people as the ultimate authority.

Billy found the balance, both leading and following. For instance, at a CTI (Christianity Today International) board meeting, in responding to a suggestion, he commented, "I don't think my board would allow me to do that." He led his board, and the trustees looked to him for leadership. He deferred to them, for "in the multitude of counselors there is wisdom." He sought accountability as protection, as a source of wisdom, as creating clear parameters for decision making.

He also aggressively sought the counsel of his teammates and of his wife, Ruth. But the essential, defining part of his followership was his giving ultimate control to someone other than himself. He constantly sought to understand the signals coming from his Coach. He may have been quarterback, but he was determined that the ultimate plays would be called by the Lord he served.

Billy's marching orders came from hours of prayer and studying the Scriptures and praying with those who shared his convictions and were in the trenches with him. He was constantly asking the question, "What is God actually saying we should do next?" He was well aware of the story in the Bible of the apostle Paul's struggling with strategic issues, and after much prayer and counsel, a decision was made only after "it seemed good to the Holy Spirit and to us."

Such sensitivity to the Spirit has typified Billy's decision-making process over the decades. Throughout his ministry, Billy *followed*. He was a highly effective leader with clarity of purpose because he was determined that nothing would short-circuit his responding to the nudges of the Holy Spirit. In facing ambiguous circumstances and hearing competing voices, the complexities pressed him to long hours of reflection, prayer, and seeking the applicable biblical wisdom.

The Team is a term that has always permeated the Graham organization. It refers to the inner circle, the vitality of which radiates out to other key players and through the ranks. The team spirit extended to thousands of participants, even out to volunteers and local leaders who made the crusades happen in their hometowns. A counselor or coordinator, a team member or recruiter felt like a vital contributor, fully engaged, following the playbook, working in tandem with the players who were up front and leading the process.

But it all started with team followership in the inner core, and that started with Billy himself.

LEADERSHIP
LESSONS | **Teambuilding**

Applying the Principles

Billy Graham built and energized his team and widely extended its spirit. But how much of his approach can we apply to our own unique challenges? As leaders, we face a huge variety of structures and strictures, some conducive to teambuilding, some not. We can't always choose our leaders or our teammates, but we can raise effective followership to a high level, often despite difficult circumstances.

Whatever our leadership opportunities and limitations, the spirit of teambuilding empowers and energizes.

Incorporate This Astounding Math

The remarkable math of teamwork challenges our usual calculations. "One shall chase a thousand," says the Bible, "and two shall chase ten thousand." G. K. Chesterton picked up on this in his novel *The Man Who Was Thursday*. A policeman confronting evil discovers an ally who tells him, "Two is not twice one; two is two thousand times one."

Whether leading a large enterprise or a small entity, teamwork multiplies effectiveness. When members of a team are rightly positioned and fully engaged, "mountains can be moved." Many leaders have drawn inspiration from sports teams that require high spirits, intense concentration on the goal, and absolute determination to excel by stretching capacities to the limit.

The test of an organization is not genius. It is its capacity to make common people achieve uncommon performance.
PETER DRUCKER

But in any endeavor, those qualities are rare. As in sports, some teammates don't live up to their potential, and unexpected events can hobble team performance. Based on their research, the authors of *Executive Teams* wrote about teams at the very top of organizations: "The composition of the executive team virtually guarantees some of the team's members will fail . . . each member [plays] multiple, complex, and central roles in concert with the CEO and with each other. That is why it is so difficult—and at the same time so crucial—to create and maintain the right cast of senior characters."

Building and energizing any team is a tall challenge and more art than science. We must be realistic about the difficulties and make adjustments as necessary. Yet teams have exponential power, and those who serve on them are often amazed at the results.

Watch Out! The Chemistry Can Empower, or Explode

Pastor Bill Hybels, in his book *Courageous Leadership,* says that earlier in his ministry he didn't rank the need for great chemistry with teammates very highly. But after many years of experience, he became "a convert to the doctrine of chemistry." He has concluded that personality and temperament, blending with other team members and with him, represents one of the top factors in building a great team.

> *Who you are is who you attract.*
>
> JOHN C. MAXWELL

Billy had the advantage of testing the chemistry of potential teammates for years before his team was formed. He knew he not only could work with them but they could bond together. It was this powerfully positive chemistry among Billy and his close associates that made possible decades of effectiveness.

The mix of chemistry must include loyalty, trust, respect, and an esprit de corps based on shared goals. When we have the opportunity to select team members, we must listen to our intuitions and best counselors. Bringing on soul mates lifts any enterprise or ministry. In contrast, the wrong chemistry can blow up the best-laid plans.

Cliff Barrows describes that chemistry on the Graham team as both professional and personal. After sixty years of working with Billy, Cliff said that Billy always showed "he is a friend of the team. He spoke of the team and team activities as 'ours,' not as 'me and mine.'"

In addition, Cliff told us, Billy's refusal to micromanage stimulated positive team chemistry. "One of my greatest resources these sixty years is the clear sense of Bill's backing and support," said Cliff, "and his belief in me and other members of the team. He respected the gifts God gave us. He never interfered with those who worked under him. He trusted the Lord and the choices he made of leaders. As a result, we would have—and did—follow him anywhere God led. We would even have laid down our lives for him."

If chemistry is measured in willingness to sacrifice for each other, then this team, for some sixty years, was a prime chemistry lab.

Face, and Admit, Your Own Limitations

Psychologist Joan Borysenko once said, "Vulnerability—being imperfect—is what makes us human, authentic, and lovable." That statement dramatically applies to leadership of a team. Accepting the brutal facts about human limitations, including our own personal weaknesses, is crucial to authenticity. And lovable? In contrast, we often think of leaders instilling fear instead of love.

A certain amount of reasonable fear is necessary. We had better fear an oncoming truck, and we'd better fear for the consequences of laziness or lackluster performance. But although fear is a powerful stimulant, it is authenticity and love that create and catalyze teams for the long haul. A leader without admitted weaknesses has no need for teammates; a leader who reveals no vulnerabilities provides no opportunities for teammates to make a significant contribution.

Books on leadership admonish us to face the facts, and the first one a leader must accept is the grid of facts that includes personal weaknesses. How can others buttress my weaknesses? Can we divide the key roles so that each player maximizes strengths? Failure is inevitable in a team when its leader doesn't see weaknesses and adapt.

Grady Wilson said of Billy, "He was painfully aware of his humanity—he has flaws, and he's the first to admit them." Billy didn't try to hide what he couldn't do. His vulnerability and style of working side by side made his team well aware of both his strengths and his weaknesses.

If You Can't Inject Humor, Laugh Anyway

When one hears laughter in the halls of an organization, when humor and good spirits enliven the breaks, when serious discussions are broken up by humor, it's a very good sign the enterprise is healthy. Teams that emphasize fun and good spirits lift effectiveness.

Billy would tell stories on himself. For instance, he liked to tell of the time in a small town when he asked a boy how to get to the post office. After getting directions, Billy invited him to come to the meeting that evening. "You can hear me telling everyone how to get to heaven."

The boy's response? "I don't think I'll be there. You don't even know your way to the post office."

Billy also liked to tell of a pastor who said in a sermon, "Apart from Christ, there never was a perfect man." Someone in the congregation interrupted him, saying, "Oh, yes, there was. My wife's first husband!"

Teams have more fun. This is not a trivial point, because the kind of fun they have is integral to their performance.
JON R. KATZENBACH AND DOUGLAS K. SMITH

Grady Wilson's autobiography, *Count It All Joy*, has an entire chapter on humor in the Graham team called "Laughing All the Way to Heaven." It describes practical jokes played on each other, and Billy's good-natured acceptance of jokes played on him—and at times, his reciprocating. Although extremely serious about their mission and the eternal stakes, the team could laugh together and play together.

Billy generally did not have the gift of making others laugh, but here's what is vital: he could join in others' humor and could laugh at himself—even when under the spotlight or on camera when he had blown a line.

Proverbs sums it up: "A merry heart does good, like medicine."

To Galvanize a Team, Articulate a Compelling Goal

Large challenges energize and coalesce teams. In sports, preparing for the Super Bowl or World Series has an amazing effect on concentration, energy, and determination. Every player is fully psyched to achieve the goal and will do whatever possible to win. In many cases individual preferences and chances for personal glory must be shoved aside for the full-court press toward victory.

In corporate life, in ministry, in any endeavor, "significant performance challenges" energize teams and make them thrive. They are essential for maximum effectiveness. Urgency, direction, mutual accountability and respect all blend as everyone on the team determines to seek the highest performance possible.

You can do what I cannot do. I can do what you cannot do. Together we can do great things.

MOTHER TERESA

It all starts with the leader. "There is a symbiotic relationship between great institutions and great CEOs," says Jim Collins, author of *Good to Great*. "The CEO is transformed by committing to a bigger purpose than mere personal success, and in doing so, the company is transformed into greatness."

Decades ago, we read a statement that has always challenged us: "A man with a burning purpose draws others to himself who help him to fulfill it." This certainly personified Billy Graham, whose burning purpose was authentic and evident to every one of his teammates. The results became obvious.

Blend Your Principles and Personalities

Over time a good team works increasingly well together because they can anticipate one another's reactions and handle the inevitable surprises in a coordinated way.

Fred Smith told us of watching the Graham team at work during a campaign when a guest musician went a bit long. "I watched Cliff and Billy," he said. "They didn't even need to exchange words. Just a glance between them was enough to signal a slight change of plan in response to what was happening."

That anticipation is also part of "chemistry," and it takes time for that to develop. But time spent working together doesn't guarantee good teamwork. It requires a blend of principles and personality—an underlying resonance. The Graham team developed guidelines for working together that were both spoken and instinctively sensed.

"We have tried to adhere to the principles that Bill himself has set as an example for us through the years," Cliff Barrows told us, "and I really believe that the principles of, for instance, our 'manifesto' that became our guide, that this was much of the reason for effectiveness in the Billy Graham Association."

"The Modesto Manifesto" (see chapter three) helped articulate the game plan, but it was consistent with the spirit of the team that was deeper than words. As a healthy team, they shared both a common mission and a common bond.

Place Confidence in the Team

The leader's attitude toward the team largely determines how strong it will become. The Graham team became strong because Billy nourished it and gave each member ample opportunity to exercise significant responsibility.

A key element is that intangible but readily detected attitude of the leader: confidence.

We asked Cliff to describe Billy's relationship to the team. He immediately pointed not to an organizational chart, but to the foundational issue—his attitude, which had a contagious effect on the team. "He was confident in God," said Cliff. "He sought God's will, he was God-dependent, motivated by his love for God and man. He was self-effacing, but he was secure in the place of God's appointment. He was anointed of God. He was considerate. He was not authoritarian. He knew that in the multitude of counselors there is safety. His decisions were based on mutual agreement rather than on a dictatorial basis. He thought about and relied on the counsel of those he trusted. He never was demeaning nor reprimanding. He trusted people and respected their contribution."

When Your Team Is Finally All Set, Expect Change!

Billy's extraordinary success with his core team raised the bar about what can be achieved. A cautionary note is in order, however. Billy was remarkably fortunate in the shaping, developing, and capacities of his core team. Once formed, he exercised the leadership that made it possible for them to work together for nearly a lifetime. However, that doesn't mean other key players on the larger team stayed with his organization. Over the decades various personnel changes—some of them painful—had to be made.

This is natural and expected. The book *Executive Teams*, by David Nadler and Janet Spencer, states, "The composition of an executive team virtually guarantees that some of the team members will fail. . . . If you stop to think about it, the odds are heavily stacked against a CEO who is trying to create an effective executive team; the equation simply involves too many variables." The book goes on to describe the many roles each member must play, and that when change occurs, some simply cannot adapt.

Organizational change inevitably results in executive team change.

EXECUTIVE TEAMS

We must accept the fact that powerful, complex forces make change inevitable. Dealing effectively and compassionately with painful changes requires continuing focus on the vision and goal, and consistency with the principles that drive the leadership.

Those who have served with Billy are quick to say that he has shown the Bible's "fruit of the Spirit: love, joy, peace, longsuffering, gentleness, goodness, self-control." In today's world, leaders must face the fact that change is accelerating at numbing speed, and that keeping a team together—or reconfiguring it—can require lots of adaptations to new realities.

POINTS TO PONDER

BILLY GRAHAM:

A keen sense of humor helps us overlook the unbecoming,
understand the unconventional, tolerate the unpleasant, overcome
the unexpected, and outlast the unbearable.

THE BIBLE:

Two are better than one, because they have a good return for
their work: If one falls down, his friend can help him up. But pity
the man who falls and has no one to help him up!

ECCLESIASTES 4:9 – 10

CHAPTER 3

Confronting Temptations

> Be thoroughly acquainted with your temptations
> and the things that may corrupt you, especially
> those temptations that either your company or
> your business will lay before you.
> RICHARD BAXTER

Today temptations massage our every move. Whether on television or movies, magazines or websites, the messages invite us to spend and indulge. Stated or suggestive, the essential lure is clear: Do what you want to do. You deserve it. Indulge the fantasy.

Compelling images, voices, and opportunities tempt us to open our wallets, minds, and bodies to what seem like natural desires but which could destroy our ability to lead. We're well aware of leaders who lost it all by giving in to the appeal of greed, sex, ego, or success shortcuts. Yet still, temptations beckon us. . . .

When Billy Graham was shaping his leadership principles and commitments, many of the temptations were, perhaps, less overt, less "in-your-face" than they are today. Yet the power of the temptations was not any less, and they were in essence the same ones we face now.

Billy had to resist the enticements that confront the traveling man. He knew of many who did not. Billy saw how spiritual enthusiasm did not make you immune to greed, pride, lust, and ambition. Indeed spiritual passion and more earthly passions often possess the same soul. During his years as a field representative for Youth for Christ in the mid-1940s, Billy traveled constantly, speaking to high school groups, college rallies, gatherings of Christian businessmen, and civic clubs. During 1945 alone, he visited forty-seven states, logged 135,000 miles flying, and received United Airlines' designation as its top civilian passenger.

All that travel put him in contact with many who succumbed to all sorts of temptations. "More than once he had to disassociate YFC from freelance evangelists who had built up extravagant expectations, then absconded in the wake of financial or moral misadventures," wrote historian George Marsden. "Seeing the terrible disillusionment trusting church folks had suffered stirred deep revulsion within him and added an increasingly dogged determination to adhere to high standards of morality and ethics."

Just a few years later, in 1948, this determination led to a fateful afternoon discussion with his newly formed evangelistic team. It would chart the course his ministry would take for the next half century. At this time—shortly before the meetings in Los Angeles that propelled him into national prominence—he and his team were holding smaller evangelistic meetings in Modesto, California.

As Billy describes it: "From time to time Cliff, Bev, Grady, and I talked among ourselves about the recurring problems many evangelists seemed to have, and about the poor image so-called mass evangelism had in the eyes of many people. Sinclair Lewis's fictional character Elmer Gantry unquestionably had given traveling evangelists a bad name. To our sorrow, we knew that some evangelists were not much better than Lewis's scornful caricature."

So one afternoon during the Modesto meetings, Billy called the team together to discuss the problem.

"God has brought us to this point," he said. "Maybe he is preparing us for something that we don't know. Let's try to recall all the things that have been a stumbling block and a hindrance to evangelists in years past, and let's come back together in an hour and talk about it and pray about it and ask God to guard us from them."

The team members went back to their rooms and listed all the problems they could think of that evangelists and evangelism encountered.

"When they returned," Billy remembers, "the lists were remarkably similar, and we soon made a series of resolutions that would guide us in our future evangelistic work. It was a shared commitment to do all we could to uphold the Bible's standard of absolute integrity and purity for evangelists."

Their discussion boiled down to four main points, and Billy has explained the thinking behind each one:

1. *Shady handling of money.* "Nearly all evangelists at that time—including us—were supported by love offerings taken at the meetings. The temptation to wring as much money as possible out of an audience, often with strong emotional appeals, was too great for some evangelists. In addition, there was little or no accountability for finances. In Modesto we determined to do all we could to avoid financial abuses and to downplay the offering and depend as much as possible on money raised by the local committees in advance."

The Graham team saw the dangers and knew they needed strong mechanisms in place that would as much as possible "lock them in" to ethical behavior.

2. *Sexual immorality.* "We all knew of evangelists who had fallen into immorality while separated from their families by travel," Billy wrote. "We pledged among ourselves to avoid any situation that would have even the appearance of compromise or suspicion. From that day on, I did not travel, meet, or eat alone with a woman other than my wife. We determined that the apostle Paul's mandate to the young pastor Timothy would be ours as well: 'Flee . . . youthful lusts'" (2 Timothy 2:22 KJV).

It may seem quaint and impractical in this day of casual relationships between the sexes to be so rigid about meeting with someone of the opposite sex—but it worked for Billy and his team. They eliminated any suspicion of problems. While on the road, the team traveled together and occupied adjoining hotel rooms, or at least rooms in close proximity. By not traveling alone, they minimized temptations. And each team member committed to never being alone with a woman who was not his wife.

When it was necessary to speak one-on-one with someone of the opposite sex, it was done in an uncompromising way. One day in 1983, Hillary Clinton, wife of then Arkansas governor Bill Clinton, requested a private conversation with Billy Graham. He agreed to have lunch with her at a table in the center of a public restaurant in Arkansas.

3. *Badmouthing others doing similar work.* "We had observed the tendency of many evangelists to carry on their work apart from the local church, even to criticize local pastors and churches openly and scathingly. We were convinced, however, that this was not only counterproductive but also wrong from the Bible's standpoint. We were determined to cooperate with all who would cooperate with us in the public proclamation of the gospel, and to avoid an antichurch or anticlergy attitude."

This relationship with local churches became a strategic distinctive of the Graham team. They would not go to a community unless the local church leaders had invited them and agreed to host their meetings. In turn, the Graham team agreed to refer those who responded at the meetings back to the churches for ongoing follow-up in the spiritual life.

They recognized that while it's often easier in the short-term to operate independently, it's better in the long run to work with others. Lone Rangers have the luxury of making decisions unilaterally; they don't have the complications of working with the varying interests of diverse allies. But Billy knew that if he could develop a coalition around his core mission, the results would be far more lasting.

4. *Exaggerated accomplishments.* "The tendency among some evangelists was to exaggerate their successes or to claim higher attendance numbers than they really had," wrote Billy. "This likewise discredited evangelism and brought the whole enterprise under suspicion. It often made the press so suspicious of evangelists that they refused to take notice of their work. In Modesto we committed ourselves to integrity in our publicity and our reporting."

Credibility is a precious commodity. Without it, people won't follow. When a leader exaggerates in one area, followers wonder if they're getting the unvarnished truth in other areas.

At Modesto and in the years since, the Graham team determined to avoid any appearance of padding the numbers. They decided to accept the crowd size estimates of local police or other officials, even when the team felt the estimates were too low. And they called those who came forward after a sermon "inquirers" rather than converts. After all, no one can know what actually happens inside a person's soul, and the Graham team chose not to presumptuously tally spiritual transactions. It was another way of fighting the temptation to exaggerate their accomplishments.

Leighton Ford, longtime Graham associate, remembers a breakfast meeting with pastors on the committee of the New York campaign, years after Modesto. An inaccuracy was being reported by the campaign committee. "Gardner Taylor spoke up," Leighton told us. "He said, 'Dr. Graham, I think we must always say just what is the truth.' Billy immediately agreed. He always insisted on total integrity."

Striving for full integrity had become a part of the organization's DNA.

Billy, in speaking of the "Modesto Manifesto" stated, "In reality, it did not mark a radical departure for us; we had always held these principles. It did, however, settle in our hearts and minds, once and for all, the determination that integrity would be the hallmark of both our lives and our ministry."

Billy's team structured the ministry to reinforce guidelines and hold themselves accountable. Cliff Barrows told us, "We were accountable to God, to our wives, to each other, the local committees, and the spiritual leadership of the community."

To ratchet up accountability, Graham formed a board of significant leaders, gave that board authority, and accepted its supervision. Bill Pollard, former CEO of ServiceMaster and a BGEA board member, remembers being impressed with how seriously Billy took his understanding of his accountability to his board.

"A few years ago when Graham was planning to be in Europe the early part of the summer," says Pollard, "there were scheduled meetings in Hungary in August. Graham's health was not great, and he was taking heavy medication at the time. At our board meeting he said, 'Between the time the first commitment in Europe ends and the beginning of the Hungary campaign the second week of August, I'd like to ask your permission to stay in Europe to prepare for the meetings and avoid the jetlag back and forth.'

"I was impressed that he wouldn't even spend the money for something like that without board approval. That's just an example of the way he has conducted himself in submission to authority.

"Graham's no milquetoast," Pollard explained. "He has strong convictions and views about many things. But at the same time, he demonstrates his genuine desire to serve under the authority of those who will keep him from stumbling financially."

A corporate vice president once observed about business realities, "The farther you climb the corporate ladder, the harder it is to get honest feedback. The more influential you are, the harder it is to find people willing to tell you the truth."

Billy knew the importance of overcoming temptation by finding people who could tell each other the truth.

"The test of Graham's soul, indeed, lay not in adversity, but in how he coped with success," wrote former *Time* magazine correspondent David Aikman. As countless leaders can confirm, the greatest spiritual challenges can come not from the times of conflict and deprivation but during heady days of triumph and reward. From the biblical King David and King Solomon to the more recent Jimmy Swaggart, Jim Bakker, and executives at Enron and Tyco, the temptations associated with success have been the undoing of many a leader who had overcome lesser temptations on the way up.

LEADERSHIP LESSONS | Temptations

Applying the Principles

Those who observe leaders soon conclude that talent and character are measured separately. Talent can take a leader far, but the accomplishments that talent brings also produce great temptations. And talent is not sufficient to sustain a leader's effectiveness if the ever-present human flaws are not addressed.

Cliff Barrows pointed out that the Bible suggests integrity may be the commodity in shortest supply. Psalm 12:1 laments, "Help, LORD, for the godly are no more; the faithful have vanished from among men." People of honor, people of their word, people who try to live in purity of mind and heart—such individuals stand out, if only because of their relative scarcity.

How do we build the will and the strength of character to confront and overcome temptations? How can we be just as savvy about protecting ourselves from ourselves as we are about leading others? Obviously, the stakes are high.

Never Underestimate a "Small Temptation"

It's easy to wink at the word *temptation*, to flirt with extramarital sex, or to shade the truth just a little, or to arrange corporate finances for just a little personal benefit. It's easy to believe the consequences of playing a little loose with temptations will be minor.

However, consider the case of some amateur Massachusetts tuna fishermen. Talk about underestimating the consequences! In 1999, for the first time in forty-seven years, the tuna were running only thirty miles off Cape Cod. And they were biting! You didn't have to be a professional to catch them; all you needed was a sharp hook and some bait. And the rewards for doing so were substantial. Rumor had it that Japanese buyers were willing to pay $50,000 for a large blue fin. As a result, many ignored Coast Guard warnings and headed out to sea in small boats. What these new fishermen didn't realize was that the problem is not catching a tuna—the problem comes after they're caught.

Reputations are fragile. They must be handled with care like a valuable vase that if dropped can never quite be put together again.
BILL POLLARD

On September 23, the *Christi Anne*, a nineteen-foot boat, capsized while doing battle with a tuna. That same day the twenty-seven-foot boat *Basic Instinct* suffered the same fate, while *Official Business*, a twenty-eight-footer, was swamped after it hooked onto a six-hundred-pound tuna. The tuna pulled it underwater.

These fishermen underestimated the power of the fish they were trying to catch. Temptation, likewise, can blindside you. A small indiscretion appears worth the risk. But as with a hooked tuna, only after we hook into temptation do we discover its strength.

Oscar Wilde said that the easiest way to get rid of a temptation is to yield to it. Maybe. In actuality, a temptation that has been given in to usually returns, only with more force. The leader who rationalizes finds himself or herself reeling in a disaster. One indiscretion can bury a leader's life work.

Minimize Secrecy; Maximize Reinforcements

When we minimize secrecy and openly admit temptations are there, we can build in safeguards against poor judgment, unconscious motivations, and self-deception. Says Bill Hybels, "Leadership requires moral authority. Followers will only trust leaders who exhibit the highest levels of integrity."

For the Graham team, the "Modesto Manifesto" put clearly on the table the issue of temptations. Ever after, the subject was no longer taboo but one that could be openly addressed. And that's the first step toward overcoming the power of temptation.

> There is no one without faults, not even men of God. They are men of God, not because they are faultless but because they know their own faults, they strive against them, they do not hide them and are ever ready to correct themselves.
> MOHANDAS GANDHI

But airing the problem isn't enough. The Graham team also recognized the need to put the right reinforcements into the structure of their work.

The book *Built to Last* describes how building mechanisms into organizations produces dynamic results. The book illustrates how in the 3-M Company mechanisms were the key factor in year after year creating new, outstanding products.

The mechanisms Billy Graham and his team built into their organization had equally profound results. Driving significant accountability stakes into the ground protected them. It then permeated their ministries and affected others with whom they were associated.

Media management consultant David Schmidt told us that the example of Billy Graham and his associates helped him resist the inevitable temptations of travel. "I'm a guy. You get tempted in hotel rooms to put something on TV you shouldn't. I knew the stories of how Billy would never be alone with a woman—how he was very careful about all this stuff—and the men around him were careful too. They weren't hiding things, they worked at personal purity. They'd say, 'You have to be in the dark what you are in the light!' That helped me to aim for a higher standard."

By openly declaring their ethical standards, the Graham team admitted the dangers and clarified the expectations. It might be well for each of us to study and apply to our own enterprises the "Modesto Manifesto":

We will never criticize, condemn, or speak negatively about others.
We will be accountable, particularly in handling finances, with integrity according to the highest business standards.
We will tell the truth and be thoroughly honest, especially in reporting statistics.
We will be exemplary in morals—clear, clean, and careful to avoid the very appearance of any impropriety.

Practice Open Integrity

The press loves to expose the juicy details of leaders who fall, and once the genie is out of the bottle, it can't be stuffed back in.

Researchers studying today's leadership dynamics put a very high premium on integrity. Of course, this is not at all a new finding. For instance, years ago President Eisenhower stated with deep conviction, "I believe deeply that every occupant of the White House . . . has one profound duty to the nation: to exert moral leadership. The President of the United States should stand, visible and uncompromising, for what is right and decent—in government, in the business community, in the private lives of the citizens. For decency is one of the main pillars of a sound civilization. An immoral nation invites its own ruin."

When we are trying to decide whether a leader is a good leader or a bad one, the question to ask is: "Is he with the Ten Commandments or is he against them?" Then you can determine if the leader is a true messiah or another Stalin.

ISAAC BASHEVIS SINGER

In today's world, it's very easy to get sucked into the allure of images from the world of entertainment that would have stunned Eisenhower. And for many today, lying and exaggerating are considered acceptable tools.

Others are only too ready to dodge financial accountability. Every leader faces situations that can lead to personal benefit: payments "on the side," manipulation of customers to maximize receipts, taking organizational resources for personal use, expanding personal perks. Conflicts of interest usually begin small and seem justified. Once started, the practice of feathering our own nests escalates. It's easy to rationalize!

To exert moral leadership as Ike admonished may be more difficult than ever. Yet it is no less essential.

Set Your Eyes on the Larger Prize

We all know that concentrating on overcoming a temptation often has the ironic effect of making it stronger. In contrast, focusing on something powerful and positive empowers mind and emotions to embrace the desired alternative. It enables the will to succeed.

Billy Graham had not only a laser focus on his mission, he was caught up in the wonder and awe of God's creation and his part in reaching out to others with his love. Don't pity poor Billy sitting in his hotel room without lively and graphic entertainment. He not only met there with colleagues and prepared for the next day's appearances, he was deeply cognizant of the vast opportunities and possibilities before him—as they are for many of us. He repeatedly spoke to his teammates about "having so much to do, so many books to write, so many invitations from all over the globe." He often expressed amazement at what had already happened and what he believed God was continuing to do through him and the team.

A good conscience is a continual Christmas.

BENJAMIN FRANKLIN

Most of us don't have opportunities on that scale, but as leaders, we know our decisions and actions and life choices powerfully affect others. Most of us can dream dreams of making a difference, fueling our positive thrusts by seeking out inspiration from others, from books and films and whatever means we individually use to enlarge our vision and hone our skills. A sense of gratitude that we can be part of significant dynamics can empower our commitments.

It would be naive to indicate all of this is easy. It never has been! Martin Luther said, "Prayer, meditation, and temptation make a minister." Interesting combination! We all struggle with temptations, even though they are different for each of us. The struggles Luther indicated continue. Yet like dawn's light chasing away shadows, becoming caught up in a great and worthy cause can illumine and brighten our mental and emotional landscapes.

POINTS TO PONDER

BILLY GRAHAM:

When wealth is lost, nothing is lost. When health is lost,
something is lost. When character is lost, everything is lost.

THE BIBLE:

And lead us not into temptation, but deliver us from evil.

MATTHEW 6:13 KJV

CHAPTER 4

Lasering In on the Mission

> Throughout history, it was the super achievers —
> and only the super achievers — who knew when to
> say "No." They always knew what to reach for.
> They knew where to place themselves.
> **PETER DRUCKER**

What's the difference between stadium lights and a laser? Stadium lights illumine an entire football field, turning night into day for cameras and spectators. They can be seen for miles.

But a laser so focuses the power of light that it can slice steel or perform surgery. Anyone who has observed an automobile assembly line with car panels being carved by the power of light, or anyone whose eyesight has been restored by laser surgery on the retina, knows the wonderful effects when energy is not diffused but intensely focused.

While broad exposure and wide-ranging interests are important, leaders who offer the most lasting contributions incorporate their exposure into a laser focus.

Without a clear purpose and well-channeled efforts, energy is diffused and power is dissipated.

"No steam or gas drives anything until it is confined," observed Harry Emerson Fosdick. "No life ever grows great until it is focused, dedicated, disciplined." The great evangelist of the nineteenth century, Dwight L. Moody, who in many ways was a model for Billy Graham, had a motto: "Consecrate, then concentrate." Billy did just that. He identified his calling, then refused to be diverted. He focused on his mission: evangelism, "to bring people out of their torpor of sin to salvation from it."

To understand Billy's focus, we need to grasp his passion. In his address to the ten thousand international evangelists he brought to Amsterdam in 2000—70 percent of them from poor, developing countries—he said, "The older I get, the more I am asked who will succeed me. Well, the fact is that I am just one of many thousands who have been called to be an evangelist. I don't need a successor, only willing hands to accept the torch I have been carrying."

In many cultures evangelists are looked down on, not only because some have been hypocrites or have failed in their personal lives, but because some people view them as mere religious salesmen. Yet in the world's churning mix of religious and secular ideologies competing for souls, the evangelist is essential. In *The Pilgrim's Progress*, it is Evangelist who points the main character, Christian, to the gate, which makes all of Christian's adventures and blessings possible. Today's deeply troubled world needs evangelists with a message of love and hope.

Samuel Shoemaker captured this in his book *I Stand by the Door*. An Anglican spiritual leader, he was deeply concerned about the sufferings and emptiness of people, and he was a primary founder of Alcoholics Anonymous, which has helped so many strugglers. Like Billy, he longed to share the Good News with searching souls. He expressed it this way:

> I stand by the door . . .
> The door is the most important door in the world—
> It is the door through which men walk when they find God.
> There's no use by going way inside, and staying there,
> When so many are still outside and they, as much as I,
> Crave to know where the door is.
> . . . The most tremendous thing in the world
> Is for men to find that door—the door to God.
> The most important thing any man can do
> Is to take hold of one of those blind, groping hands,
> And put it on the latch—the latch that only clicks
> and opens to man's own touch.

Billy Graham has spent a lifetime pointing to the door and praying for those who hear his invitation to put their hands on the latch, to walk into a life of reconciliation, purpose, and joy. No other role, for his life, has loomed larger; other goals have never been compelling enough to deflect him.

George Brushaber, president of Bethel University in Minneapolis, sees Billy's focus as a vital ingredient of his leadership. "There was something about the central passion of his life that attracted his people," he told us. "Even though many times they were older or had higher education credentials or business success, they held him in awe. There's an anointed, unique quality about him hard to describe, a transparency so people could look into his soul—his commitment to his mission was so strong and so clear. The utter simplicity of his agenda is a powerful factor."

Even so, for Billy, as for almost every effective leader, distractions and potential diversions continually confronted him.

Christian apologist Ravi Zacharias observed, "Billy never changed his calling. Many times it could be said, 'God loved him and *others* had a wonderful plan for his life.' But he kept his focus. Many good things can stand in the way of fulfilling your calling just as much as bad things can. But Billy remained clear on what he was called to."

But that calling was tested. Early in his career, Billy's charisma and good looks led to an offer from Paramount Pictures Corporation to become an actor. He declined. In the late 1950s, NBC offered him a million dollars a year to host a show opposite the highly popular Arthur Godfrey. He turned it down.

During a citywide campaign at a press conference with some aggressive and somewhat hostile reporters, Billy was grilled about the finances of his organization and was asked, cynically, whether he expected to make substantial money from the city. As he continued to be pushed on the issue, Billy reached into his coat pocket and pulled out a telegram he'd received from Hollywood, making a highly lucrative offer for him to star in two movies. "If my interest was in making money," he said with a smile, "I'd take advantage of an offer like this."

Grady Wilson describes the time in the 1960s when Billy was swimming with President Lyndon Johnson at Camp David, and the president said in front of several staffers, "Billy, I think you ought to run for president when I'm finished with my term. If you do, I'll put my entire organization behind you."

Billy answered with a laugh, "Mr. President, I don't think I could do your job."

"Billy, I know you think I'm joking," said the president, "but I'm serious. You're the one man who might turn this country around."

Later, Billy revealed that President Richard Nixon offered him an ambassadorship, a cabinet post, "any job I wanted." Earlier in 1952, Texas billionaire H. L. Hunt offered Billy six million dollars if he would run for president. As attractive as these options may have been, Billy realized they were not part of his mission. To each he said, "God called me to preach, and I do not intend to do anything else as long as I live."

Billy's focus was clear.

During the late 1970s, after feeling stung by the revelation of Nixon's statements on Watergate tapes, Billy had to further clarify his focus on evangelism from even informal political involvement. "I'm out of politics," he said in an interview in 1981, partly as a reaction to the perception that he had been too involved in politics through his friendships with Lyndon Johnson and Richard Nixon. He clearly separated himself from the Moral Majority, a conservative religious movement seeking to steer America's political path to the right.

"I'm for morality," he said, "but morality goes beyond sex to human freedom and social justice. We as clergy know so very little to speak out with such authority on the Panama Canal or superiority of armaments. Evangelists cannot be closely identified with any particular party or person. We have to stand in the middle in order to preach to all people, right and left. I haven't been faithful to my own advice in the past. I will be in the future."

Billy openly admitted he had allowed some blurring of his focus in the past. "It was a mistake," he said, "to identify the Kingdom of God with the American way of life."

After that, he would frequently respond to questions about politics with "I'm not for the left wing or the right wing. I'm for the whole bird."

John Akers, one of Billy's closest aides, told us, "Billy's principle was that you shouldn't do anything that would shut the door to the gospel. I can't tell you how important that is. People are constantly wanting him to sign a petition about something, and he declines. He's been called a moral coward for not taking this stand, or that stand, or the other stand. But from his standpoint, to do so was to unnecessarily close doors to the gospel."

■ ■ ■

Yes, it's easy to lose focus, not just with forays into political causes, but also with tasks that are closely related to your core mission. For instance, in the overall process of reaching people and helping them become faithful followers of God, Billy has focused on one element—connecting with broad audiences and bringing them to the point of decision. That means he primarily leaves to others the task of helping people grow in faith.

That is precisely what impressed the skeptical British commentator George Scott during Billy's 1954 campaign in London. Scott wrote:

> If the people will not go to the Church, the Church must go to the people. . . . One of the strongest things in [Graham's] favour, the fact most likely to overcome the national prejudice against him, is that he does not pretend to be a one-man Church. He sees his mission primarily as that of the fairground barker who will first win the eyes and ears of the public so that they will be attracted into the tent.

Scott had been especially impressed when Billy observed that evangelism is only 5 percent of the task, and when Billy's work is done, the other 95 percent is just beginning—"to keep [the convert] resting in Christ and growing into maturity in Christ and in the Church."

Billy lasered in on the 5 percent, explaining the decision a person needed to make regarding Jesus. When a person makes that decision, Billy encourages local churches to follow up with the elements of the 95 percent for spiritual growth.

Billy's associate Rick Marshall describes Billy's role as the obstetrician, not a pediatrician. "I have four children," says Marshall. "They each had an obstetrician, but I only got two things from the OB—a baby and a bill. I never expected the OB to treat my children as they grew up." Billy, the spiritual obstetrician, understood his role, even as he appreciated the many pastors who, like pediatricians, would be required for the subsequent follow-up care.

■ ■ ■

In *The Screwtape Letters*, C. S. Lewis masterfully and imaginatively constructs the correspondence between a senior devil, Screwtape, and his protégé, Wormwood. In one letter, Screwtape instructs Wormwood in the art of gaining souls for the Devil by diverting their energies in multiple directions. For instance, he tells him to entice people to exaggerate their everyday interests and worries, thereby making those diverse concerns "the main thing," and thus preventing anything of significance from being accomplished.

Billy kept his focus on the core mission, but this was tested most seriously in the late 1960s when he was asked to help start a Christian university. Strong voices urged him to consider founding a graduate university, solidly Christian, with academic credentials that would rival Yale or Harvard. But should it be part of Billy's mission? In 1966 he told a reporter, "If someone came along with $10 million to invest in such a school, I'd consider it."

A year later, the conditions were met, and he had to consider it—and make a difficult, and ultimately painful, decision.

The opportunity became a real one when insurance financier John D. MacArthur offered a thousand acres in Palm Beach Gardens, Florida, along with a pledge of millions of dollars to launch the project. When others heard that Billy would be involved, additional millions of dollars were offered, and planning for

Graham University began. But the price for the Graham organization would also be high—approximately $10 million during the first year and $3 million per year for the next five years.

"I consider this a major decision in my life," Billy said, as he wrestled with the pros and cons.

Clearly, Billy was concerned about education. He supported others in their efforts to provide quality Christian education—most notably through the Graham Center at Wheaton College in Illinois and his efforts as a board member to strengthen Gordon-Conwell Divinity School in Massachusetts and Fuller Theological Seminary in California. He placed high value on the life of the mind.

Ultimately, after long discussions with coworkers and members of his board, he decided the university would divert too much energy and funding away from his primary mission, evangelism. He backed out of the project, a decision that offended MacArthur and alienated the directors of the foundation that administered his wealth.

At times, maintaining focus is costly, but ultimately the decision enabled Billy to move forward with many major initiatives, including bringing tens of thousands of evangelists together in Amsterdam in 1983, 1986, and 2000, and to put his resources and energies into evangelistic campaigns all over the world.

Jay Kesler, longtime president of Youth for Christ and later president of Taylor University, told us "Billy's great strength is his ability to intuitively go to the center of things. German pastor Helmut Thielicke has written about the difference between the evangelist and the philosopher-teacher-pastor," Jay said. "Thielicke says the evangelist is like a man hunting a stag. If you want to hunt stag, you can't shoot at rabbits. If you shoot rabbits, you'll never see a stag. In my mind, Billy Graham was no rabbit shooter. He was always going for the stag."

■ ■ ■

Billy was so focused on bringing his message in every venue, whether with Jack Paar, Johnny Carson, Larry King, Diane Sawyer, or a sitting president, that he would somehow always find a way to do it. His use of the microphone check illustrates the intensity of his focus.

The A. Larry Ross firm handled media and public relations for more than twenty-three years for the Graham organization. Ross says, "One of the distinctives of Mr. Graham's ministry has been his ability to make positive points for the gospel in any situation. You can ask Billy Graham how he gets his suits dry-cleaned on the road, and he'll turn it into a gospel witness.

"I cut my teeth in the corporate world before I worked with Mr. Graham," says Ross, "and I set up numerous media interviews. Almost always before a TV interview, they do a microphone check, and they ask the interviewee to say something— anything—so they can adjust the audio settings. Often a corporate executive, for that check, will count to ten, say their ABC's, or recite what he had for breakfast. Mr. Graham would always quote John 3:16—'For God so loved the world that he gave his only begotten Son, that whosoever believeth in him shall not perish, but have everlasting life.'

"When I asked Mr. Graham why he does that, he replied, 'Because that way, if I am not able to communicate the gospel clearly during the interview, at least the cameraman will have heard it.'"

Even the preinterview time is focused on his overriding purpose.

LEADERSHIP LESSONS | Lasering

Applying the Principles

Leaders must identify the essential goal and continually move toward it. In this, Billy learned well from his predecessor, Dwight L. Moody, who said, "Give me a man who says 'This one thing I do,' not 'These fifty I dabble in.'" Not that there aren't times when leaders must multitask; it does mean simplifying the issue until the single ultimate objective is clear.

As someone put it, "If you chase two rabbits, both will escape."

Management literature frequently notes the polarity between big-picture people and detail people. While someone must pay attention to details, the most effective leaders tend to be consumed by one overriding concern. In 1953, Isaiah Berlin wrote a famous essay, "The Hedgehog and the Fox," which distinguished between the monist and pluralist visions of the world. Taken from the Greek poet Archilochus's observation that "the fox knows many things, but the hedgehog knows one big thing," the fox epitomizes management that is constantly aware of a multiplicity of options, contingencies, and competing interests, while the hedgehog represents leaders who see the One most important thing and constantly burrow in that direction.

This principle has been picked up more recently by Jim Collins in *Good to Great*, which suggests that a leader who identifies one unifying "hedgehog principle" and bases all decisions on that is more likely to achieve "greatness" than a leader who does many things.

The presidency of Jimmy Carter, for instance, has been criticized for not distinguishing the One Thing from the multiplicity of details. By contrast, in the 1992 presidential race, James Carville clearly defined Bill Clinton's campaign with the pithy phrase, "It's the economy, stupid."

Identify the One Thing

Ronald Reagan was a big-picture leader. As political commentator Richard Brookhiser put it, "The economist Milton Friedman daydreams about an income tax return so simple it could be printed on a postcard. Reaganism could be jotted down on the back of a business card."

It was essentially "Defeat communism and cut taxes." What didn't fit on the card, Brookhiser said, could safely be ignored.

Reagan speechwriter Patrick Buchanan remembers sitting in on a cabinet-level debate over grain exports. While a heated argument raged between Secretary of State George Shultz and Secretary of Agriculture John Block, Reagan concentrated on a bowl of jellybeans, picking out his favorite colors. Buchanan remembers thinking,

"What in heaven's name is with this guy?" Reagan caught Buchanan's eye and winked, which Buchanan interpreted to mean, "They're having an argument here, and I'm not getting into it."

Billy, of course, was a prime example of a leader with a one-point agenda. Over the years he focused more and more carefully on the core. "I used to talk on every subject," he admitted. "If somebody asked me anything political, I'd talk on it. I've learned through the years that I'm much better off keeping quiet on certain subjects in order that I may appeal to a wider group of people in my presentation of the gospel."

Don't Hunt Rabbits

Jay Kesler's point from Helmut Thielicke about hunting stags, not rabbits, meant Billy knew his target. This affected hundreds of small decisions. For instance, in 1970 Billy admitted that his hair was "a little longer" than it had been the year before—a full inch over the collar. He was identifying with the younger generations, those most likely to respond to the gospel. Amid the conflict between parents and their young people over appearance, Billy said, "It's ridiculous for parents to engage in bitter battles with their children over the haircut issue . . . long hair or short hair is a matter of personal taste, not a basic moral question." He recalled that his grandfather, a Civil War veteran, "Had a beard down to his chest and a mustache and very long hair . . . and he was one of the most wonderful Christian men I ever knew."

Billy didn't want to be diverted by secondary targets.

Cast the Vision; Make "Big Asks"

In addition to keeping the vision uncluttered, the leader must recognize what limits its fulfillment, and that may require soliciting help. Bill Hybels summarizes it this way: "The leader continually casts the vision and makes 'big asks.'"

Cliff Barrows told us about sitting with Billy in Shreveport, Louisiana, in 1952, when they both realized they needed help handling all the people who came forward at the close of Billy's sermons.

"We were concerned about giving the right counsel to the people who were making decisions," said Cliff, "and it was wearing us out. We would stay after the service and go to the inquiry room where we'd talk about the decision they had made, the importance of prayer and Bible reading, identifying with a church, and sharing your faith. By the time we were done, it took all our energy out of us."

As Cliff and Billy talked about the need, the name of Dawson Trotman came up. He'd earlier been a colleague of Billy's and had recently started a ministry called the Navigators, which emphasized systematic growth in the spiritual life. Cliff knew Dawson, respected him highly, and said, "Let's call him."

Billy asked Dawson to come to Louisiana to advise them. When he arrived and observed what they were doing with inquirers, he said, "You're going to kill yourselves and wear yourselves out trying to do all this. Let some of the rest of us study this and see what we can do."

With Billy's encouragement, Dawson developed packets of Scripture verses and basic explanations of the Christian life. "That was the beginning of our follow-up and counseling materials," said Cliff. "Billy didn't try to do that himself. He gave himself to preaching and his calling as an evangelist." But while lasering in on his mission, he made a "big ask" for help in preparing for those who responded.

Broaden Your Base of Help

Having clarified his primary mission, Billy could welcome help from others, even from some who differed on other issues. This has been the source of some of the most vocal criticism of Billy Graham over the years. Only his laser-sharp understanding of his central calling has enabled him to navigate these issues.

One example arose during his 1987 meetings in Denver. Colorado Governor Richard Lamm was a platform guest on opening night. Lamm was known as a liberal Democrat who had recently made controversial statements about euthanasia and the obligation of the terminally ill to expedite their deaths, thus freeing up resources for others.

Graham's longtime media and public-relations director A. Larry Ross remembers this generated a lot of controversy. Many people were asking, "Why is Mr. Graham endorsing the governor? Why are you allowing him on the crusade platform?" Over and over Larry had to explain, "We're not endorsing the governor; rather, the governor is endorsing Mr. Graham and these meetings. He's welcoming us to the community and saying, 'This event is a good thing for this city and our state; we welcome Billy Graham to Colorado.'"

The dog has four feet, but he does not walk down four roads at the same time.

HAITIAN PROVERB

Billy's clarity of focus allowed him to keep relationships in perspective.

Maximize Mission Clarity

The leader with a crystallized calling can lead with resolve, urgency, and persistence.

In his book *On What Leaders Really Do*, John Kotter claims that infecting others with a sense of urgency is the difference between effective and ineffective leadership. Urgency is more important than even the leader's own work ethic. "Sooner or later, no matter how hard they push," writes Kotter, "if others don't feel the same sense of urgency, the momentum . . . will die far short of the finish line."

Billy's predecessor, Dwight Moody, was an example of personal commitment to urgency. An associate of Moody's, R. A. Torrey, reports how a friend once told Moody, "It remains to be seen what God will do with a man who gives himself up wholly to Him." Moody's response: "Well, I will be that man."

Our greatest fear should not be of failure, but of succeeding at something that doesn't really matter.

ANONYMOUS

Torrey's conclusion: "I, for my part, do not think 'it remains to be seen' what God will do with a man who gives himself up wholly to Him. I think it has been seen already in D. L. Moody." Billy's pattern, like Moody's, was to devote himself to the urgency of his cause with a lifetime of persistence. As Calvin Coolidge observed, "Nothing in the world can take the place of persistence. Talent will not; nothing is more common than unsuccessful men with great talent. Genius will not; unrewarded genius is almost a proverb. Education will not; the world is full of educated derelicts. Persistence and determination alone are omnipotent."

But persistence cannot endure without a clear sense of purpose, a laser-etched mission.

POINTS TO PONDER

BILLY GRAHAM:

I just want to lobby for God.

THE BIBLE:

One thing I do: Forgetting what is behind and

straining toward what is ahead . . .

PHILIPPIANS 3:13

CHAPTER 5

Loving Harsh Critics

> Get a friend to tell you your faults, or better
> still, welcome an enemy who will watch you
> keenly and sting you savagely. What a blessing
> such an irritating critic will be to a wise man.
> **CHARLES HADDON SPURGEON**

All leaders get criticized. It's their response to criticism that sets them apart.

Our natural reactions to criticism include emotions ranging from woundedness and indignation to desire for revenge. Deserved or undeserved, inane or thoughtful, criticisms hurt. We may realize they're inevitable, but when they hit, we feel it. One researcher on a broad range of leadership dynamics declared, "Emotions rule!"

Today our culture conditions us to amplify our reactive emotions, to use our verbal weapons against others. News and talk shows use lively invective. Electronic games invite us to spend hours stalking the enemy, reacting instantly to menacing movements, skillfully shooting or crushing—with vivid, bloody results—our "enemies."

Sitcoms are often games of Stick in the Verbal Knife—duels of ridicule and counterridicule. In politics, the more verbal jabs and vitriol, the livelier the coverage. Revenge movies depict outrageous acts that must be avenged, then with explosive action, deliver the message: Revenge is sweet.

This constant undercurrent flowing into our subconscious affects us more than we may realize. Media may be a mix of the coarse and the cerebral, but too much of it urges "Sue 'em! Out 'em! Retaliate!"

The strategy of Billy Graham has been the polar opposite of this dark undercurrent. Anglican rector John Stott commented about Billy, "He has loved his enemies who have vilified him, bearing the pain and declining to retaliate." To even his harshest critics he genuinely reached out in love, thereby redeeming many a volatile situation but also empowering his own soul.

Did Billy get angry with his critics? Of course he did. As the Bible says about Jesus himself, "He was a man of like passions as we are." Billy may be viewed by many as all sweetness and light, but his life and spirit are the results of gritty determination to love God, to lead from that love, and to forgive, and even learn from, his "enemies."

In his later years, media and commentators have been mostly kind to Billy Graham. But early in his ministry, he often felt the sting of criticism. His wife, Ruth, recalled that in their pastorate in a Baptist church in Western Springs, Illinois, they felt plagued by "resident troublemakers" who "generated a cackle of criticism about the minister and his non-Baptist wife, swooping in to catch the slightest sliver of glittery gossip or detail. They fell soundly into John Calvin's category of those determined to take offense."

Many times over the decades, Billy was attacked by critics who would say scathing things, even when they were dead wrong about the facts. Still, inaccuracies didn't stop millions of people from reading their accusations.

Billy has been described by liberal and secular writers as being a "moral dwarf," of being "psychologically sick," and telling "sanctified lies." His prayer at one president's inauguration was termed a "raucous harangue," and one liberal seminary described his ministry as "spiritual rape." Religious conservatives, angry at his alliances with Catholics and liberals, were equally vicious, and because he came from a conservative upbringing, he particularly felt the sting of their criticisms.

One former ally told a local television station that Billy "is doing more to harm the cause of Jesus Christ than any living man," and suggested that Billy's supporters pray by reciting, "Dear Lord: Bless the man who leads Christian people into disobeying the Word of God, who prepares the way for Antichrist. . . ."

This savage criticism pained Billy not just because of its blistering tone, but because on a majority of their theological beliefs, he still concurred with conservative antagonists, admiring their respect for the Bible.

His response to these critics? For the most part, Billy simply brushed off their disapproval. He feared engaging them would ultimately detract from his mission. "Satan would like nothing better than to have us stop our ministry and start answering critics, tracking down wretched lies and malicious stories," he said of his policy in 1952. "By God's grace I shall continue to preach the gospel of Jesus Christ and not stoop to mudslinging, name-calling, and petty little fights over nonessentials."

Pastor Leith Anderson recently observed, "Unlike many religious leaders before and since, Graham refused to attack his critics and those with whom he disagreed. Most of those people and their issues have long been forgotten, but Graham's legacy is long-lasting. If he had chosen to attack those with whom he disagreed, he would have been lost in the dust of forgotten controversies."

■ ■ ■

Billy's restraint was severely tested during preparation for his 1957 campaign in New York City. Key fundamentalist leaders turned on him when he included Catholics and liberals on the platform. In addition, his stance didn't protect him from attacks from the left—liberal theologians added to the chorus of criticism. One theologian in particular—the prominent Reinhold Niebuhr—ridiculed Billy for presenting Jesus as the all-sufficient answer for man's ills. Writing in *Life* magazine, Niebuhr argued, "Perhaps because these solutions are rather too simple in any age, but particularly so in a nuclear one with its great moral perplexities, such a message is not very convincing to anyone—Christian or not—who is aware of the continuing possibilities of good and evil in every advance of civilization, every discipline of culture, and every religious convention."

Some leaders embrace controversy, seeing it as a means to prominence and press coverage. Billy did not. Instead, he tried to meet privately with Niebuhr. The renowned theologian had no interest in dialogue and refused to see him, so Billy simply complimented him, yet set his own context. "I have read nearly everything Mr. Niebuhr has written, and I feel inadequate before his brilliant mind and learning," Billy told reporters. "Occasionally I get a glimmer of what he is talking about. . . . If I tried to preach as he writes, people would be so bewildered they would walk out."

Even before he entered the national consciousness with his 1949 meetings in Los Angeles, Billy showed great wisdom in dealing with critics. During a preaching campaign in Birmingham, England, in 1947, Billy had faced intense opposition from skeptical local pastors. Through the years itinerant revival preachers had passed through Birmingham and drummed up local support by denouncing the local clergy. So before Billy even arrived, these pastors, sure that he was just another religious opportunist, convinced the city council to prohibit him from speaking in the city auditorium.

When Billy showed up, he didn't grouse about this prohibition. Instead, he made appointments with his detractors, one by one, admitted his weaknesses as a young preacher, and assured them he wanted only to help them reach the city for Christ. He asked them calmly to explain and pray about their opposition. Soon the hostility morphed into fervent support.

"Billy called on me," recounted one pastor who had been critical of "America's surplus saints." "He wasn't bitter, just wondering. I ended up wanting to hug the twenty-seven-year-old boy. . . . I called my church officers, and we disrupted all our plans for the nine days of his visit. Before it was over, Birmingham had seen a touch of God's blessing. This fine, lithe, burning torch of a man made me love him and his Lord."

■ ■ ■

Billy faced an even greater challenge when he visited London in 1954. As in Birmingham, controversy awaited him when he stepped on Britain's shores. To raise money for the trip, Billy's organization had produced a fund-raising brochure in the U.S. that described the spiritual condition of postwar England with less-than-precise language: "And when the war ended, a sense of frustration and disillusionment gripped England, and what Hitler's bombs could not do, Socialism, with its accompanying evils, shortly accomplished."

The phrasing may not have been inflammatory in America, but Billy's aides did not know British politics and had unwittingly criticized Britain's ruling Labour Party, also known as Socialists. An article appeared in a London *Daily Herald* newspaper entitled "Apologise, Billy—Or Stay Away!" A British journalist wrote, "Billy Graham has more gravely libeled us than anyone has dared to do since the war. . . . Socialism, indeed, by ushering in the Welfare State, saved Britain from degradation of poverty and injustice that might have brought about a revolution." And in the *Daily Worker* newspaper, another British writer said, "This fast-talking American . . . confessed with a light laugh that many people had said to him: 'Stay at home.' It is excellent advice he would have done well to heed."

Although alarmed and discouraged about the damaging publicity, Billy employed the same tactics that worked so well in Birmingham. He surprised the critics with a prompt and clear apology for the mistake. He and his team feared the snafu would keep people away; instead, for twelve weeks audiences packed every venue where he preached.

Journalists learned they had misjudged him. A writer with the *Daily Express* newspaper confessed, "To be honest, I was prejudiced about him. We have heard so much here about these American hot gospellers and their methods of selling religion, which they seemed to have picked up from the salesmen of insurance. And then, just after breakfast yesterday, I met him. I had better say straight away . . . I may be making a mistake, but I think he is a good man. I am not so sure that he isn't a saintly man. I just don't know. But make no mistake about this . . . Billy Graham is a remarkable man."

Amid the crusade frenzy, Billy also sent a brief note to William Conner, who had harshly criticized him in the *Daily Mirror* newspaper. He diplomatically complimented Conner: "While your articles about me were not entirely sympathetic, they were two of the most cleverly written that I have ever read."

He offered to meet Conner, who accepted and impishly suggested they meet at a pub called "Baptist's Head." Following the meeting Conner said, "I never thought that friendliness had such a sharp, cutting edge. I never thought that simplicity could cudgel a sinner so damned hard. We live and we learn. . . . The bloke means everything he says."

In assessing Billy's approach to handling criticism, Lon Allison observed, "His seemingly preferred mode is to go directly to the people causing him the most pain and basically say, 'Teach me.'"

LEADERSHIP LESSONS | Critics

Applying the Principles

Fred Smith, who has been a mentor to countless leaders, advises, "Turn your critics into coaches." His point: all of us need all the insights we can get about ourselves and our challenges, and if we look at our critics as sources of insight, we can leverage even painful and mean-spirited critiques.

Critics can sharpen the mind, clarify parameters. They can force us to evaluate what we really believe about ourselves and our mission. How we respond to critics reveals a lot about our sense of calling and our composure.

As Thomas à Kempis observed six hundred years ago: "It is good that we at times endure opposition and that we are evilly and untruly judged when our actions and intentions are good.

Often such experiences promote humility and protect us from vainglory. For then we seek God's witness in the heart." Thomas, of course, was a saint, more concerned about refining his soul than developing his leadership. But his insight about the astringent value of unfair criticism also applies to leaders.

Criticisms are an ingredient in the leadership mixture we're forced to deal with; courageous and intelligent response can lift us to a new level. Our first reaction to critics may be to blast them, but like a quarterback under pressure, an effective leader looks for the opportunities this opens up and develops alternate strategies.

Expect to Be Criticized

Leadership, by definition, means change, which makes criticism inevitable. Even if the road ahead is progress, change produces disequilibrium, uncertainty, and a reluctance to part with the past.

Fred Smith points out that a leader must expect criticism much as an Olympian would expect and plan for pain. "I listened to Bob Richards, the Olympic gold medalist, interview younger Olympic winners of the gold," said Fred. "He asked them, 'What did you do when you began to hurt?'

"None of these Olympians was surprised by the question; all had a specific way of handling the pain. After the interviews, I asked Bob why he had asked about handling pain, and he said, matter-of-factly, 'You never win the gold without hurting.'

"Likewise, every leader has to develop a plan for handling criticism, because criticism will come in any dynamic organization."

Leaders like Billy accept the challenge of criticism rather than let it become a threat. Jerry Beavan, an early Graham associate, recalls the time he was upset at someone who had attacked Billy. "I was really mad," he told us. "I was talking to Billy and said, 'Bill, they can't say these things about you!' He said, 'Jerry, they're not talking about you! Why should you get mad?' Billy stayed positive."

> Leaders take people where they want to go. A great leader takes people where they don't necessarily want to go, but ought to be.
>
> **ROSALYNN CARTER**

When criticism is a threat, a leader becomes defensive, but when it is viewed as a natural occurrence and a challenge, it can become a source of constructive energy.

Be Realistic about Our Dual Natures

Billy understood human nature. He was well grounded in the Christian theology that teaches even the best people are still inhabited by an "old self," as the Bible describes it, which often expresses itself in contentious ways. To survive in leadership, we need a healthy understanding of the dual nature of human beings.

Criticism is stirred up because leadership initiatives cost money, cause inconvenience, require effort, or produce a shift in power or recognition. We should never be caught by surprise at people's negative behavior but accept it as a reminder that our work as leaders is not done.

A wise older pastor once observed, "The qualifications of a pastor are to have the mind of a scholar, the heart of a child, and the hide of a rhinoceros." That's true of any leader as well. Especially the part about the hide.

Embrace Three Essentials

If anyone had severe critics, it was Abraham Lincoln. He was inaugurated as the most deeply hated American president in history. *Harper's Weekly* called him a "filthy storyteller, despot, liar, thief, braggart, buffoon, usurper, monster, ignoramus Abe, old scoundrel, perjurer, swindler, tyrant, field-butcher, land-pirate." Even his hometown newspaper castigated the new president. The *Illinois State Register* in Springfield called Lincoln "the craftiest and most dishonest politician that ever disgraced an office in America." The intense opposition created what must have seemed to be an impossible leadership conundrum: How do you save a Union that apparently doesn't want to be saved? How do you withstand a continuous flow of criticism?

Consider these three strategies from the lives of Lincoln and other leaders:

1. *Settle on your deepest convictions about your mission.* Lincoln's goal was to save the Union. No matter how harsh the criticisms, on this issue he refused to be swayed. That goal was nonnegotiable. Criticisms of strategy and personnel were welcome, but not criticism of this central commitment.

Bill Waugh, owner of a restaurant chain, was asked to become chairman of the Salvation Army. He chose as his theme "Keep the main thing the main thing." By that he meant, "Keep the purpose of the organization clearly in mind and do not get diverted from it."

A leader must seek the depths of conviction so that when the fierce storms come, priorities and stance are clear. One way to filter criticism is to reject any that distracts from the organization's main purpose.

Billy Graham frequently would hear out a critic, then explain his calling and his determination to fulfill that mission, inviting the critic to help with what he was compelled to do.

2. *Ignore most of it.* Lincoln often chose to ignore criticism. Knowing the almost irresistible temptation to dwell on negative comments, he chose to limit his intake. "As a general rule," he said, "I abstain from reading the reports of attacks upon myself, wishing not to be provoked by that to which I cannot properly offer an answer."

We can overcredit criticism, and we can turn a cold into a cancer. Some criticisms sting more than they damage, and every bee sting is not a snake bite.

Fred Smith's homey analogy: "Sometimes if a racehorse pays too much attention to a horsefly, it makes the fly too important. Some people's only taste of success is the bite they take out of someone whom they perceive is doing more than they are. Those of us who have known Billy Graham for many years have admired the way he has not let his critics divert him from the goal."

It's helpful to have a friend or two who can help you sort the criticisms to ignore from the ones to be carefully considered.

3. *Don't respond reactively.* Many times Lincoln would write a heated letter of response to critics, but then he would hold it and just leave it in his desk. For instance, during the 1864 election, a

New York newspaper claimed that while touring the Antietam battlefield in 1862, Lincoln, despite the grisly scene, asked a friend to sing cheerful songs. That was a lie. The story infuriated Lincoln's friends. They spurred the president to compose a refutation, but Lincoln didn't send it. He knew that issuing a heated denial would most likely just fuel the controversy.

> If the end brings me out all right, what is said against me won't amount to anything. If the end brings me out wrong, then ten angels swearing I was right would make no difference.
>
> **ABRAHAM LINCOLN**

Billy frequently took several days before responding to criticisms. He knew the importance of avoiding a knee-jerk reaction. At times he didn't respond at all, especially when they ridiculed him personally or attacked his motives. "People didn't understand his heart," Cliff Barrows told us. "He could never answer those criticisms, for he told me that trying to answer those kinds of charges drained him of his energy. He would not defend any attack that was toward him personally. I think God honored that in a special way."

Instead of being defensive, Lincoln often used humor to diffuse the tension. When one speaker droned on about Lincoln's shortcomings, he responded by observing that "the oratory of the gentleman completely suspends all action of his mind." Lincoln's witty statements underscored his refusal to take criticism too seriously.

Treat Critics Better Than They Deserve

Even if unfair criticisms are made publicly, it's rarely wise to counterattack publicly. The result is usually a spraying match with a skunk. It doesn't produce an atmosphere that makes anyone—friend or foe—want to linger.

"Billy had a practice never to speak disparagingly of another person publicly," said Cliff Barrows. He recalled a situation during the Los Angeles meetings, when a local pastor's members were very involved in the campaign, but the pastor felt the meetings were hindering his church ministry, infringing on the Wednesday night prayer services.

"For eight weeks, this pastor called Billy personally to complain that his work was being hindered, and that Billy didn't care about local churches," recalled Cliff. "Billy told him we were trying to follow the Lord's leading, and that he wanted to encourage his church members, not hinder them. The congregation told the pastor they wanted to promote the meetings and be part of them, but they sensed his hostility.

"On the last weekend Billy called him and said, 'Sir, I want to thank you for the leadership your church has provided in this series of meetings, and you would do me a great honor to sit with me on the platform. I'd like to introduce you and ask you to lead in prayer.' The pastor was overwhelmed."

> There is a kernel of truth in every criticism. Look for it, and when you find it, rejoice in its value.
>
> DAWSON TROTMAN

Later, according to Cliff, the pastor asked Billy to forgive him. "He told Billy that if he ever preached within a hundred miles of his church, he would be there, as would his congregation. They became good friends."

Sometimes the best way to get rid of a critic is to turn him into a friend. Through a grace-filled and humble response, leaders can sometimes do that.

Accept the Gift of a Good Enemy

Every once in a while someone will be honored at an awards gala, and the honoree will thank his friends and then say this: "I also want to thank my enemies."

The audience is jarred. Enemies? What's he saying? Why is he thanking his enemies?

"Without my enemies," the person of high achievement says, "I never would have been challenged to reach the next level, never would have found the determination to excel."

Sometimes we need enemies to press us to new heights, just as a football team needs a challenging opponent to drive them to extraordinary effort. Billy did not let his critics control his agenda or his emotions. He personified his commitment to the gospel of love.

POINTS TO PONDER

BILLY GRAHAM:

Hot heads and cold hearts never solved anything.

THE BIBLE:

A fool shows his annoyance at once,

but a prudent man overlooks an insult.

PROVERBS 12:16

PART THREE

CREATING MOMENTUM

You have to set the tone and the pace,
define objectives and strategies, demonstrate through
personal example what you expect from others.
STANLEY C. GAULT

Four questions

Billy Graham has always been seen by the public as a positive leader, but is that his natural personality?

As a preacher, did Billy hand over financial matters to trustees and managers so he could concentrate on his mission?

How did he lead and energize his teammates when he was so pressured by being in the spotlight?

As Billy grew in understanding the complexity of issues, how did he set a course, and how did he communicate that to his conservative constituency?

■ ■ ■

We found unexpected answers to these questions, which we explore in these four chapters. Billy turns out to be very human, like the rest of us, but with a powerful intuitive grasp of what's required to lead effectively.

CHAPTER 6

Communicating Optimism and Hope

> Leaders are dealers in hope.
>
> **NAPOLEON**

Longer than anyone else, decade after decade after decade, Billy Graham has been included in *Good Housekeeping*'s most-admired list. Over the years, presidents and other luminaries have appeared, then faded. But Billy has always been at or near the top of the list.

One day Fred Smith, who had chaired one of Billy's Cincinnati crusades, asked us, "Have you thought about the *Good Housekeeping* list?"

"Not particularly."

"Take a close look. Every person on it is *positive*."

When thinking about those who have appeared on the list, images come quickly to mind. Dwight Eisenhower's big, broad smile. John F. Kennedy's vigor and crinkly-eyed humor. Billy Graham's warm gaze beside his wife, Ruth. Yes, year after year, virtually everyone on the list is positive, including Billy Graham. He may talk about sin and its tragic effects, but we resonate with his positive message of new life and hope.

But here is a remarkable thing we learned. His family nicknamed him Puddleglum.

Puddleglum?

When we first read that fact in a publication from Billy's own organization, we were taken aback and puzzled. Puddleglum is a character in C. S. Lewis's book series, the Chronicles of Narnia. A

93

dour Marsh-wiggle, Puddleglum is a brave but glum creature, always expecting the worst. When he says "good morning" to the children in Narnia, he immediately adds, "Though when I say *good*, I don't mean it won't probably turn to rain, or it might be snow, or fog, or thunder." The Marsh-wiggle always talks about what could go wrong and how many difficulties and reversals might lie ahead.

Billy's family uses the nickname for him with humor and affection, but how could it really fit?

Most of us, sensing a rightness about Billy's being chosen most admired and often being called "the beloved evangelist," would never dream of his being nicknamed Puddleglum. His family and closest friends saw a side the public did not—a dubious, pessimistic tendency that he had to fight constantly.

Yet most of us never dream of the realities leaders live with. "Ebullient" Teddy Roosevelt, trying to keep riding too fast for "dark care" to catch up. Behind Franklin Roosevelt's jaunty grin and optimistic Fireside Chats were heroic but agonizing strains from his polio, his life in a wheelchair, and weighty depression. JFK, for all his youthful vigor and optimism, endured major chronic pain. Lincoln battled significant depression. They all projected a gritty, can-do, optimistic spirit.

One historian concluded, however, after studying world leaders who had accomplished the most, that melancholics were significantly overrepresented. Whatever one's personality, leadership—as explored in chapter 1—is continually forged in the furnace. The heat, the messiness, the human tragedies all weigh against and counter the optimism and hope that must be communicated. Those American presidents on the most-admired list carried the weight of world leadership while enduring harsh criticism and disastrous reversals—yet like all effective leaders, they inspired others. Despite the worst, the leader must personify hope for the best.

Long before Dwight Eisenhower became president, Billy forged early ties with him—the start of a long and fruitful friendship. Both men projected the positive, and Ike did so as a specific leadership strategy. It was at a time early in World War II, when the likelihood of victory was slim, that he embraced it. If he had not conceptualized the principle at that time and then internalized it, his leading the Allies during the crucial years of the war in Europe may have floundered.

Eisenhower was in the dank tunnels under Gibraltar when he came to view communicating optimism as a requirement of leadership. Deeply discouraged by military reversals, his depressing quarters, and the power of the enemy, he realized he couldn't allow the troops to be further demoralized by his mood. The Rock was a personal crucible, but his men needed a powerful antidote to their own discouragements. As a student of leadership, he believed it could be developed by "studious reflection and practices." As he thought through his situation, he concluded he had to share enthusiasm—first, so he himself would not be demoralized; second, to inspire others.

"With this clear realization," he wrote in his diary, "I firmly determined that my mannerisms and speech in public would always reflect the cheerful certainty of victory—that any pessimism and discouragement I might ever feel would be reserved for my pillow. I adopted a policy of circulating through the whole force.... I did my best to meet everyone from general to private with a smile, a pat on the back, and a definite interest in his problems."

Eisenhower saw it not as hypocrisy but as calling forth his own best impulses and vision, then personifying them for his troops. His famous grin from the European war theater was a trademark throughout the conflict and his presidency. He never let exhaustion or discouragement extinguish it.

Stephen Ambrose writes in his book, *Eisenhower*:

> In public, Eisenhower had a remarkable ability to shed his weariness, self-pity, and pessimism. He held weekly press conferences and was consistently cheerful in his assessment of the situation. As he explained to Mamie, when "pressure mounts and strain increases, everyone begins to show the weaknesses in his makeup. It is up to the Commander to conceal his; above all to conceal doubt, fear and distrust." How well he was able to do so

was indicated by a member of his staff who wrote at this time, "[Eisenhower] was a living dynamo of energy, good humor, amazing memory for details, and amazing courage for the future."

Like Eisenhower, Billy Graham has had plenty to discourage and exhaust him. Yet his colleagues are full of stories about Billy that mirror Ambrose's description of Ike's shedding weariness and pessimism when up at the plate. Billy has always been known for communicating hope.

James Loehr, who coaches athletes and corporate executives, has struggled with the paradox of leaders feeling emotionally down but needing to personify optimism. For years he resisted using the word "acting" because it seemed to suggest something phony done on a stage. But once he understood how our thoughts physically control our emotions, and that our chosen "script" determines our feelings and bodily responses, the concept of acting no longer seemed phony. In his book *Stress for Success*, Loehr writes, "Each of us spends as much as 90 percent of our days modifying, filtering, and adjusting our emotions and behavior to fit the most appropriate scripts for particular moments—in other words, we are acting."

In one sense, everyone is "acting" all the time. Each day we choose the "script" we communicate to our bodies, and our bodies respond. Says Dr. Loehr, "The ON switch for an emotion can be fully activated regardless of whether it fits reality as judged by the rational brain. . . . Once the targeted neurons in the amygdala are turned on, the corresponding physiology rolls out."

So, do we just let our emotions rule us? Or do we choose what we believe, how we want to feel and act, and what "script" we want to personify and communicate? By those choices, we can significantly alter our resulting emotions.

New brain research shows how mental training can literally help to wire and rewire neurological circuits. Whether we are by nature melancholic, choleric, or sanguine, the more we write and implement our own scripts, the more we become what we purpose to be.

Ronald Reagan, as an actor, understood this. He had deep convictions but was as subject to emotional fluctuations as anyone else. How could he consistently communicate his passionate beliefs? He knew that a smile could change his body chemistry. His personifying his hopeful vision was not just a matter of words but of embracing it personally—whatever his feelings at the moment—then communicating it.

The extreme example of this was when he was shot, just seventy days after his inauguration. At the hospital entrance, despite the bullet lodged near his heart, he waved off Secret Service agents and slowly climbed out of the car. He stood and buttoned his jacket, then walked in. Only after getting inside, after collapsing on one knee, did he allow agents to help. And during the medical procedures, he famously quipped one-liners: "Honey, I forgot to duck," and to the surgeon about to operate, "I hope you're a Republican."

James M. Strock writes of Reagan, "One looks in vain for photographs that show him without full control over his physical presence.... The head erect and the shoulders thrown back; the purposeful stride; the jaunty wave; the empathetic listening to another's need; the respectful, confident, vigorous military salute.... The nod and the wink and the wave—these all became part of Reagan's ongoing communication with the American people."

Is all of this genuine? Of course. The optimistic, thoughtful leader is well aware of the brutal realities, the questions, the what-ifs. The leader may feel jangled nerves or malaise but *chooses* the way of faith and hope, knowing he must communicate that to others.

Billy Graham endured attacks, rough-and-tumble opposition, lots of reversals, as seen elsewhere in this book. Did this make him despondent?

At times, yes, but Billy's associates also speak of his "undiluted enthusiasm" and his "constant air of expectancy." He has always been eager to learn and to move on to the next challenge. At the same time, Billy carried his heavy responsibilities with extreme seriousness.

His colleague John Akers admits, "Yes, he could be pessimistic; probably it's simply his nature." He explained it like this: "A way to look at this is that he has a wife who is exactly the opposite. A mirror image. The other day she was slumped in her chair, her speech slurred because of pain medication. 'How you doing, Ruth?' Her response: 'I'm doing fine.' The family jokes that remark will be on her tombstone—'I'm doing fine.' But if you ask Billy in private the same question, you'd get an extensive answer."

"We've heard," we interjected, "that Ruth described Lewis's 'Puddleglum,' and therefore Billy, as having 'the boundless capacity for seeing the grim side of every situation.' She tells the story of how Billy cautioned her with an endless number of problems she might face on her flight from Miami through Atlanta to Asheville."

John nodded, with a smile. "It's just that his natural mindset is, *What could go wrong?* Remember, he was a kid of the Depression. His father, a farmer, worried like that, and his sister tells me Billy's always been that way."

We've long been intrigued by this paradox. Can a natural pessimist be ultimately an optimist, even though it strains his nature? Genetics, nature, and culture shape our personalities—we are who we are. But must the leader transcend this? And if melancholics are more highly represented in great leadership, does that mean natural optimists must also make adjustments?

One thing is clear. Billy Graham has plenty of reasons to see life's downsides. As a perceptive human being, he feels his vulnerable position in the public eye, and he can foresee possible backlashes from his decisions and actions. The pressures on him affect him physically. But he has determined to live by his convictions and the gospel of hope, and to communicate that confidence to others.

■ ■ ■

Perhaps the greatest personification of this paradox is Mother Teresa of Calcutta.

When we think of Mother Teresa, we remember pictures of her radiating purpose. From her devotional life flowed a peace and happiness and a sparkle in her eye.

All of that, and more, was true. But this was not because she simply plugged into joy each morning in her personal time with God, then moved through the day with a steady euphoria. In fact, it was quite the opposite.

Professor Carol Zaleski, with deep appreciation of Mother Teresa, writes in *First Things*, "The missionary foundress who called herself 'God's pencil' was not the God-intoxicated saint many of us had assumed her to be."

She explains: "Throughout 1946 and 1947, Mother Teresa experienced a profound union with Christ. But soon after she left the convent and began her work among the destitute and dying on the street, the visions and locutions ceased, and she experienced a spiritual darkness that would remain with her until her death."

"My smile is a great cloak that hides a multitude of pains," wrote Mother Teresa in 1985. At times she felt "that God does not want me." Because she was "forever smiling," people assumed "my faith, my hope and my love are overflowing. . . . If only they knew."

Zaleski muses, "It is hard to know what is more to be marveled at: that this twentieth-century commander of a worldwide apostolate and army of charity should have been a visionary contemplative at heart; or that she should have persisted in radiating invincible faith and love while suffering inwardly from the loss of spiritual consolation."

Most of us are surprised that Mother Teresa, this great soul whom all India and all the world mourned at her death, struggled with feelings of doubt, loneliness, and spiritual abandonment. Yet despite that, she chose to personify and communicate the way of faith, love, and hope, whatever her feelings.

Zaleski continues, "Faith must supply what is lacking to our feeble senses." Humanly Mother Teresa sometimes felt burnt out, but faith supplied what was lacking to troubled faith; spiritually she was often desolate, but her vow endured and her visible radiance—to which so many attested—was undiminished.

"'Keep smiling,' Mother Teresa used to tell her community and guests, and somehow, coming from her, it doesn't seem trite.

For when she kept smiling during her night of faith, it was not a cover-up but a manifestation of her loving resolve to be 'an apostle of joy.'"

In the same way, Billy Graham has been an "apostle of love," even when his natural feelings may have tempted him to give in to anger or despair. Colleagues who have traveled with him when he lay slumped with exhaustion and discouragement have been amazed at the way he could come alive with full vigor to meet the challenge of a press event or a meeting with dignitaries or connecting with his staff. People see in Billy—even when he may be weary and discouraged—that warm, gracious, and upbeat spirit that lifts their own hearts.

This is not to say it's all "grit your teeth" and override your emotions. The fruit of the Spirit includes love, joy, and peace, but the Bible also describes the Spirit as the *Ruach*, the Hebrew term for the unpredictable wild wind. The Spirit brings ecstasy and exuberance at times but ultimately works through the will. Billy Graham continually concentrated his will into the service of the gospel.

Staff member Rick Marshall recalls the spring of 1991 in Edinburgh, Scotland. Billy had been visiting with dignitaries, and Marshall came to escort him to preach. He found him completely exhausted.

"Dr. Graham, it is time to take the stage," Marshall said.

"I can't do it. I'm so tired."

Marshall looked for a smile, thinking he was kidding. He wasn't—he was physically spent.

The young associate sat down beside him and they prayed together. Marshall, who as crusade director was in charge of the meetings, felt desperate. *This mission is finished before it begins*, he thought.

Somehow, Billy got to his feet and slowly made his way to the stage. Yet when he took the pulpit, Marshall recalls, "I could not believe the strength of the man's voice and the ability God gave him that evening."

Much of that amazing resiliency is due to his choice of scripts and his determination to lead with optimism and hope.

LEADERSHIP LESSONS | **Optimism**

Applying the Principles

Military historian John Keegan, in his book *The First World War*, comments about the war's most horrific battle: "The Somme (together with the battle of Ypres in July 1917, where 70,000 British were killed and 170,000 wounded) marked the end of an age of vital optimism in British life that has never been recovered."

Gordon MacDonald, who pointed us to this quote, reflected, "I found myself thinking about a society that had, for more than a hundred years, enjoyed a wild run of vital optimism and then, overnight, according to Keegan, lost it. And worse: never recovered it. Think about it! One terrible battle with catastrophic losses and the cultural momentum (centuries in the making) of a great nation is arrested, dissipated."

Optimism is not living in a fantasy world where nothing tragic ever happens; vital optimism is a confidence that tragedy is not the last word, that the best is yet to be. Optimism is being able to acknowledge brutal realities and to point to an even greater reality—that our experiences are not in vain, our responses are not futile, and our efforts are going to be worthwhile.

Christian leaders like Billy Graham most often link this optimism and hope to an abiding trust that history is going somewhere and that God, who specializes in redeeming flawed situations, is powerfully directing it. But hope is also basic psychology and biology.

Most of us have heard all our lives about positive attitudes and how they lead to success. Books, conferences, and videos all emphasize optimism. It's easy to shrug it all off, but the leader who aspires to high effectiveness incorporates the positive. Sometimes bringing hope to a dispirited group is the most important thing a leader can do.

In studies of the brain, much has been learned recently about how and why negative thinking drains us, but the positive energizes and raises our capacities. The old adages have turned out to be based on chemistry and physiology as well as faith.

Respond with the Math of Hope

In Mother Teresa's India, the hopeless and the dying are like an endless sea of despair. Someone asked her how, considering this enormity, she could continue day after day, year after year with her ministry to the dying. How could she not be overwhelmed when her efforts were contrasted with the needs? She could do only a little.

She responded that looking at it that way applied the wrong math. She used *subtraction*. Every time she loved and cared for a destitute and dying man, every time she rescued a girl from prostitution, she was subtracting from the despair and adding to hope.

Author and scientist Loren Eiseley in his book *The Star Thrower* describes someone who in this regard thought like Mother Teresa. On a beach in Costabel, Eiseley saw great numbers of empty shells, "the debris of life." He watched gulls cut a hermit crab to pieces and wrote, "Death walks hugely and in many forms."

One dawn, he surveyed what the night's ocean had deposited. "Long-limbed starfish were strewn everywhere." Eiseley knew the tiny breathing pores of the starfish were stuffed with sand, and the rising sun would shrivel their bodies.

Rounding a bluff, he discerned the star thrower. It was a man who stooped to pick up a starfish, then loft it far out to sea. Eiseley approached him. "It may live," the man said of the starfish, "if the off-shore pull is strong enough."

The man stooped again and threw another starfish back to its natural habitat. "The stars," he said, "throw well. One can help them."

Eiseley saw in the man's skimming the starfish out into the water "the posture of a god." Yet he also wrote, "The star thrower is a man, and death is running more fleet than he along every sea beach in the world."

Despite that fact, the star thrower kept at his task. "One can help them," he reasoned.

Does death win it all? Is life meaningless? Or is there hope? Each of us must choose the math of subtraction—of reducing despair—or the math of being overwhelmed and sinking into cynicism.

■ ■ ■

A leader's task, we're told by businessman Max DePree, is to define reality. That requires more than projecting short- or long-term goals or declaring a multiyear focus. To cast a positive vision, a leader must wrestle with enough of life's enigmas to not get blindsided by the unforeseen. To define reality and lead effectively, one must discover a reality resonant with hope.

Said Martin Luther, "Everything that is done in the world is done by hope." The truth Luther expressed is timeless. His namesake, Martin Luther King Jr.—though separated by centuries—applied it to modern times: "We must accept finite disappointment, but never lose infinite hope."

Stay on the Horse

As a college president, Jay Kesler found that if he went public with discouragement, the whole campus could be affected. Just saying he felt "down" one day could cause groups to buzz with the news, "Jay's discouraged. We're in trouble."

Jay learned he had to stay "up," or at least limit voicing his discouragements to those capable of hearing them and helping. "The larger group needs leadership," Jay says. "It's not deception or subterfuge to be optimistic, to be excited, to encourage others to believe in God. It's just one of the elements needed in a leader."

Jay uses the illustration of the film "El Cid." Charlton Heston, in the title role, was leading the Spanish army in a series of battles against the invading Moors. Just before the climactic confrontation, he was mortally wounded. His presence on the battlefield, however, was so important to the morale of his army that his officers fastened him in his

> Hope is the power of being cheerful in circumstances which we know to be desperate.
>
> G. K. CHESTERTON

saddle and propped him upright so he could lead his troops into the fray. Seeing their leader before them, the Spanish soldiers took heart and fought on to victory.

If El Cid had not been there, or if he had slumped in the saddle, his army might have lost heart and gone down to defeat.

"That's the way it is with much of life," Jay said to us. "There are so many battles won or lost depending on whether the people involved hang on just a little bit longer. So the leader has a primary obligation not to declare doubts or failures at the drop of a hat."

Fred Smith agrees. "Leadership means plugging away until the breakthrough comes." He also makes this pungent observation: "The energy needed to retreat might have been just the amount needed to succeed."

Never Underestimate the Power of the Positive

U.S. Secretary of State Colin Powell once said, "Leadership is the art of accomplishing more than the science of management says is possible." Jesus said that all things were possible if we would believe.

In a period of distress, a leader's outward display of courage and confidence is vital. The lack of it can cause a group's resolve to melt.

"Confidence and optimism are essential," writes Michael Useem in *Fast Company*. "It's not faking it. It's remaining optimistic through the most trying times, even when it looks pretty dark. Think about Nelson Mandela. Twenty-seven years of prison. I have to imagine he got a little discouraged, but from all accounts, he never wavered in his confidence that one day South Africa would be a multiracial democracy. I am sure a few African National Congress people in prison with him said, 'Nelson, you're full of it. This is ridiculous. Your optimism is misplaced here.'

"And in his deepest inner moments, I am sure Mandela had doubts. But outwardly, it's critical to have that sense of optimism. As long as you believe it's true and communicate that back to the people you lead, you overcome any inauthenticity."

In contrast, an absence of hope permeates today's affluent societies. Billy Graham has expressed strong concerns about this, going beyond simply wringing his hands. He has spoken out with a call to embrace hope, quoting noted physicians who prescribe hope as curative, based on clinical studies. "Hope is both biologically and psychologically vital," Billy stated. "Men and women must have hope."

Leaders understand this. If doctors see hope as dramatically effective medicine, leaders need to also wisely and liberally dispense it to those who look to them to "define reality."

All this comes down to day-by-day leaders, when we touch others who catch our spirit. Says Amway founder Richard M. DeVos, "Few things in the world are more powerful than a positive push. A smile, a word of optimism, and hope."

Brood Not; Confront Catastrophe

Crises in some form come to every leader. Those caused by evil intent can create anger and thirst for revenge. But responding in kind chills a leader's ability to deal with the new realities.

David Sarnoff, former head of RCA, advised, "Let us not paralyze our capacity for good by brooding over man's capacity for evil."

In 2001, after the tragic events of 9/11, many felt paralysis as on television they saw over and over the results of "man's capacity for evil." Billy Graham was called on to bring hope and meaning to his stunned fellow citizens.

What could he say? He knew his message in the National Cathedral just three days after the devastation would be viewed by millions around the globe.

Billy spoke with a mature empathy born from experience. He not only felt the shock and dismay himself but put himself in the place of his listeners. He assured them God understood their feelings about the terrible carnage. He spoke of tragedy and evil and suffering, but that God is a God of love, mercy, and compassion. "Who can understand it?" he asked, honestly.

Then he communicated hope. "I've become an old man now," he said, "and the older I get, the more I cling to that hope that I started with many years ago." Billy spoke of Ambassador Andrew Young, who, after the tragic death of his wife, quoted from the old hymn "How Firm a Foundation": "We all watched in horror as planes crashed into the steel and glass of the World Trade Center. Those majestic towers, built on solid foundations, were examples of the prosperity and creativity of America. When damaged, those buildings eventually plummeted to the ground, imploding upon themselves. Yet underneath the debris is a foundation that was not destroyed. Therein lies the truth of that old hymn that Andrew Young quoted: 'How *firm* a foundation.'

"Yes, our nation has been attacked. Buildings destroyed. Lives lost. But now we have a choice: whether to implode and disintegrate emotionally and spiritually as a people, and a nation, or, whether we choose to become stronger."

Billy identified with those who long for leadership in the maelstrom. He gave them both specific responses to the obvious questions and a basis for hope. Among his concluding words were these: "My prayer today is that we will feel the loving arms of God wrapped around us."

Never flinch, never worry, never despair.

WINSTON CHURCHILL

We may not be called on to speak to large audiences in crisis, but the small audiences we do have—maybe just one person— need to hear in context the positive messages so necessary. As Billy has said, "Men and women must have hope."

POINTS TO PONDER

BILLY GRAHAM:

I've read the last page of the Bible. It's all going to turn out all right.

THE BIBLE:

Surely goodness and love will follow me all the days of my life,

and I will dwell in the house of the LORD forever.

PSALM 23:6

CHAPTER 7

Mobilizing Money

> If a person gets his attitude toward money
> straight, it will help straighten out almost
> any other area of his life.
> **BILLY GRAHAM**

Said his younger brother Melvin, of Billy Graham, "I've never seen a man in my life that cares as little about money as Billy Frank does."

True? Yes, in that Billy has given away millions of dollars of royalties and said no to countless offers to enrich himself. Yet in many ways, he also cares a lot about money. He recognizes that leaders can fall hard over it, that it can seduce or blind or entrap. On the other hand, he knows money has remarkable power to accomplish great ends.

If asked about Billy Graham and money, most of us would assume his high-capacity business advisers handle all that for him, and, to a large degree, that's the case. Yet as CEO, and as the man who has to answer questions from the press, and from his own conscience, he knows he carries the ultimate responsibility.

Graeme Keith, BGEA treasurer and Billy's longtime financial counselor, says Billy was the first to admit business was not his strong suit. Yet as chairman of the audit committee, Graeme understood his concern for the very highest financial accountability. "We all felt his charge," he said, "and it made you want to work for him. After Billy gives you a responsibility, you feel that sense of trust he has in you. Integrity is critical. He sets the expectations."

What were his financial expectations? "Billy is a realist," Graeme told us. "He has seen the economy go both ways. He has a great gut feel for the future. He wasn't led by in-depth business analyses but always had a vision of what God wanted him to do— and he knew how to convey his vision to his board and employees."

We had heard from others that if anything, Billy was often more conservative on money than his trustees. Graeme affirmed that, quoting Billy as saying, "Whatever God provides, we will live within the budget."

Long ago, when Graeme and others were planning a Charlotte campaign, they wanted to use Panther Stadium. Billy, however, was more cautious and wanted a smaller venue. "Billy didn't think that many people would want to come. Expenses would be very large because of the special construction needed. The budget would be $3.1 million." Graeme then said that Billy had gone along with the Panther Stadium plan, and then he was able to conclude his story with a smile, "We raised $4.1 million and sent one million after the crusade to the BGEA."

The picture from our research was clear: Billy listened intently to his advisers. In fact, someone observed, "He listens so loud you can hear him." Yet sometimes he stuck with his own gut; other times he followed his counselors. Invariably, he was determined to sense God's will—and he often judged that by unanimity on his board.

"His last great vision was Amsterdam 2000," Graeme said. "The analysis indicated it would cost $35 million, which was a huge amount. Billy believed we needed to do it to get the message out. He always kept his focus. Top CEOs often get wrapped up in airplanes and other toys, but not Billy."

Here we sense the complexity of his determination not to waste money, yet his equal determination to use even large sums to further the vision. His focus on the vision clarified his allocation of funds and kept him from distractions.

We asked Graeme about Billy's approach to personal finances.

"His idea was to give his resources away. He told me, 'I'd like to die with nothing.'"

Graeme's descriptions of Billy's attitude toward his own finances echoed the observation from his brother.

■ ■ ■

Mel Graham began our interview with him by telling about his and Billy's ancestors who fought in the Civil War. "When they came back, they farmed—nothing but poor red soil here, depleted by cotton. The South was considered very poor; in the thirties this was a terribly depressed area. But my daddy, he took over his father's farm, and he paid it all off."

Mel obviously had learned a lot from his father, operating the dairy farm until he was forty, then finding additional success in related ventures.

"Was running the dairy farm a tough business?"

"It was tough! Seven days a week; Sunday almost like Monday. Something every hour, it seems—like a cow trying to calve. We milked a hundred head by hand twice a day—no machinery—three of us. Billy had to do it too."

Mel said Billy didn't like the milking, but he was eager to work as a Fuller Brush salesman. "The first week Billy Frank set an all-time record as a rookie in the whole company—working in one of the poorest places in America. By the end of the summer he was one of the best they'd ever had."

"Was Billy cautious about money?"

"He would never borrow a dime."

"So he had to scramble from the very beginning?"

"He moved furniture. He did everything."

We talked to Mel about Billy's caution in spending organizational money. Melvin described how Billy would cut some projects "way down. He's just conscious of God's money." Melvin told us a complicated story about Billy's extreme generosity to another ministry in settling a financial matter.

"Why did he insist on being so generous?" we asked.

"Just the way he is. Doesn't care a thing about money. When we divided up our dairy farm years ago, Billy said, 'Give me whatever you want, it doesn't matter to me.' That was his attitude."

We'd heard Billy was uncomfortable being seen in fancy cars. Melvin told us stories of his refusing gift cars and about his simple tastes. "Unless he was with somebody like President Kennedy, he wouldn't even want to use a limousine. Today, over at the hotel, I said, 'Billy Frank, let me take you to the nice restaurant here.' He said, 'No, drop me over to McDonald's.' He got that from our momma and daddy."

We could see in many ways how the legacy imprinted on Billy in his youth stamped his approach to finances. His not wanting to in any way misuse "God's money." His working very hard to secure adequate resources to fulfill his ever-expanding vision. His intuitive grasp as to how ordinary people would react to symbols of wealth.

Billy had reached young adulthood as a farm boy during the Depression, a sure formula for a man's taking money very seriously. During the Depression, Billy learned that to survive, you had to generate cash flows, starting with his selling brushes and moving furniture. We asked Bill Pollard, chairman of Graham's executive committee and former CEO of ServiceMaster, if Graham was concerned about money.

"He sure was. He's concerned that the size of the organization can be supported by the revenue—a fundamental principle he's always held."

"How did he make that happen?"

"When it comes to touching the hearts and minds of people, Billy Graham has a special skill and genius of being able to speak to the individual, regardless of the size of the audience. In business, we would call him a marketing genius. Graham would have been successful running a business or any other venture. He may not have gone to a business school and thought about channels of distribution, but the economic model of the community carrying local costs and the BGEA carrying onsite team costs; his vision to expand the gospel in radio, films, TV, and now videos; the content of the direct mail letters—it's all part of his genius, a gift from God."

Pollard's mention of the donor letters brought to mind a phone conversation with Billy many years before. He had told us he thought his greatest contribution to the organization was writing his regular letters to his supporters. We were a bit jarred by that statement. Billy Graham's greatest contribution writing fundraising letters? Yet Billy's observation fit. He understood that resourcing the organization was vital. The letters were pure Billy Graham in tone and substance. He carefully shaped each one, pouring out his heart to his thousands of supporters who, for the most part, were like Mel's and Billy's neighbors in Charlotte.

When we asked Bob Cooley, longtime president of Gordon-Conwell Seminary, to describe Billy as a leader, his first point was that Billy saw the gospel as supra-cultural. "The second thing," Bob said, "was not only did he understand the gospel as a unifier, but he also understood the interface between mission and economic vitality. That was critical to his leadership."

Most ministers—or writers or scholars or musicians—become so absorbed in their craft and mission, they don't think much about the necessary fiscal structure. Those few who do, geometrically expand their influence.

For instance, we have all read of Thomas Edison's intent absorption in his more than one thousand attempts to invent the light bulb and his creating hundreds of other inventions. Yet Edison's mind also was on business and money. Before applying for patents, he would plan each invention's business application. He thought big—so big, he conceptualized the entire electrical industry, from the simple light bulb to the municipal grids necessary to bring electricity to every home. He insisted on both craft and business.

"Billy understood that his mission wouldn't succeed without economic vitality," Cooley explained. As the seminary's president, Bob had served under Billy, who was chair of the trustees. "If you look at his leadership in many organizations, Billy led with his strengths, but he also made sure businessmen were in place and carrying fiscal responsibility."

We asked Bill Pollard how, in setting the financial tone for his own organization, Graham worked with his trustees. Pollard described mutual give-and-take, accountability on Graham's part, yet great respect by trustees for his leadership.

We thought about how over the years this must have included tension points, then remembered a story John Corts, former BGEA president, had told us. At the Boston campaign in 1950, Billy wanted a television in his room, but it cost three dollars a day, a significant amount then. The executive committee said it would not pay that expense. Billy, knowing he had to keep up with what was happening in the news and in the world, paid for it out of his own pocket.

That was then. What about after decades of success?

Although our interviews made clear Billy was the driving force in generating the revenues, he consistently accepted the board's role in making financial decisions. Many CEOs in that position—enjoying friendships with presidents and top media coverage—would have leveraged their power for personal privileges. But Billy did not do that. With these high-capacity, soul-mate trustees, he welcomed genuine partnership and proper board dynamics. This allowed them to woodshed difficult issues and to ensure both accountability and effectiveness.

Said George Bennett, who as Harvard's treasurer as well as treasurer of the Graham organization would have an informed perspective, "I've never known an organization that has better financial management than the BGEA. How that happened, I don't really know, except that Billy had an outstanding ability to pick people. He picked the right people. They had outstanding financial control."

Billy's vision for accountability was not for his own organization alone. In 1979 in the wake of financial scandals among some nonprofit organizations, his business manager, George Wilson, took the lead in founding the Evangelical Council for Financial Accountability (ECFA), with Billy's blessing. The BGEA drew key organizations together to address the need, and today, earning the ECFA's seal of approval has become essential for Christian organizations to demonstrate their financial integrity. The ECFA reassures donors by holding Christian organizations to many of the same standards of accountability implemented by Billy with the BGEA, including financial transparency, board governance, and fund-raising honesty.

■ ■ ■

Sterling Huston, who serves as director of North American ministries for the BGEA, had his first experience with Billy Graham and money in 1956 before he joined the Graham team. "I was visiting Jack Wyrtzen's camp (Word of Life Camp, Schroon Lake, New York) on July 4. Billy preached, and Jack took up an offering for Billy and his ministry. After it was collected, however, Billy got up and said to the audience, 'With your permission, I want to give this to Jack for his dining room.' A fire had just damaged that part of Jack's main camp facility. Billy's magnanimity in giving the money to Jack left a deep impression on me. The generosity of spirit was typical of Billy. Because of his love and care for people, he's generous almost to a fault. And there was always transparent integrity about money."

"And was Billy sensitive to appearances?"

Sterling affirmed that he was. "His strong concern was the ministry not be hurt by giving the wrong appearance about money. For instance, many years ago some of his board members offered to buy him a plane and pay for all expenses so he wouldn't have to fly on commercial flights with all the hassle. 'Billy,' they said, 'you don't have to worry about all this. This won't have to come out of the budget; we'll take care of it.' He later called the chairman of the executive committee, however, and said, 'I can't do it. I haven't slept all night. I know it's paid for, but people just won't understand.'

"It wasn't that it was improper," Sterling explained. "The apostle Paul said, 'All things are lawful,' but not all things speed the gospel along. Billy's sense of that truth was more important to him than his own comfort."

"In this instance was Billy right?"

"I believe he was. When you look at 1987, for example, when some televangelists were in the headlines, it was very helpful to be able to say to the inquiring press that Billy didn't have a private plane, that he was driving an eleven-year-old car, that his home on the side of a mountain was a glorified log cabin, and that he gave away royalties to his books. That added greatly to his financial credibility."

We asked Sterling about Billy's financial risk-taking.

"He attempted bold things, like the Amsterdam conferences, but he was always determined never to run into debt. He's managed the ministry with conservative principles ever since it started in a little basement office. If we were running behind in donations, he would cut expenses."

"Sterling," we asked, "it's said a leader can't lead unless he cares about money, about resourcing the vision. How do you see Billy's role here?"

"He strongly felt his responsibility. When you're head of a large organization with many employees, you have that on your mind all the time. He was aware of the income flow and the need to pay the bills. In board meetings he would turn to George Bennett and say, 'George, talk to us about the economy.' When we were setting the budget, he would call George, listening, seeking wisdom. If he thought the economy was in a downturn, he would say, 'We're going to cut back.' And he would take the initiative, even at the last minute saying, 'We're going to cut everything by 10 percent.' Yet other times when he knew we had enough revenue, he would increase the budget. He was in touch with reality."

■ ■ ■

Perhaps Sterling's succinct "he was in touch with reality" provides the most astute summation of Billy's approach to money. Coming of age in the Great Depression showed him the consequences of inadequate resourcing. Tragic examples of leaders who used money selfishly made him viscerally opposed to feathering his own nest. Although he had many wealthy friends, he was acutely aware of the Bible's warnings about the love of money, and he was determined not to become personally entrapped. His own skills with money were unexceptional, but he saw money as a vital, God-given asset to be wisely employed. And, he knew that even with the best of intentions, financial sloppiness could spell disaster.

Billy had always been concerned that he do nothing to cause the media to attack his financial integrity. Despite his efforts, an attack came anyway. In 1977, headlines all over the country declared that Billy had a "slush fund" of about $20 million in a Dallas account, with the implication that here was another evangelist enriching himself and his cronies.

Two investigative reporters at the *Charlotte Observer*, who in 1976 pored over the BGEA's financial records and declared the operation clean, had felt misled when they later learned of that account, which was called the World Evangelism and Christian Education Fund (WECEF). "Breaking" the story, they accused the BGEA of misleading its donors by not disclosing the fund's existence.

Actually, the BGEA had disclosed the fund during a news conference in 1970 and also had filed a publicly accessible IRS report. The BGEA planned to use the money to train evangelists at what later became the Billy Graham Center in Wheaton, Illinois, to build a layman's training center in Asheville—what is now the Cove—and to assist student-focused ministries like Campus Crusade for Christ and the Fellowship of Christian Athletes. Billy even discussed the fund in 1972 with a reporter from the Akron *Beacon Journal*, which is owned by the same parent company as the *Observer*.

Still, the fund's relatively low profile jarred reporters accustomed to Billy's complete financial disclosure. Why didn't Billy offer information about the WECEF when talking with the *Observer* reporters one year earlier?

"We didn't mention the fund because it was a separate corporation," Billy later explained. "And they didn't ask about it. That was a little bit on the fence line, I think. We should have said, 'We have another fund down in Texas that we are going to do thus and such with.' We told the government about it, but we didn't think the newspapers necessarily had a legitimate right to know about everything. I've changed my mind on that. I think they do. We should be publicly accountable for everything."

Yet Billy's graciousness wasn't shared by all his family and friends. Some were incensed at how the story had been blown far out of proportion and were frustrated that the huge slush fund newspaper headlines were corrected later by small paragraphs buried in the back of the paper.

Billy, however, even had positive things to say about the *Observer* reporters afterward. "Bob Hodierne and Mary Bishop taught us some good lessons. We have learned some things from them."

Sterling, in describing the incident to us, said, "He was really forgiving. You know Billy's spirit—he was gracious simply because he felt that was what God wanted him to be."

"Even though it was unfair?"

"Yes, Billy looks at difficult events as things God permits for some reason and asks, 'Is there a lesson to be learned? If so,' says Billy, 'I'm teachable.'"

Unlike some leaders who bristle at financial inquiries and think of investigative reporters as enemies, Billy's attitude was to listen and learn, always preparing for storms to come. That meant not only full financial disclosure but maintaining integrity in many areas.

John Corts tells of traveling with Allan Emery to see Billy about an issue that was troubling them. Plans had been made that they felt uncomfortable with, sensing that in some ways they lacked integrity. When they laid this before Billy, explaining their concerns, he immediately agreed with them, saying, "Of course!"

John and Allan knew the BGEA value was to avoid the very appearance of evil. When the press investigated in-depth in 1977, they found both a clean house and a forgiving spirit.

LEADERSHIP LESSONS | **Money**

Applying the Principles

Great volumes of advice about money come at us via print, electronic media, educational offerings—and counselors eager to advise us. The subject is vast and complex.

Jesus, it's said, spoke far more about money than about sex, violence, or heaven and hell. The subject is obviously important.

Leaders, especially, must exercise great wisdom about finances, for their decisions have such wide impact on others and on institutions, as well as on their own families. Here we explore some thoughts on how each of us might shape our economic thinking.

Establish Your "Money DNA"

Greed in any organization can devastate it. In contrast, if the bottom line trumps other values, it can also devastate. Some organizations scrimp and cut every possible cost; others spend to build momentum and create new realities.

A person of wisdom and conscience will pay serious attention to the philosophic issues raised; yet not everyone will come to the same conclusions.

Ron Wilson, who spent many years as an entrepreneurial editor and then leader of the Evangelical Press Association, tells of an experience that dramatized the polar-opposite approaches similar organizations have toward money. In the mid-1960s, he visited the offices of Operation Mobilization (OM) in Zaventem, near the Brussels airport. OM had a similar evangelistic mandate as the BGEA, but different methodologies. "They had taken over an old factory building," Ron told us, "and I used to joke that they went fourth class because there wasn't any fifth class." Ron remembered its founder, George Verwer, while he was a student at Moody Bible Institute, coming into its bookstore and pulling out of the trash some evangelistic tracts that had been damaged and discarded. "No doubt," Ron said, "he went into Chicago's streets and passed them out."

> When I have any money, I get rid of it as quickly as possible, lest it find a way into my heart.
>
> **JOHN WESLEY**

From Belgium Ron then went to Paris and stopped in at the Billy Graham office on the Champs-Elysées. "The contrast was startling," Ron said, "from fourth class to first class. I thought of it in terms of the organization, not personalities—and Billy's desire to do things well. Each organization had its style."

Similar missions. Essentially the same theology. Yet dramatically different approaches to money.

Actually, Billy Graham and his team aimed not to go first class but "in the middle." When David Schmidt first went to dinner with the Graham team, he was told, "Now, Dave, Billy taught us that we don't order the best thing on the menu, and we don't order the cheapest thing. We order in the middle." David says, "The rest of my days working with them, I just ordered in the middle. Middle hotel. Middle car. That was a formative financial value they instilled in me."

David talked about the value of a person and the need to eat reasonably well. "At the same time, these were not our dollars, they were given under God's prompting and entrusted to us by donors who trusted Billy. His organization models a sense of stewardship, a strong sense of ethical concern."

Integrity in "the middle way" contrasts with integrity in fifth class. Each of us must wrestle with what's right for our organizations. Are our values ethical in the highest sense? Do they bear the light of scrutiny? Every organization develops a financial DNA created by its leaders.

Refine Your Personal Ethic

The quote by Billy that leads off this chapter is worth pondering: "If a person gets his attitude toward money straight, it will help straighten out almost any other area of his life." Certainly that applies to the leader.

Developing our personal financial ethics requires significant soul-searching and application of our deepest values. And it is a continuing process.

Maxey Jarman, who was one of Billy's advisers and who also led the major conglomerate Genesco, was a wealthy man when he attended Billy's first Lausanne Conference in 1974. He had already given millions to charity but was challenged by Lausanne's statement that we should live "simply." He came back to the U.S. and started driving a small, cheap car—so he could give away more. "The only money I get to keep," he said cheerfully, "is what I give away," referring, of course, to eternal rewards.

Ken Taylor, a friend of Billy's and founder and chairman of Tyndale House Publishers, has also given away many millions; to economize, Ken also drove a small car, a tiny Chevette. Friends continually urged him to drive something bigger and therefore safe. Eventually he did.

> Money has become the grand test of virtue.
>
> GEORGE ORWELL

What do we need for ourselves? Should we all drive small economy cars? If we are among the fortunate, to what degree should we sacrifice? How can we genuinely help the poor?

The answers are far from simple. Billy Graham has given away millions, but he has always wrestled with the fact that he has been given so much and the world's needs are so great.

In a world of consumerism and constantly changing economic vectors, defining a financial ethic is a lifetime task—one that leaders should approach head-on with application of their best logic and commitments.

Match Financial Harnesses That Fit

Once we have developed our personal convictions about money, we need to evaluate our personal skills. Here is where a team approach is critical. Generating funds, administrating them, strategizing their use—all are vital components. Strong, able players must be put into the best-fitting harnesses and given clear mandates.

Recognizing what we *don't* do well and must leave to others is as crucial as recognizing our strengths.

"Billy has always clearly seen he is a poor fund-raiser," one of his colleagues said about him. "He hates to ask people for money if he feels they are friends—hates to impose on their friendship. He doesn't want them to think he's interested in them for their money." It's likely Billy's feelings are not just personal hesitance but his "off-the-charts emotional intelligence" kicking in. His networking and pastoral roles to national leaders and others could easily be jeopardized by coming off like a salesman.

Yet Billy knew it took money to make things happen. Ted Engstrom, who later served as president of Youth for Christ and then World Vision, was chair of his very first citywide meetings in Grand Rapids in 1947. "In 1948 he came to our city to raise funds for me to go and participate in the Youth for Christ World Congress on Evangelism," he told us. "Billy was willing to personally make sure the vision was resourced."

His sensitivity to the danger of coming off like a salesman meant he faithfully wrote those fund-raising letters, not just for the money but to communicate with authenticity. Fred Smith quoted Billy as saying in regard to money, "My daddy was a dairyman, and he knew he had to milk the cows every day or they'd go dry." Fred explained, "He felt that you needed to keep asking for small amounts of money on a regular basis." Bottom line: Billy did what he did best, he built his constituency and made sure trustees and managers were in place to cover all the financial bases.

In contrast to Graham, Bill Bright, who founded and led Campus Crusade for Christ with its budget of $374 million and staff of 26,000, was well known for his ability to ask face-to-face for major contributions. Leaders must assess their own capacities and those of associates and blend the team into complementary roles.

Scout People with Money Clues

Here's a provocative bit of advice from author Robert J. McCracken. "Get to know two things about a man. How he earns his money, and how he spends it. You will then have a clue to his character. You will have a searchlight that shows up the inner recesses of his soul. You know all you need to know about his standards, his motives, his driving desires, his real religion."

Whether you're evaluating a man or a woman, McCracken's advice could reveal vital insights. Thoughtful observance may reveal where that boss or that employee or that applicant's heart really is, what attitudes bleed through, and what will drive him or her in the future. Values may clash and be ultimately disruptive, or they may fit well your leadership style and commitments.

Incorporate Billy's Essentials

Every individual organization faces unique and often complex financial challenges. But the essentials we see in Billy's approach to money are clear, as we review this chapter. Essentials such as: be accountable to qualified others; be transparent; take money seriously. But, perhaps above all, don't love it!

At least that's the Bible's advice, which says, "For the love of money is a root of all kinds of evil."

We are to love God and people, not money.

POINTS TO PONDER

BILLY GRAHAM:

There is nothing wrong with men possessing riches.

The wrong comes when riches possess men.

THE BIBLE:

A good name is more desirable than great riches;

to be esteemed is better than silver or gold.

PROVERBS 22:1

CHAPTER 8

Empowering Soul Mates

> Leadership consists in getting people to work
> with, not for, you — particularly when they are
> under no obligation to do so.
> **FRED SMITH SR.**

Executive Max DePree begins his book *Leadership Jazz* with a very personal illustration. His granddaughter Zoe was born premature at one pound, seven ounces. Because Zoe's father had "jumped ship," a nurse suggested DePree become surrogate father. She told him to come to the hospital every day and "rub her body and her legs and arms with the tip of your finger. While you're caressing her, you should tell her over and over how much you love her, because she has to be able to connect the voice to your touch."

DePree uses the story to say, "At the core of becoming a leader is the need always to connect one's voice and one's touch," emphasizing the "mysterious energy" in the connection.

Then DePree explains his title, *Leadership Jazz*: "Jazz bandleaders must choose the music, find the right musicians, and perform—in public. . . . A jazz band is an expression of servant leadership. The leader of a jazz band has the beautiful opportunity to draw the best out of the other musicians . . . to integrate the 'voices' in the band without diminishing their uniqueness."

A. Larry Ross, who had directed Billy's media and public relations for decades, applies this concept to Billy's management style. "A lot of people define leadership as functioning like a symphony conductor. He mounts the podium, lifts his baton, and the musicians raise their instruments to play. Everybody's ready, and they play in harmony, directed with passion and precision by the conductor.

"But there's a type of leadership that's more like a jazz band-leader, who stands in front of the ensemble tapping his foot to set the rhythm. He points to the piano player to take a few bars; then he points to the saxophonist and he does a riff. Likewise with the drummer and bass player. They're all playing the song, but at different times, different people take the lead doing different things, which enhances but doesn't eclipse the group's overall sound.

"For fifty years the BGEA's mission statement has been to support the worldwide ministry of Billy Graham," Ross explains. "He definitely is the leader, setting the direction and the pace, but at various times certain ministries or emphases come to the forefront. Whether semiannual crusades, periodic telecasts, a weekly *Hour of Decision* radio broadcast, monthly *Decision* magazine, or the release of a World Wide Pictures film—all are part of the band, channeling audiences to the same goal. There's an obvious harmony, but it's not because Mr. Graham is up in front waving his arms around, keeping everybody together. He brought good people to the team and devised the basic strategy and overall direction, but he gives them room to do what they have to do for their particular aspect of the ministry."

The broad freedom Ross says Billy gave to "good people" on the team is widely affirmed by other colleagues. They could "find their own voices." Like DePree's finger and voice communicating love to Zoe, Billy has personally touched his many associates with vitality and his own vulnerability, empowering and inspiring them.

Ross's reference to *Decision* magazine provides a compelling example. Like so many on the extended team, Sherwood Wirt, as its first editor, was indeed a soul mate to Billy, and an illustration of a leader's choosing an appropriate "musician." A pastor, an Edinburgh Ph.D., a journalist, and a free spirit, Sherwood Wirt brought to the magazine far more than the usual competence of a house-organ editor. In *Decision* magazine he published Billy's sermons and ministry news, but he also included articles such as a thoughtful yet accessible series on Russian author Fyodor Dostoyevsky, complete with compelling original art. He knew Billy's vision was to take the magazine to a higher level, and he stretched to do so.

Early in the preparations for this book, we contacted "Woody." In his nineties and still vigorous, he supplied excellent insights and advice and also pointed us to his own book, simply titled *Billy*. It gives detailed insights into how Graham connected with respected teammates, how he cultivated them, worked beside them, inspired and entrusted them.

First, Billy had to recruit Woody. He called him late one night at his parsonage, said he had read his writings, and that he had been talking with others who had connected with him. Billy asked him over the phone to become editor of his "new paper."

Soon Billy had Woody with him in Melbourne, Australia. It was the start of "jazz music" à la DePree and Ross. Here are some of the ways Billy led this particular "musician":

He immersed Woody in the vision, the dream, the action. A few months after Billy's invitation over the phone, the evangelist was experiencing the largest crowds of his career in Australia, and he brought his new editor right into the middle of it. Once, although he wasn't invited, Woody added himself to the team's travel roster for a flight to Tasmania. He felt apprehensive that he'd been too bold and, on boarding the plane, met with Billy, who was surprised at his presence. Still, Billy gave him a squeeze (the value of touch) and said, "Bless your heart," assuring him he was welcome.

He prayed with him. The core reality of Billy's leadership centers in prayer. Billy called Woody to his hotel room to give details of his new position as editor; then they prayed together. The effect on Woody of those few minutes on their knees had its own power: "I rose, feeling greatly refreshed. A final word, a handshake, and I was out the door and on my way to the airport and across the Pacific, bursting with anticipation of what the Lord was about to do."

He gave him detailed instructions. Billy sent Woody copies of British church magazines and wrote a lengthy, well-constructed letter with many specific ideas. He told his editor he "was convinced profound truths could be expressed in simple language," that he "wanted the magazine to be relevant, thought-provoking, timely, spiritual, devotional, yet with a breezy, easy-to-read style." Along with detailed instructions, he ended a letter with both a challenge and warmth. "This is quite a big order; however, I believe it can be done and will meet a real need. I believe the Lord has led you to this important ministry and am thankful for your willingness to obey His voice in this matter. With warmest personal greetings, Billy Graham."

This letter and other communiqués sparked Woody to lift his horizons and give it his all. Billy had freed him to create the new publication but within the parameters of Billy's vision.

In addition, Billy wrote a long purpose statement about the magazine's mission, its audience, its tone, and its content, which appeared in the first issue. He focused personally on the tasks with the greatest impact.

He kept up the drumbeat of communication. Billy continued to write to his new editor with all sorts of ideas about style, length, theological emphasis. "These early issues," he wrote, "will be of strategic importance, as they will be analyzed and studied by religious leaders around the world. I hope you will put the best of everything into it."

The letter made Woody realize the high stakes involved and kept him focused on the quality expected.

After the first issue came out, Billy wrote, "Dear Woody: Just a note to say I have read through your manuscript for the first issue of *Decision*. I think it is terrific!" That simple declaration lifted Woody's spirits and kept him energized for the next issues.

He supported and defended him. On one occasion, Woody had interviewed a prominent person, then sent the edited version to the interviewee—who strongly objected to a deletion! He said the interview must run in its entirety or not at all. Unfortunately, Woody believed the deleted material was not acceptable, yet he faced an immediate deadline. He went ahead and published the edited interview.

When that issue of *Decision* came out, the man was furious. He immediately called Billy to object. In responding to the irate man, Billy didn't put Woody in a bad light. He told the man that he'd always seen his editor act with integrity, then apologized for the incident. In a later discussion with Woody, he reassured him, but he also counseled, "Next time, Woody, don't get caught so close to the deadline. Protect yourself."

Billy sought the balance of praise blended with expectations for learning and growth.

Other colleagues doing different types of work knew the Graham voice and touch as well. Billy would intently focus on new projects, thinking far out ahead and sometimes neglecting continuing projects. Yet whenever he did touch base with his colleagues, he guided and encouraged them. When describing their accomplishments to others, he would praise them highly—another way of ensuring they understood how much he valued them.

Billy's voice communicated optimism, love, and a strong sense of purpose. In modern parlance, he was "high-touch."

■ ■ ■

In contrast to Sherwood Wirt, who worked with Billy from very early days at the heart of his ministry, a much younger David Schmidt says he's had only a handful of face-to-face conversations with Billy. His work as a consultant for the BGEA was often not right in the team center. Yet Billy has had a profound influence on him.

David says it's because of Billy's DNA.

Having worked closely with crusade director Sterling Huston for many years, David says the Graham DNA has permeated Billy's organization, imbuing its leaders with the same values and strengths Billy himself shows. The DNA in Billy's colleagues has added up for David to the kind of leadership guidance and motivation Woody perceived firsthand from his boss.

"Billy trusted those around him," David says, "and those people in turn found people they could trust. That became what I would call 'cascading trust.' It ultimately came from Billy through the organization, touching my life, and allowing a trust that empowered me."

"Interesting phrase, *cascading trust*," we said.

"When you have a great leader," David responded emphatically, "and his character and worldview cascade through the enterprise, the enterprise can accomplish great things! Billy surrounded himself with people who cared for him, told him the truth, and got results. He modeled the bonding. In turn, the bond was extended through Sterling to me and others—simply put, they took us in."

"So how has that affected the way you run your own organization?"

"I look for people who will tell me the truth, who will show compassion for me and the cause we're about, people who will get results. When I find those people, I try to treat them the way I was treated by Billy Graham. For Billy to trust others, he had to be trustworthy himself. That meant loving others and telling the truth. Billy delivered on his promises and got results. All that challenges me to do the same."

"So Billy's DNA . . ."

"You sense it in the people he surrounded himself with," David said, and he named nearly a dozen team members. "Most of them did not have a lot of face time with Billy, but he instilled in them a strong sense of mission. The DNA was mission focused, and full of compassion. They always treated me lovingly . . . ," David paused, then added, "if firmly. No one's perfect; we make mistakes and have to be corrected. You must work hard. You won't be kept if you're deadwood. But focus was on the cause. You can't do that if you don't see cause and compassion blended in the leader. We didn't need to meet personally with Billy on projects because we could emulate that blend of cause and compassion. Our entire firm's motivation stayed intense."

Another aspect of the DNA David told us about was Billy's

drive toward excellence, which required thoroughness and hard work. "In creating media and print tools," David explained, "we wouldn't spend a dollar on production until we had sign-off on the audience and the purpose of the communication. What were the outcomes we wanted? What would constitute success? We'd pass ideas around, involve the team, and they would all weigh in on it. Only after all that thinking was done would we spend money on photos and recordings. That kind of work took products and ideas to higher levels, because there was no 'Billy has to approve everything' or 'I woke up this morning feeling I wanted to do this.' Many organizations never put in that level of thinking."

"Did this DNA convey a sense of empowerment?"

"Clearly. Once Billy put something into motion, it went. People had tremendous spending authority, and this goes back to trust. Billy had too many irons in the fire and too high an agenda to review the details. If Sterling needed to do a project, he didn't have to check with six people. Billy's trust in those with spending authority cascaded to us and gave us freedom. In turn, we could act with our vendors in the same way. It called out of us standards—you raise the standard and it pulls everyone up."

"We've noted that Billy and his organization have shown great ability to deal with crises. How have they been able to do this so well?"

David nodded. "My short answer is, the systems. He had systems in place; they had matured organizationally. People knew how to move right in, and information didn't lollygag at a lower level. People had the discernment to know 'This can bite us! Let's get it right up.'"

We explored with David various mechanisms of Billy's organization, and he kept returning to the way Billy's vision and values had influenced his colleagues. Several of them have recently faced health challenges or changes in position, and in describing their responses, David said, "These are grace-filled people! That's Billy's DNA. They model grace, and they have a sense of cause. They emulate Billy in saying, 'I'm called to do this, no matter what the challenges. Join me!'"

LEADERSHIP LESSONS | **Empowering**

Applying the Principles

At the core of leadership is guiding and empowering those we lead. When we do so with skill, love, and grace, the effects radiate far beyond those we personally touch.

But it takes skill and empathy. Here are ideas on how to go about it.

Unleash and Multiply

When we interviewed Graham biographer Bill Martin, he told us that what had impressed him most when he talked with people who had worked with Billy over the decades was the way he selected and delegated. "He chooses people whom he trusts," Martin said, "then delegates a great deal of the authority to do the task. Their own dedication to him and confidence in him causes them often to rise to the occasion."

He observed that often people without qualifications for the tasks would, with Billy's confidence in them, rise to the challenges. "Pastor Lane Adams told me that Billy is rather like a master artist. He says, 'Here is the easel. Here are a few lines. Now, you go ahead and fill in the blanks.'"

Martin also quoted T. W. Wilson's insight: "He gives you a task, and then says, 'Don't bother me with the details; we can talk about it from time to time—but come back and tell me when you have it done.'"

The leader with a large vision knows the means of accomplishment is to select those with great capacities who can slash their own trail through the thickets and get the job done. But it's far more than mere selection and assignment. Delegation means providing clear, simple "lines" and freedom, but also generating strong loyalties and a sense that each person's contribution is highly valued. "Billy not only delegates authority," says Martin, "but he gives credit to those who do their jobs and shares the credit very generously; that makes others feel appreciated. They have confidence he is what he claims to be—that he is a man of integrity and he's not going to disappoint or embarrass them. All this lifts them to a higher level. Carl Henry told me, with a kind of chuckle, 'When Billy asks you to do something, you kind of want to find a way to do it. You don't want to let him down.'"

Inspiring and challenging others, and watching them rise to their full potential, is the complex yet enormously rewarding role of the leader. Warren Bennis observes that the successful leader is not the "one with the loudest voice, but the readiest ear," and that "the real genius may well lie, not in personal achievement, but in unleashing others' talents."

When the talents of others are unleashed, it multiples the leader's impact. The truth is, leaders must work not only with Ph.D.'s like Woody Wirt and Carl Henry and brilliant businessmen like Allan Emery and George Bennett. Ordinary people too must be inspired and mobilized. Bill Pollard cautions, "Build your

> *I'd rather get ten men to do the right job than to do the job of ten men.*
>
> DWIGHT L. MOODY

team around the talents and skills of the ordinary person, not just around the special skills and talents of those few extraordinary people." Every person has been created in the image and likeness of God, with the potential of the extraordinary and with the reality of their immortality. Leadership's responsibility is to unlock this potential and to respect and nurture this immortality.

Similarly, Peter Drucker—always realistic about the limitations of human beings—has written that an organization's test is "its capacity to make common people achieve uncommon performance." In *The Effective Executive*, Drucker balances these dynamics with an astute analysis of leadership strategy: "The effective executive knows that it is easier to raise the performance of one leader than it is to raise the performance of a whole mass. He therefore makes sure that he puts into the leadership position, into the standard-setting, the performance-making position, the man who has the strength to do the outstanding, the pace-setting job."

Drucker goes on to explain: "The task of an executive is not to change human beings. Rather, as the Bible tells us in the parable of the Talents, the task is to multiply performance capacity of the whole by putting to use whatever strength, whatever health, whatever aspiration there is in individuals."

Don't Dominate—Lead!

Here's a statement that merits considerable thought by anyone in a leadership capacity. Psychiatrist David Cooper says, "Perhaps the most central characteristic of authentic leadership is the relinquishing of the impulse to dominate others."

Many have that problematic impulse, often arising from their own insecurities. Is Cooper right?

On first reading the statement, one might object that countless leaders of great accomplishment have powerfully dominated others. Yet if a leader today is to unleash the full potential of others, domination will severely limit the soaring of the followers' spirits and effectiveness.

Billy Graham never dominated, but in thousands of connections he inspired and led. At the same time, he understood the need for an adequate level of control. Obviously, a certain degree of control is necessary for a leader to function.

Leighton Ford, in thinking back over the many years he worked with Billy, remembers him as always empowering and encouraging, without pulling rank. But he does remember one time when he did.

He, John Corts, Sterling Huston, and John Dettoni had a bright idea. They thought they could learn by surveying members of the team. They developed questions and put together forms for them to fill out.

Billy, when he saw the forms and how they were to be used, said, "This has to be thrown out!"

Leighton tried to explain why they were doing it, and why they thought it would be helpful. He now recalls it as one of those very rare times when Billy pulled rank in a strong, confrontational way. "I'm running this organization," he said. "I've seen people whose organizations were taken away from them."

Billy understood the dangers of leadership giving up its authority. Leighton learned that any incipient sense of usurping Billy's authority was stepping over a line.

"That was the only time he spoke out that strongly," he told us.

It does not take multiple confrontations to set parameters. When a leader is secure in knowing his or her authority, capacities, limitations, and shared goals, then domination is unnecessary.

In *Management of the Absurd*, business consultant Richard Farson says, "Effective leaders and managers do not regard control as the main concern. Instead, they approach situations sometimes as learners, sometimes as teachers, sometimes as both. They trust the wisdom of the group. Their strength is not in control alone but in other qualities—passion, sensitivity, tenacity, patience, courage, firmness, enthusiasm, wonder."

When the essential leadership positioning is in place, we believe David Cooper's admonition is worth careful study—that "the most central characteristic of authentic leadership is the relinquishing of the impulse to dominate others."

Light Fires, Communicate Trust

Jesuit philosopher Baltasar Graciàn advises, "Know how to put fire into your subordinates." Leaders try to do that in many ways, some effective, and some not. At times, a leader lights fires under people that singe and burn, or flames blast down on them as "heat from the boss." Graciàn advises getting the fire within the person, where it will drive and energize in a positive way.

Putting fire into others starts with integrity and a significant cause. Yet the flames need to be fanned regularly, and a primary way to do that is through praise.

Wise Ben Franklin understood that, and in a bit of fascinating correspondence to John Paul Jones, he advised, "If you should observe an occasion to give your officers and friends a little more praise than is their due, and confess more fault than you can justly be charged with, you will only become the sooner for it, a great captain."

John Paul Jones, of course, did go on to become a great captain, perhaps by heeding Franklin's advice. With Billy, there's no perhaps. Benjamin Franklin's counsel to John Paul Jones describes Billy's practice of leadership perfectly. If anything, he would praise people a bit more than they might deserve. He

> *You may be able to compel people to maintain certain minimum standards by stressing duty, but the highest moral and spiritual achievements depend not upon a push but a pull.*
>
> **REINHOLD NIEBUHR**

would claim more of the fault for problems as his own. But this was not manipulation. His colleagues knew he really felt that way about their contributions, as well as their importance as persons, and that he saw his own role in a humble light.

Billy's friend, the highly successful businesswoman and entrepreneur Mary Kay Ash, said, "Everyone has an invisible sign hanging from his neck saying, 'Make Me Feel Important!' Never forget this message when working with people."

She understood the emotional dynamics of leadership and the necessity of praise as a regular ingredient. An English proverb observes, "Old praise dies, unless you feed it." People need reassurance and a regular flow of encouragement.

That's especially true during the rough times, and when someone has messed up. Mary Kay has advice for handling that: "Never giving criticism without praise is a strict rule for me. No matter what you are criticizing, you must find something good to say—both *before* and *after* . . . criticize the act, not the person."

Set the Pace!

The leader raises the bar and knows that he or she must be first to meet its demands. The leader must set the pace and communicate enthusiasm for running the race.

Fred Smith illustrates this with the spirit of a music director: "One of the toughest bandmasters I ever knew was Willy Fenten, a German who produced a championship high school band year after year. I can still hear him hollering at the trumpet player, 'You can't play like that and play in this band! This is a championship band!' Fenten didn't emphasize his own personal displeasure. He emphasized the student's contribution to the organization, and the quality of the organization."

A commitment to championship goals in any endeavor sets all eyes on the significant challenge.

It is far more than just enthusiastic bombast. Field Marshall Bernard Montgomery, who led his troops to many strategic victories in World War II, understood his own life had to demonstrate depth of character. "Leadership is the capacity and will," Montgomery stated, "to rally men and women to a common purpose and the character which inspires confidence."

Model Team Spirit

Andrew Carnegie once said, "No man will make a great leader who wants to do it all himself or get all the credit for doing it." When we read that, we think, "Of course. That's obvious."

Yet in practice, many leaders try to do all the major lifting themselves, and then bask in the limelight. It's a constant temptation.

To keep our roles in perspective and to apply our gifts appropriately is a larger challenge than we might think. And it all starts with attitude.

When we talked with David Schmidt about Billy's experiences, he said, "I wish I could help your readers understand what it's like to have the state and local police pull up in a motorcade and escort you to the lower bowels of a stadium through a back door. There's so much that says, 'You, you, you. You're a rock star! You're it!' Billy goes down the line shaking hands, meeting dignitaries, and everything is saying, 'You're important.' But Billy kept saying, 'No, it's not for my glory. God won't share his glory, so I need to get down so he can get up.' When you have a leader at the top who says, 'This is not about me,' that's big!"

Billy knew he could accomplish nothing without God, and next to nothing without a team. Those who followed him over the decades, from trustees and employees to counselors and local pastors, knew he wasn't grasping for his place in the sun. And they knew without doubt that he loved them.

Love? That word may come easily in the context of Billy's leadership. Yet what about business, politics, and sports?

Actually, love is the mark of truly great leadership, whatever the venue.

Consider the rough-and-tumble of football, where quarterbacks are brutally sacked and linemen drive mercilessly into their opponents. Love seems far removed. Yet the great coach Vince Lombardi declared, "You've got to care for one another. You've got to love each other. Most people call it team spirit."

POINTS TO PONDER

BILLY GRAHAM:

God has given us two hands, one to receive with
and the other to give with.

THE BIBLE:

Then make my joy complete by being like-minded,
having the same love, being one in spirit and purpose.
Do nothing out of selfish ambition or vain conceit, but in humility
consider others better than yourselves.

PHILIPPIANS 2:2 – 3

CHAPTER 9

Expanding the Growing Edge

> In periods where there is no leadership, society stands still. Progress occurs when courageous, skillful leaders seize the opportunity to change things for the better.
>
> **HARRY S. TRUMAN**

Talk about being caught in a vise! In the 1950s Billy Graham was building momentum as a national leader just as an issue that was increasingly dividing the country was rumbling toward full-blown crisis. His advisers were divided, and he was out there on the visible point.

Leaders often find themselves not only caught between forces but struggling to come to their own conclusions. Then they must form convictions strong enough to drive stakes in the ground— stakes that if wrongly chosen, or driven into the wrong ground, could impale instead of support the necessary weight. In today's acceleration of change and emergence of global ideas and methods, sharp divisions put leaders in precarious positions.

For Billy, in the 1950s, the gathering storm of racial issues forced him to search deeply the Scriptures and his own soul. From our perspective a half century later, we may wonder why he would have any question whatsoever about "the right thing to do." But immersed in the churning currents of beliefs in America at that time, he truly was caught in a dilemma. He needed the wisdom of Solomon and the courage of David to navigate the roiling, dangerous waters.

Billy grew up in the segregated South. His first two college stops were Bob Jones College and the Florida Bible Institute, neither of which admitted minorities. But then he enrolled at Wheaton College, a school founded by abolitionists.

He chose, at Wheaton, to major in anthropology, hoping to obliterate "any condescending notions I might have toward people from backgrounds other than my own." Yet within Wheaton in the 1950s were many currents of thought about solutions to racial issues. Northern evangelicals were largely unprepared for the Civil Rights Movement. In fact, it was only much later that most evangelical leaders thought seriously about the issue. It was not until the mid-1960s, for instance, that black intellectual Bill Pannell was hired as a Youth for Christ staff member, who began educating and sensitizing the YFC leadership about the painful experiences of black Americans.

But the majority of such education came a decade later. In the 1950s, Billy was still developing his own convictions. Some of his closest mentors believed in the "integrity of the races" and that segregation was ordained by God. These pietistic, seasoned elders had often wisely counseled, but on this they were divided.

Although Billy has often said he is no intellectual, his "emotional intelligence" has been described as "off the charts." For someone as sensitive to the nuances and feelings of his mentors and allies, it was another crucible of growth.

■ ■ ■

At first Graham tried to carve a middle ground that opposed both forced integration as well as forced segregation. He relied on the example of Billy Sunday, who had followed local custom by preaching to integrated audiences in the North and to mostly segregated audiences in the South. So, in many of his earliest meetings, Graham followed suit.

But the dramatic times left little maneuvering room for moderates. Reporters demanded to know why he could not speak to integrated audiences in South Carolina and Georgia just as he did in California and Massachusetts. They asked why he never addressed racism in the South.

Billy chose to make his stand in the heart of the segregated South. He initially agreed to segregate the audience during his 1952 campaign in Jackson, Mississippi, but rejected Governor Hugh White's suggestion to conduct separate meetings for blacks. Meanwhile Billy prepared to make a much bolder statement. Holding segregated events had always struck him as wrong, but he'd never chosen to take decisive action—until now. Walking toward the ropes that separated blacks and whites, Billy tore them down.

Mystified and uncomfortable ushers tried to put the ropes back up. Billy personally stopped them.

This symbolically powerful gesture marked a major ministry watershed. He never again led a segregated campaign.

"There is no scriptural basis for segregation. It may be there are places where such is desirable to both races, but certainly not in the church," Billy told his Mississippi audience. "The ground at the foot of the cross is level, and it touches my heart when I see whites standing shoulder to shoulder with blacks at the cross."

Nearly two years before the famed *Brown v. Board of Education* decision, when the U.S. Supreme Court declared "separate but equal" arrangements unconstitutional, Billy threw his clout behind the Civil Rights Movement. Though tearing down the ropes in Jackson seems in retrospect a simple decision, his action earned the respect of many blacks and the enmity of segregationists. In so doing, he signaled to his followers that racial inequality should not be tolerated in the church.

Long-term colleague Sherwood Wirt in a letter to us said of Billy Graham, "He outgrew Southern racism much earlier than his Southern colleagues did. He thought like a large ruler. His vision outstripped all of us."

■ ■ ■

It may be that had it not been for a black man, we would never have heard of Billy Graham. On the Charlotte dairy farm, as he was growing up, his family employed an African-American foreman and treated him as a valued member of the family. In 1933 when evangelistic meetings were being held in town, young Billy didn't want to go. He had no interest in it—but as a new driver, he did have a strong interest in driving the foreman's truck.

"Tell you what. I'll let you drive my truck if you'll go to the crusade with me," the older man offered.

Billy accepted the deal, and that led to his conversion. The concerned foreman, who was like family, represented one of the roots of Billy's sensitivity on racial issues. As he continued to minister throughout the country, he widened his contacts with the black community. At the same time, he knew where the growing edge of the white community was, and if he went too far ahead of it, they would write him off and he would lose all influence. He had to strategically communicate his message of love and hope, including his vision of racial harmony and reconciliation, to a wide range of constituents.

His stance had its effect. Charles Marsh, author of *God's Long Summer: Stories of Faith and Civil Rights*, grew up in the South. In his memoir, *The Last Days: A Son's Story of Sin and Segregation at the Dawn of a New South*, he tells the story of how his father, a pastor in a small Mississippi town, was influenced in his pilgrimage "from a son of the segregated South to preacher of the sermon 'Amazing Grace for Every Race.'" Writes Marsh, "Billy Graham had long refused to hold meetings before segregated audiences, and this conviction stirred my father's willingness to change, if not to see racial equality as ordained by God. 'The ground at the foot of the cross is level,' Billy liked to say."

Yet for all those who resonated with his convictions, there were many who did not. Segregationists continued to disparage his efforts, and then he had to factor in church leaders from the other side of the spectrum like Reinhold Niebuhr, who criticized him for not moving quickly enough.

Billy's 1957 New York City campaign illustrates just what he faced and the tactics he employed.

During the first few nights, critics and supporters alike noticed a disturbing trend: the audiences looked more like a cross section of Middle America than the diverse streets of New York City. Especially notable was the absence of African Americans. Lamenting this fact, Billy called Cleveland pastor Howard Jones, an African American, and asked him how to reach the city's minorities. Jones pulled no punches and told Billy to go where the blacks lived—Harlem. Jones even left his job in Cleveland to organize this effort. Eight thousand people attended the first event there. One week later at a similar event in Brooklyn, Billy for the first time voiced his support for civil rights legislation. Though Billy focused his efforts on spiritual change and emphasized the necessity of inward transformation, he also lobbied for institutional reform. Billy's leadership tactics reflected his belief that a variety of devices would be needed to coax change.

Jones later noted Billy's leadership with admiration. "For better or worse, the church has typically followed the lead of secular society when it comes to our attitudes about race," he reflected. "When Billy approached me to join him in New York, it was more or less understood that white Christians worshiped with white Christians and black Christians worshiped with black Christians. Our evangelical churches seemed to believe that heaven too would be 'separate but equal.' We recited the Lord's Prayer and prayed: 'Thy will be done on earth as it is in heaven' but then proceeded to bow at the altar of Jim Crow. Talk about being countercultural; what Billy did was radical. There's no getting around it. He weathered the barrage of angry letters and criticisms. He resisted the idea of pulling the plug on the whole thing and playing it safe. There was never any hesitation on Billy's part. He remained faithful to his convictions."

Billy's brief foray into Harlem produced the intended result of involving African Americans and marked the beginning of an important relationship. Two rally organizers were close friends and advisers of Martin Luther King Jr. Together with King, they huddled with Billy in private strategy meetings and even swapped dreams of conducting joint evangelistic crusades. But the union was not to be. King's approach was too political for Billy's taste, and they agreed to seek change in separate spheres.

Billy did invite King to give a prayer at the meetings, a symbolic move that further solidified his commitment to the movement toward racial equality. "A great social revolution is going on in the United States today," Billy said as he introduced King. "Dr. King is one of its leaders, and we appreciate his taking time out of his busy schedule to come and share this service with us tonight."

Billy's relationship with King affords a telling glimpse into Billy's strategy. He sympathized with King's motives and admired his peaceful tactics, but he also recognized that much of his own core constituency was not ready for civil disobedience. Billy broke custom and tradition where necessary, but he would not break the law. This cautious approach doesn't impress many modern observers, who eagerly point out how much more Billy could have done to aid King's cause. At the time, however, Billy bolstered King's agenda among a constituency not yet reached by civil rights activists. Billy knew his followers and their limitations, identified their growing edge, and helped shape their perspectives on race relations.

New York City was not the end of King's and Graham's collaboration. In 1962, while Billy conducted a crusade in Chicago, his media adviser, Walter Bennett, offered advice to some of King's senior aides. Bennett deconstructed their approach to event organization and media relations. He warned that King would burn out if the minister continued his breakneck pace of speaking at small churches before modest audiences. Bennett suggested that King should bide his time and gear up for fewer, more spectacular events. Some of the advice may have influenced them. One year later, King exhibited exceptional media savvy and organizational acumen during his defining moment, the March on Washington, where he made his historic "I have a dream" speech.

LEADERSHIP LESSONS | **The Growing Edge**

Applying the Principles

Today, commentators often lament the way polls, not leaders, set the direction and the pace. National leaders can seem captive to the latest currents of thought and emotion, their convictions seemingly irrelevant in the quest to take the pulse of the people and therefore "lead them."

It's easy to lament and critique leaders; but it's another thing entirely to skillfully, and with integrity, lead without losing one's followers or convictions.

On racial issues, as on many others that confronted him during his career, Billy had to constantly search his soul. He had to drive stakes in the ground that would maintain his integrity yet not jeopardize his primary mission.

Whatever our own leadership challenges, we face the same core dynamics. How can we effectively lead in this area?

Establish Convictions

Billy would listen carefully to a multitude of counselors before he formed his own convictions on racial justice. A conviction is but a shallow idea if it is simply reflective of how one was raised or as a response to persuasive voices. Issues are complex, and forming conviction takes depth of analysis and careful probing of one's soul.

Once established, convictions must be nurtured by fresh evaluations as new circumstances and information arise. Sometimes new realities require they be modified. Leaders must seek that mature space between being doctrinaire and bullheaded versus wishy-washy and checking every wind of change.

Know the Edge

If we don't have a good grasp of people's intensities and beliefs on an issue, we face two limitations. First, we won't know how to articulate our convictions in ways that communicate effectively

143

to those who waver or disagree. Second, we will be blindsided by unexpected reactions.

Billy was sensitive to others' viewpoints, always probing for additional insights. After all, he was an anthropology major. At the same time, he didn't let his information paralyze him. In his 1957 crusade, he knew certain fundamentalists would react viscerally to his having Catholics and Protestant liberals on the platform, but he did it anyway. In Jackson, when he took down the ropes segregating black from white, he knew how upset many of his Southern supporters would be, but he did it anyway. He was prepared for the results.

Bill Martin, in assessing Graham's approach on issues, told us, "Billy is typically ahead of his own unit, but never at the head of the parade. That's where he was on race, the war on poverty, and all those things—in front of the position taken by most evangelical Christians."

Graham knew that if he moved too far ahead, he would lose his "unit," and he would have been forced into a different role. He understood his constituency and their growing edge. Martin pointed out that many people saw Billy as "backward and not prophetic." But Billy kept his laser focus on his primary calling, and in various ways stretched other leaders. And in a related strategy, he founded *Christianity Today* magazine, which dealt more frontally with issues.

Sometimes when we form a conviction, we're tempted to "preach the unvarnished truth" and let the listeners take it or leave it. But they may not have the background and information to accept such straight talk. Leadership, by its nature, requires strong convictions but also the skills to effectively communicate those convictions and to back off emphases that will deflect from the main thing. As the saying goes, "Let the main thing be the main thing."

Be Patient Like Lincoln and Roosevelt

Political analyst David Gergen points out that our most effective presidents have carefully brought the public along on controversial issues. In *Eyewitness to Power*, he cites both Abraham Lincoln and Franklin Roosevelt. "Lincoln decided in the summer of 1862 to issue the Emancipation Proclamation, but kept it locked in his desk until Union forces could win a significant victory in the field, giving him enough political capital to hold the Union together. Meanwhile, he dropped a series of public hints, including a well-publicized letter to Horace Greeley, foreshadowing his announcement. Massive Confederate casualties at Antietam gave him the moment he had been awaiting, and he finally went public with his decision in September. Even then, he waited until January 1 to sign the Proclamation, giving the country three additional months to ready itself. A man of extraordinary insight into public psychology, Lincoln was always patient, allowing issues to ripen and events to move in his direction before he moved."

Garry Wills, writing in the *Atlantic*, makes a similar point. "In order to know just how far he could go at any moment, Lincoln had to understand the mixture of motives in his fellow citizens, the counter-balancing intensities with which they held different positions, and in what directions those positions were changing moment by moment. The leader needs to understand followers. . . . This is the time-consuming aspect of leadership."

Roosevelt too prepared the American people. Gergen writes, "Franklin Roosevelt foresaw as early as 1937 that the United States would very likely be drawn into war with Europe. But he didn't issue a series of presidential decrees or seek bold initiatives because he knew the country was sleeping under a blanket of isolationist sentiment and would resist being jerked out of bed. Instead, he slowly awakened the public mind to the dangers outside and prepared it for eventual sacrifice. . . . Most historians rightly believe that one of FDR's greatest achievements was to arouse the country out of isolationism gradually, preparing it psychologically and militarily."

These macroexamples illustrate what leaders on every level face: it often takes time and patience to communicate tough and controversial necessities, yet both are needed to generate enthusiastic support.

Use Natural Forces

Often it's not arguments but positive natural dynamics that break down barriers and bring understanding to people alienated from each other.

Gerald Strober interviewed both black and white clergymen in Jackson, Mississippi, after the 1976 Graham campaign there. Had Billy's meetings made an impact on race relations? One responded, "A year ago, people who didn't know each other started praying together, started studying together, started planning together. Now you see integration in the choir, on the platform, in the stands." Another said, "This has been the first time that many black people have entered white churches. They have begun to know one another." And the future? "Normal problems will crop up," said one, "but we now have a precedent, and when problems occur, the people can say, we worked together on the Billy Graham campaign, we can work together on this."

Obviously, Billy's 1976 efforts in Jackson did not solve the city's racial problems. But his nurturing the growing edge of people's racial understandings by bringing them together had a powerful effect. It was one of many good seeds that years later, among other good things, resulted in "Mission Mississippi," a ministry that today fosters interracial harmony and positive action.

Respect the MLKs

You never know when someone who sees things quite differently will go on to make a huge impact—and will have been right about many things. Martin Luther King Jr. shared Graham's roots in the gospel but had been trained in a liberal seminary and had a different agenda. Billy could have simply avoided him and dodged a lot of criticism from many in his constituency. At the same time, he had developed convictions in tune with King's, and he sought common ground.

Howard Jones recalls Martin Luther King Jr. telling Billy, "I believe your crusades are doing more to break down racial barriers and to bring the races together than what I'm doing. Your work is helping me."

After King's death, Billy continued his efforts for racial justice. For instance, when in the late 1960s he met with black leaders in New York and heard of their difficulties with the Nixon administration, he arranged for several of them to meet with President Nixon in the White House. As a result, significant funds were reinstated for impoverished black neighborhoods.

> There is a spirit and a need and a man at the beginning of every great human advance. Each of these must be right for that particular moment of history or nothing happens.
> **CORETTA SCOTT KING**

The Reverend John Williams, a pastor from Kansas City and NAACP leader who would later become a member of Billy's board, told Nixon that the construction of a hospital near his church had been stalled. Two days later, the funds began flowing as a $1 million federal grant enabled workers to complete the Martin Luther King Hospital.

Billy has always shown respect for others who have wished to better the world but see priorities and solutions differently. He insists that if asked to give the invocation at the Republican National Convention, he also would do so at the Democratic Convention, and vice versa. It is no fluke that when Congress voted to give the Congressional Gold Medal to Billy and Ruth, the vote was unanimous.

In a world increasingly polarized and bitter, Billy Graham has shown how one can maintain integrity, continue to grow personally, and to carefully communicate the fruit of that growth to others' growing edge.

At times we may be tempted to use the pit-bull tactics so prevalent around us. But Billy shows how respect for those he leads and respect for those with whom he disagrees can result in growth and great progress in fulfilling a mission.

POINTS TO PONDER

BILLY GRAHAM:

The test of a preacher is that his congregation

goes away saying not, "What a lovely sermon!" but,

"I will do something."

THE BIBLE:

Thank God for you, brothers, and rightly so,

because your faith is growing more and more, and the love

every one of you has for each other is increasing.

2 THESSALONIANS 1:3

PART
FOUR

GROWING THROUGH FIRE AND ICE

Just pray for a tough hide and a tender heart.

RUTH GRAHAM

Over the years, any leader out on the point will come up against events that either dramatically deepen the person or generate bitterness of soul. As Colin Powell and others have said, "Command is lonely."

Billy Graham has experienced plenty of the travail common to leadership. These chapters candidly explore very human dynamics:

Summoning Courage

Learning from Failure

Experiencing Trauma and Betrayal

Redeeming the Ego

In each of these four chapters we see how he responded to realities, then kept on leading. Clearly, he has been among those whom the process has humbled, sensitized, and deepened.

CHAPTER 10

Summoning Courage

> Courage is the first of human qualities because
> it is the quality which guarantees all the others.
> WINSTON CHURCHILL

Leaders are on the point. Out in full view, each one becomes a target, and each must anticipate being shot at. Sudden shifts in events, jarring betrayals by allies, or decisions gone awry make any leader feel fear and often confusion. Leaders must sense the challenge to rise above the natural reactions to lash out or shrink back, to summon courage and tenacity to lead when the stakes are high and the results could be failure or humiliation.

Billy Graham has been out on the point, highly visible in the press, every statement and response and off-the-cuff comment evaluated and major decisions assessed. He has often found himself in the bull's-eye in a great many ways.

In fact, sometimes a literal bull's-eye. All through the decades of his ministry, Billy has had to live with the constant awareness that at any time he could get shot at with real bullets. Hate mail would arrive at his office. The FBI and police would inform him about death threats. He was always in the public eye, knowing that at any moment some crazed person could shoot at him—as they did John and Bobby Kennedy, Martin Luther King Jr., John Lennon, and Ronald Reagan.

One man called Billy at his hotel and told him, "Mr. Graham, some of us are going to kill you before midnight tonight." We can imagine how that would affect his ability to go to sleep that night.

Early in his ministry he was leading a service when, in the middle of it, he was told a pastor had called to warn him a man was coming to murder him. Billy told the audience about it but continued with the service.

This was one of many realities that demanded courage on Billy's part. Stepping into the lion's den to dialogue with hostile intellectuals or cynical reporters; facing angry conservative critics; making decisions he knew would cause consternation among friends.

At times on major initiatives, he diligently and with great thoroughness sought wisdom and counsel, then devoted full energies to implementing a plan of action—only to see his efforts assaulted.

Perhaps no greater example of that was his experience on his return from his historic trip to Russia in 1982.

His vision for ministry in the Soviet Union had begun long before. In 1959, though unable to get permission to hold meetings there, he visited the Soviet Union as a tourist. Sitting with friend and ministry partner Grady Wilson, Billy gazed across the vast expanse of an empty Lenin Stadium in Moscow. The great coliseum, site of Soviet athletic triumphs and numerous Communist Party celebrations, felt strangely impotent without the throngs of Russian spectators. He envisioned standing before those masses, preaching the good news of Christ in a country where God had been outlawed. Communist officials had barred him from speaking publicly, so instead Billy simply bowed his head and prayed that God would one day bring him back to the Soviet capital and allow him to share the gospel.

"And yet for decades, it seemed as if that was one prayer God would never answer, an unrealistic pipe-dream that could never come true," Billy wrote in his autobiography. "The barriers were too great, the wall erected by Communism against religion too impregnable."

Yet Billy kept probing. In 1978, PepsiCo CEO Don Kendall arranged for him to meet Soviet ambassador Anatoly Dobrynin. When they met in a Washington hotel, Dobrynin queried Billy with characteristic Russian directness. "Why do you want to come?"

Billy deferred the question to Dr. Alexandr Haraszti, a Hungarian Baptist who won Billy's trust when they ministered together behind the Iron Curtain in Hungary and Poland. Haraszti spoke of a faithful remnant of Christians both within and without the Orthodox church, whom Billy wanted to encourage. He pointed out that Billy would be a positive force in relations between the U.S. and the Soviet Union. Dobrynin agreed to do what he could.

Eventually, after long and complex negotiations, Communist authorities gave a green light, with some conditions. Billy would not be permitted to preach in any of Russia's great stadiums, as he had prayed in 1959, but he would be able to speak in both Baptist and Orthodox churches. There was just one catch: he would also be expected to participate in a gathering called "The World Conference of Religious Workers for Saving the Sacred Gift of Life from Nuclear Catastrophe." That was a problem. Despite the noble-sounding purpose and religious sponsorship, such meetings were infamous for being Communist-manipulated, anti-American propaganda events. How could he participate and give his implied endorsement to such a farce? The Reagan administration and his conservative supporters back home would surely be opposed.

Billy agonized over the decision. Two years before, the U.S. had boycotted the summer Olympics in Moscow to protest the Soviet invasion of Afghanistan. President Ronald Reagan had delivered hard-line addresses and would soon use the "Evil Empire" phrase to describe the Soviet system. Would Billy be undermining his country?

When Billy asked their advice, Allan Emery and George Bennett counseled him not to go, believing the risk to his reputation was too great if the Soviets used him for political gain. In contrast, Haraszti adamantly said he should go, arguing that "the Lord has opened the door, and we must enter the door." Haraszti pointed out that if Billy's reputation suffered, it wouldn't compare to the sufferings of Russian Christians. He urged Billy to take the long view: "You must not jeopardize the ten years to come. This is the beginning. . . . This will be your first coming to the Soviet Union but not your last one. If you accept the invitation, all the other satellite countries will fall in line. These things are interwoven. No Moscow, no satellite countries."

But Billy's friend, Vice President George H. W. Bush, called him to tell him the U.S. ambassador to the Soviet Union did not want him to go. Billy was torn by compelling arguments on both sides.

Finally, he decided to accept the invitations, and his ministry in Russia turned out to be remarkable. Baptists and Pentecostals and Orthodox all welcomed him. He presented the gospel clearly and without restriction in his preaching and in private conversations.

Two events, however, tested his patience, courage, and diplomatic skills. At the infamous peace conference, one of the speakers railed on and on that the U.S. was the sole cause of the world's unrest and nuclear threat. The speech's length and one-sidedness eventually prompted Billy to remove his translation headset in protest.

Also, when Billy visited the dissident "Siberian Seven," Pentecostals who had sought asylum in the U.S. embassy, becoming a worldwide symbol for religious freedom, many anti-Communists criticized Billy for not denouncing the Soviet Union on their behalf. Throughout the trip, Billy's comments, meant to be gracious and evenhanded, were interpreted as naive. Back home in the U.S., the media was sharply critical.

The *Baltimore Sun* editorialized, "Billy Graham has a God-given right to make a fool of himself in Moscow. He's doing a pretty good job of it while attending a propaganda show...."

Political cartoonists depicted Billy abandoning persecuted Christians, many of whom labored in Siberian work camps like Aleksandr Solzhenitsyn before them. Even his hometown newspaper, the *Charlotte Observer*, posed him in a cartoon next to a Soviet-looking Julius Caesar and remarked, "Billy Graham never met a Caesar he didn't like!" The rhetorical firestorm triggered *Christianity Today* to observe, "Never before in all his career has the evangelist faced such condemnation from the American press and from evangelical leaders."

Because he moved on to England after his trip to the Soviet Union, Billy remained largely unaware of the tumult back home.

He did not know that about fifty protesters had been marching around the Billy Graham Center at Wheaton College carrying signs like "Graham Eats Caviar as Russian Christians Suffer in Jails." Unlike the American commotion, the European press had reacted more favorably to Billy's Russian venture. They applauded his address to the peace conference.

But Billy became acutely aware of the controversy when he agreed to appear via satellite from London on *This Week with David Brinkley*. He was immediately startled by the pointed and presumptuous questioning of Brinkley, Sam Donaldson, and George Will. Mark Azbel, a Jewish Soviet dissident, and Edmund Robb, an evangelical Graham ally, joined the tag-team fray to heap even more criticism.

Will: "What makes you think that you're going to cause the Kremlin to begin dismantling the apparatus of thought control that's the basis of their regime?"

Graham: "I don't think I'm going to do it. I don't think I'll even live long enough to see that. But I know what the power of the gospel can do."

Donaldson: "Why not preach here at home? Aren't there people in the United States who need your ministry? Your critics say your ego requires a worldwide ministry."

Graham: "It's not my ego; it's my calling. Jesus said, 'Go ye into all the world and preach the gospel.' He didn't say, 'Go into the capitalist countries only.' I've been in countries with right-wing dictatorships. I've been in countries that have left-wing dictatorships. But I've tried to stay right with the gospel of Christ and stay out of the various political situations."

Robb: "We feel like impressions have been made that are unfortunate. I love you, I believe in you, and I shall continue to be your supporter. But I am convinced you've made a serious mistake in your visit to the Soviet Union, and if some of the things you've been quoted as saying are true, they've certainly compromised you with a great deal of the evangelical community."

Graham: "Well, I'll tell you one thing. I'll continue to preach the gospel whether there are many or few there."

■ ■ ■

It was a harrowing experience to face so much withering criticism. And in America, he learned that the media had isolated the most incendiary and perplexing observations in Moscow, removing them from any context that could have explained them. Soon after returning from his trip, Billy traveled to Chicago to chair a Christianity Today board meeting. He looked exhausted and discouraged. At the meeting, he shared with the trustees a report by journalist Ed Plowman, which put the statements and events in Russia in context. Still, everyone was acutely aware that the American media continued to be hostile.

When leaders take risks and find themselves not only in the bull's-eye but deep in the pits, it takes courage to go out and continue to face the assaults. But Billy did.

He weathered the emotional hits and stayed the course. He avoided petty defensiveness because his confidence in the mission did not depend on media approval. His decision to go to the Soviet Union had been carefully considered and prayerfully discerned.

Ultimately, Billy was vindicated for his historic 1982 trip, but he couldn't know that at the time. He had to simply keep soldiering on and accept the harsh realities of the assaults. For Billy, the only critic who really counted was God. Billy remained certain that God had wanted him to preach in the Soviet Union. He was anything but naive about the trip; he knew Soviet leadership would exact temporary gain from his presence there. "Of course they are using us," he said, "but we are using them as well, and my message is stronger than theirs."

History proved Billy correct. No one can definitively gauge the degree to which Billy contributed to the Iron Curtain's demise. However, in 1990 President George H. W. Bush praised Billy's prescience: "You know, eight years ago, one of the Lord's great ambassadors, Reverend Billy Graham, went to Eastern Europe and the Soviet Union and, upon returning, spoke of a movement there toward more religious freedom. And perhaps he saw it before many of us, because it takes a man of God to sense the early movement of the hand of God. And yet, who could predict that in 1989 freedom's tide would be economic, political and intellectual or that the walls of bayonets and barbed wire, the walls of tyranny, would come tumbling down."

Dan Rather of CBS, who had joined in the chorus of criticism, later acknowledged that Billy alone had looked past the atheistic Soviet propaganda to see a nation eager for change. "Before anybody else I knew of, and more consistently than anyone else I have known, of any nationality, race, or religion, Reverend Graham was saying, 'Spirituality is alive in the Marxist-Leninist-Stalinist states.' . . . Frankly, there were those years when I thought he was wrong, or that he didn't know what he was talking about," said Rather. "It turns out he was right. And give him credit—he also took the time to go and see for himself."

Just as Billy had hoped, the visit to Moscow opened the door for him to preach without censorship behind the Iron Curtain. He returned to the Soviet Union in 1984 and 1988; he toured Hungary and Romania in 1985; he preached in China in 1988 and North Korea in 1992 and 1994.

In 1992, Billy stood again in Moscow's Olympic Stadium, where he had prayed as a tourist in 1959. Only now, the stadium was not empty. This time Billy shared the message of God's love with 50,000 people crammed in a stadium built for 38,000. Between 20,000 and 30,000 additional people stood outside watching the crusade on projection screens.

■ ■ ■

Martin Luther King Jr. once said, "Courage is an inner resolution to go forward in spite of obstacles and frightening situations." Billy Graham in 1982 not only went forward but tenaciously persevered when the battle grew hottest and the outcome was still in doubt.

LEADERSHIP
LESSONS | **Courage**

Applying the Principles

Leadership and fear—the two seem opposites. A leader steps out boldly, "fearlessly." Yet fear and leadership are intertwined—not just in the "great moments" of high danger. We daily must make the decisions and take the risks that call for courage.

Embrace Courage—In the Ordinary, and in Chaos

When we read about Billy Graham's taking the risk of going to Russia and experiencing the drama of the international fallout— or we read of Eisenhower at Gibraltar or Churchill calling the nation to courage as the Nazis bombed London—we may feel far removed from their experiences. Yet the essential principles that enabled them to rise to the challenges are available to all who lead.

We all experience fear. It is not just the soldier on the battle-field who knows how vulnerable he is; we intuitively sense how even our body language—wrongly interpreted—can incite criticism, or a fumble of words can humiliate us, or the wrong decision ruin what we value most.

Research says the most common fear among us is of public speaking—something every leader must do at one time or another. In contrast to life-and-death situations, some may condescendingly smile at that fact. Yet the research makes sense. Up in front of a crowd, a foolish slip of the tongue or an embarrassing blank response can intently focus all those eyes on our failure. And we know the more we think about such unpleasant possibilities, the more likely we'll get tongue-tied or empty-headed. The consequences can be severe.

If we have courage, it means we are overcoming fear, and leaders—in addition to natural human fears of cancer and head-on collisions—have the added weight of communicating unpleasant realities or being misunderstood. For instance, one young man who reluctantly agreed to lead a meeting afterwards heard himself criticized. He felt angry. "If they don't like it, let them get up on the platform!" he thought. "I didn't ask to do this." Like many young leaders, his first taste of being misunderstood felt bitter. Fortunately, he didn't give in to his anger and fears. Over the ensuing decades, he learned to face lots of criticism, recognizing it "comes with the territory."

Tom Peters wrote a book for leaders titled *Thriving on Chaos*. Some of us wonder how anyone can thrive on chaos, but today we're often required to do just that. The problems and challenges keep growing, and the acceleration of change at times turns our decisions and plans into disaster. But courage means we count the cost, make our best decisions, and lead on.

Recognize Fear as a Catalyst for Courage

The stream of leadership over a lifetime runs over small rocks and large, meanders through a few sunny meadows, and often plunges down steep gorges, through dark caves, and then into tight little crevices. There's plenty of occasion for fear.

But fear is an ally. Fear is a catalyst. Fear wakes us up to realities. Fear helps equip us to lead.

Novelist I. A. R. Wylie says that in looking back at her life, she found an unexpected insight: "I had enjoyed myself most when I had been at my best, and I had been most often at my best when I'd been badly scared." She recalls that experiencing adventure or danger ultimately empowered her. "I found that fear has aroused in me unsuspected powers."

Fear rouses unsuspected powers? In his book *Out Front Leadership*, trainer Joe Reynolds agrees. He considers fear an indispensable ally. "The sweat of fear has its distinctive smell, and I know it well," he says. "But few actions cleanse and revitalize the spirit as well as facing the fear of risk." He explains that courage is "recognizing and coping with fear positively and responsibly." Then he quotes George Bernard Shaw: "It is courage, courage, courage that raises the blood of life to crimson splendor."

> *Life is a battle in which you are to show your pluck.*
> HENRY DAVID THOREAU

If that sounds over-the-top—admittedly, Reynolds served in the Marine Corps and competed in rodeo bull-riding through age fifty-four—think about not only such physical occasions for fear but also the necessity of dealing with it. In all the ordinary demands of leadership, fear emerges, and we can either make it a catalyst or a culprit leading to subtle cowardice.

Brace Yourself—And Take Action

It takes courage to face brutal facts. To require accountability. To deal wisely and decisively with a failing employee. To quit a job that violates our integrity. It takes courage and tenacity to year after year confront our own temptations and weaknesses and to constantly shear off what limits us. In short, it takes courage to lead.

One major way we siphon off courage is by avoiding the conflicts we dread.

Linus and Charlie Brown know about this. As they discuss how to deal with their difficulties, Linus tells Charlie Brown that he has a definite philosophy: "No problem is so big or complicated that it can't be run away from."

We may smile at that, but our emotions kick in, and we often feel just the way Linus does.

The key, whether it's facing a life-threatening event or a speaking engagement, is to confront what we feel. Colin Powell's leadership rule number 12 is "Don't take counsel of your fears. . . ." Eleanor Roosevelt advised, "Look fear in the face . . . you gain strength, courage, and confidence . . . you must do the thing you think you cannot do."

> *Avoiding danger is no safer in the long run than outright exposure. Life is either a daring adventure or nothing.*
>
> **HELEN KELLER**

Life is full of fearsome things, and the requirements of leadership increase our risk. Courage comes when we swallow our fears, sensing within how much our response changes everything—even when the worst happens.

"Mishaps are like knives," Herman Melville wrote, "that either serve us or cut us, as we grasp them by the blade or the handle." We may wince as we think of firmly grasping a knife by the blade.

Yet when we experience our mishaps or suddenly find ourselves in the bull's-eye, we may impulsively grab its sharp edges. We must have not blind reactive courage but the boldness of mature intelligence, which can assess and also access all the resources available. Our minds can put events into perspective and dramatically affect our bodies' responses to sources of fear. Commitments and faith energize the essentials of courage.

John Maxwell has observed, "What's ironic is that those who don't have the courage to take risks, and those who do, experience the same amount of fear in life."

An old saying sums it up:

> Fear knocked,
> Faith answered;
> No one was there.

Build "Dikes of Courage"

Martin Luther King Jr. had plenty of fears to face. Like Billy, he received death threats, but in his case they ultimately led to his murder. In addition to all the hatred spewed at him by segregationists, the FBI tracked his every move, looking for evidence against him. He had experienced arrest and imprisonment, and he realized how dangerous his leading the Civil Rights Movement really was.

The night before he was murdered in Memphis, he talked about the threats from "some of our sick white brothers." Then he said, "Well, I don't know what will happen now. We've got some difficult days ahead. But it doesn't matter with me now. Because I've been to the mountaintop. And I don't mind. Like anybody, I would like to live a long life. Longevity has its place. But I'm not concerned about that now. I just want to do God's will. And He's allowed me to go up to the mountain. And I've looked over. And I've seen the promised land. I may not get there with you. But I want you to know tonight, that we, as a people, will get to the promised land. And I'm happy, tonight. I'm not worried about anything. I'm not fearing any man. Mine eyes have seen the glory of the coming of the Lord."

The next day he was shot.

It took lots of courage for King to continue leading, and we see his call for courage in the midst of continuous danger. "Courage," he said, "is an inner resolution to go forward in spite of obstacles and frightening situations." Clearly, he constantly experienced both, even dying for his cause.

It's not hard to imagine King in "frightening situations" mentally repeating his own statements about courage, statements that are like a drumbeat of affirmations to strengthen resolve.

> "Courage breeds self-affirmation; cowardice produces destructive self-abnegation."
>
> "Courage faces fear and thereby masters it; cowardice represses fear and is thereby mastered by it."
>
> "Courageous men never lose the zest for living even though their life situation is zestless; cowardly men, overwhelmed by the uncertainties of life lose the will to live."

King was well aware that the alternative to courage was cowardice, and he was not afraid to name it. In fact, there is power in naming these opposites, courage and cowardice, and then determining to choose the first.

Said King, "We must constantly build dikes of courage to hold back the flood of fear."

King led with enormous courage, though he surely felt "the flood of fear." We may not face challenges as dangerous or tragic, but we can apply his drumbeat of affirmations to a wide range of our own leadership challenges.

Fear the Right Things

The word *courage* comes from a Latin word for "the heart." It shows what we are at the core.

Billy Graham has always found sound advice about courage in the Bible. "God has not given us the spirit of fear," it says, "but of love, power, and a sound mind." Angels in the Bible are quick to call for courage.

"Fear not," Gabriel said to teenaged Mary when he told her she would soon be pregnant by the Holy Spirit.

"Fear not, Zacharias. Your prayers have been heard," Gabriel said as he announced that John the Baptist would be born.

"Fear not," said the angel of the Lord to trembling Gideon, soon to lead his people in warfare.

Yet the Bible also tells us fear can be very good if we fear the right things. Fear of falling bricks or botulism is common sense. Fear of God is even more essential.

Fear God? Isn't he a God of love? Isn't that the God Billy has invited people to receive?

Yes. But the Scriptures say God is holy and hates the evil that visits horrors on his people and his creation. So throughout the Bible we read a drumbeat of commands to "Fear God." And it's a remarkable paradox of fear and joy. In the Psalms we read:

> Happy are those who fear the Lord.
> Praise the LORD, all you who fear him.
> Serve the LORD with reverent fear and rejoice.

A strange mixture, rejoicing in fear. Yet it's a matter of rightly placed fear. In this case, it's the ultimate fear that the Scriptures say gives ultimate joy.

Billy Graham fears the right things. He reads Proverbs daily, which tell him, "The fear of the LORD is the beginning of wisdom," and "The fear of the LORD teaches a person to be wise." That "reverent fear" is an essential ingredient of Graham's leadership. It results in courage.

Fearing God puts into perspective the intimidation of sparring with Boston intellectuals or clever diplomats or hostile "crazies," as Graham had to do. It gives power to face situations in which one feels overpowered or underequipped.

As theologian Karl Barth, who had faithfully ministered during the Nazi rule and knew about the need for courage, put it: "Courage is fear that has said its prayers."

POINTS TO PONDER

BILLY GRAHAM:

Courage is contagious. When a brave man takes a stand,
the spines of others are stiffened.

THE BIBLE:

Even though I walk through the valley
of the shadow of death,
I will fear no evil, for you are with me;
your rod and your staff, they comfort me.

PSALM 23:4

CHAPTER 11

Learning from Failure

Success is going from failure to failure
without loss of enthusiasm.
WINSTON CHURCHILL

As a middle manager was receiving a promotion, his vice president cryptically said, "You know what being promoted means, don't you? It means your bad decisions do more damage."

Our having positions of influence means more opportunity to do good. But it also means that the costs are higher for failure.

No one likes to fail, especially leaders, whose failures produce magnified consequences. Our errors of judgment, and our failures of nerve or vision, affect not just ourselves but also our followers and our cause. Clearly, failure is nothing to take lightly.

Yet as ski instructors frequently tell their novice students, "If you don't fall now and then, you're probably not pushing yourself enough."

Failure is the inevitable companion of a large vision. No one can take on a significant and difficult challenge without stumbling a few times. The important thing is how we respond. The goal is not a fail-safe record but a pattern of increasing effectiveness.

David Aikman, analyzing great individuals who shaped the twentieth century, said it well: "Virtue, after all, often consists not so much in the absence of fault altogether as in the speed and grace with which fault is recognized and corrected."

■ ■ ■

One of Billy's early failures, an embarrassing gaffe following a meeting with President Truman, showed him to be one who recognized and corrected his mistakes with speed and grace. This humiliating moment, interestingly, is the incident Billy uses to begin his autobiography, *Just As I Am*. This failure prepared him for a lifetime of significant encounters with world leaders.

It happened in 1950, when Billy was thirty-one years old and still emerging as a national figure.

After two successful campaigns in Los Angeles and Boston, Billy thought it was time to make contact with the highest levels of political power. He hoped to gain the president's support for his evangelistic efforts, especially one he dreamed of bringing to West Berlin.

He wrote the White House to request a visit with President Truman. When his initial request was rebuffed, he persisted, writing the president's secretary to ask that Mr. Truman be assured that "over 1,100 students at these Northwestern Schools [where Billy was then serving as president] are praying daily that God will give him wisdom and guidance" and that "we believe our President to be a man of God. We believe him to be God's choice for this great office."

A bit later, after Communist forces invaded South Korea, Billy sent a telegram to the president: "Millions of Christians praying God give you wisdom in this crisis. Strongly urge showdown with communism now. More Christians in southern Korea per capita than in any part of the world. We cannot let them down. Evangelist Billy Graham."

Then, working through Massachusetts Congressman John McCormack, Billy renewed his efforts to visit Truman, and he finally got an invitation for a twenty-minute appointment for July 14, 1950.

Billy pressed for more, asking that he be able to bring three colleagues along—Grady Wilson, Cliff Barrows, and Jerry Beavan. Somewhat surprisingly, permission was granted.

"We four young men were so excited," Grady remembered, that "we were jumping up and down." Their thoughts turned to what they should wear to make a good impression on the president. Grady pointed out that Mr. Truman was photographed in white buck shoes while on vacation in Key West, and maybe their delegation should meet him in white bucks of their own. Billy loved the idea and commissioned Grady to find identical shoes for the whole delegation.

On the day of the appointment, the team donned what they had been wearing at their most recent Bible conference at Winona Lake, Indiana—flamboyant cream-colored suits, hand-painted ties, and the unmistakable white bucks. "People probably thought we were a barbershop quartet," Billy later said with a smile.

President Truman greeted them cordially, saying that he'd heard some good things about their meetings.

Billy told him about Los Angeles the previous fall, where an unprecedented 350,000 had attended the fifty days of meetings, and about the New England meetings, including the 50,000 who had gathered in Boston Common to hear him speak. Billy reported that he had told the gathering that because of the recent news that the Soviet Union was building a nuclear arsenal, he had publicly called on the president to proclaim a day of national repentance and prayer for peace.

Mr. Truman nodded but said nothing.

Then Billy reaffirmed his support for swift reaction to North Korea's invasion of South Korea, even though the recent news from the battlefields was not encouraging.

"Our allotted time was quickly running out," Billy reported later, "and what I really wanted to talk to him about was faith."

"Mr. President," Billy said, casting about for an opening, "tell me about your religious background and leanings."

"Well," the president replied, "I try to live by the Sermon on the Mount and the Golden Rule."

"It takes more than that, Mr. President," the evangelist said, now on familiar ground. "It's faith in Christ and his death on the Cross that you need."

The president then stood up, the visit apparently over. Billy and the others stood up too, and Billy asked, "Mr. President, could we have prayer?"

The president, not known for his spiritual side, said, "I don't suppose it could do any harm." So Billy put his arm around the shoulders of the president of the United States of America and prayed, while Grady and Cliff chimed in with "do it, Lord," and hearty "amens."

"When we left the Oval Office," Billy said much later, "I looked at the clock; my prayer had taken another five minutes."

Upon emerging from the White House, the press corps descended on them: "What did you tell the president, and what did he say?" Billy, not knowing he was violating diplomatic protocol, told them everything he could remember.

Photographers asked them to recreate the pose they had struck with the president for the prayer. Billy replied that he considered it improper to simulate prayer, but wanting to please the press, he said: "My team and I were planning to thank God for our visit with the president, and now is as good a time as any. I suppose you could take a picture of that."

So the next day, newspapers across the country ran stories of the meeting, accompanied by photos of four men in white suits, down on one knee with heads bowed, who had prayed with the president.

"It began to dawn on me a few days later how we had abused the privilege of seeing the president," said Billy. "The president was offended that I had quoted him without authorization."

Billy tried to make amends. But Truman had informed his aides that "when, as, and if a request comes for Billy Graham to be received at the White House, the president requests that it be turned down."

By January 1952, as plans were being finalized for the Washington, D.C., crusade, Billy invited the president to bring words of greeting to the crusade. But a White House memo reported that "the president said very decisively that he did not wish to endorse Billy Graham's Washington revival, and particularly, he said, he did not want to receive him at the White House. You remember what a show of himself Billy Graham made the last time he was here. The president does not want it repeated."

Only many years later, while in retirement at his home in

Independence, Missouri, did Truman agree to see Billy. "I recalled the incident and apologized profusely for our ignorance and naiveté," Billy said.

"Don't worry about it," Truman said graciously. "I realized you hadn't been properly briefed."

Billy vowed that it would never happen again if he was given access to a person of influence. And true to his vow, after the embarrassment with Truman, Billy was circumspect regarding his conversations with prominent persons.

During the London meetings in 1954, for instance, Billy met privately with Winston Churchill for forty minutes. What did they talk about? Journalist George Burnham, who traveled with the Graham team, reported that the question was still unanswered a year later. All Billy would reveal during Churchill's lifetime was that it was Bible-centered.

When he was invited to preach at a private chapel service attended by Queen Elizabeth, the Duke of Edinburgh, the Queen Mother, and Princess Margaret, he was queried by reporters about what he said. Billy revealed only that he had spoken for about twenty-five minutes and used Acts 27:25 as the text for his sermon.

■ ■ ■

He eventually became a confidant of popes and presidents and prime ministers because he had learned to keep conversations in confidence. Further confirmation that he had learned something from his failure in 1950 was revealed more than thirty years later.

In 1981, he visited for half an hour with Pope John Paul II. Afterward he would speak only in general terms of their conversation, saying that they talked about "inter-church relations, the emergence of Evangelicalism, evangelization, and Christian responsibility toward modern moral issues." His assessment was homey but guarded: "We had a spiritual time. He is so down-to-earth and human, I almost forgot he was the pope."

Only after almost twenty years did Billy feel free to reveal a more personal aspect of their conversation, by then knowing it wouldn't prove an awkward revelation for either the pope or for Billy. The pope had grabbed him by the thumb and pulled him close to whisper intensely, "We are brothers."

He had made an error of judgment in revealing the content of his conversation with President Truman. He would not make that mistake again.

That's not to say he didn't make *other* mistakes. During his otherwise wildly successful visit to South Africa in 1973, with an unguarded comment he shot himself in the foot, or, as William Martin described the episode, it was "a shot that hit his foot and ricocheted around the world."

Since the United States Supreme Court had recently handed down the *Roe v. Wade* decision, upholding the legality of abortion, a reporter asked Billy if he considered abortion the taking of human life. Billy said yes, he did, but that such a procedure might be justified in certain situations, such as pregnancy caused by rape.

Billy's unfortunate tendency to allow a key word or image to send his mind down a "rabbit trail" then led him to make an unprompted comment about a newspaper article he had read the day before about the gang rape of a twelve-year-old girl. He said he advocated strict punishment for rape, and then added, "I think when a person is found guilty of rape, he should be castrated. That would stop him pretty quick."

Billy immediately knew that he had gone too far. "It was an offhand, hasty, spontaneous remark that I regretted almost as soon as I said it."

South African papers paid it little attention, but in America it created an uproar. The comment was considered both barbaric and racist. Despite the fact that Billy had insisted his South Africa meetings be integrated, a first for South Africa at the time, the comment was considered evidence of Billy's being a racist, because in America a disproportionate number of convicted rapists were black.

American readers were surprised at how quickly Billy put out this media fire by admitting he had spoken unwisely. "I unfortunately used a word which, in our sex-saturated culture, was emotionally charged and did not clarify my true thoughts." He explained he had been deeply moved by the victim's situation— doctors were saying she'd been so traumatized that she would be a psychological invalid for the rest of her life. He also pointed out that he realized any penalty "should be administered fairly, objectively, equally and swiftly to all, without regard to race or wealth."

But again, Billy didn't break a confidence that could have shed even more light on the statement. Only thirty years after the event did one of Billy's staff reveal where the unguarded thought originated.

"You know how that happened?" said one staffer who had traveled to South Africa with Billy. "He had ridden from the hotel to the press conference in a car with a black Anglican minister, and the conversation turned to how they could handle the problems of crime and punishment, and the minister said, 'Well, I believe in castration.' So that vivid conversation was on Billy's mind, and when the question in the press conference led to the mention of rape, he just blurted out what they'd talked about in the car. Now Billy could have blamed someone else for suggesting the idea, but he didn't. He took the heat for it."

In the sweaty arena of leadership, failures and gaffes are inevitable. A slip of the tongue, the wrong person hired for a key position, a regrettable decision—Billy experienced all of these and more. He knew how to take the heat and admit mistakes.

He was a fast learner, and he learned especially quickly from failures.

LEADERSHIP LESSONS | Failure

Applying the Principles

How can we learn from failures and apply the lessons to new challenges? Failures can lead eventually to great accomplishment, but of course they can also stop a leader cold and destroy his or her effectiveness. Much of it depends on whether or not we have, at the critical times, the fortitude and wisdom to embrace the central principles.

Use Failure as an Asset

Thoughtful observers have always recognized failure's contributions to leadership. Said Henry Ford, "Failure is the opportunity to begin again, more intelligently." J. M. Barrie observed, "We are all failures—at least, all the best of us are." And with brutal realism, Evan Esar advises, "If you can't bear to have your face stepped on, don't try to climb the ladder of success."

Gail Sheehy writes in her book *Pathfinders*, "Although it is difficult to believe, great men and women often feel helpless and afraid. . . . It is the rare leader who at some point in life does not become convinced that he or she has failed."

There is the greatest practical benefit in making a few failures early in life.
THOMAS HUXLEY

Sheehy goes on to quote Lord Randolph Churchill's description of Benjamin Disraeli's career as "failure, failure, partial success, renewed failure, ultimate and complete triumph." Then she describes Randolph's son Winston's career, which, at age sixty-five, appeared to have ended in total failure. Yet all those Churchillian failures prepared him for his magnificent leadership in World War II.

Most of us are familiar with the long list of Lincoln's failures before he became president. They contributed greatly to his realism, his strategies, and his character—all of which made him one of our greatest presidents. Failure is painful when it happens, but it can become one of our greatest assets.

Train Yourself for Failure!

John C. Maxwell has written an entire book on learning from failure titled *Failing Forward*. Page after page, it's a steady drumbeat of advice on how to persevere and rise above failures, with illustrations of people from all walks of life who turned failure into success.

He quotes former White House aide J. Wallace Hamilton in CTI's *Leadership* journal as stating, "People are training for success when they should be training for failure. Failure is far more common than success." Maxwell says that this concept—training for failure—prompted him to write the book. "Most people try to avoid failure like the plague. They're afraid of it. But it takes adversity to create success. Basketball coach Rick Pitino states it even more strongly. 'Failure is good,' he says. 'It's fertilizer. Everything I've learned about coaching I've learned from making mistakes.'

"People who see failure as the enemy are captive to those who conquer it. Herbert V. Procknow says, 'The fellow who never makes a mistake takes his orders from one who does.' Observe any high achiever, and you'll discover a person who doesn't see a mistake as the enemy. That's true in any endeavor. Musicologist Eloise Ristad emphasizes that 'when we give ourselves permission to fail, we at the same time give ourselves permission to excel.'

"There's an old saying in Texas: 'It doesn't matter how much milk you spill as long as you don't lose your cow.' In other words, mistakes are not irreversible. Keep everything in perspective. The problems come when you see only the spilled milk.

"'Mistakes are not permanent markers,' continues Ristad. I love the perspective of the late Senator Sam Ervin Jr., who remarked, 'Defeat may serve as well as victory to shake the soul and let the glory out.' That's the way we need to look at failure."

Take Risks

Giving in to our fears of taking risks stunts our capacity for growth. A leader cannot simply tread water.

When Billy Graham decided to go to Russia against the advice of the State Department and many high officials, as well as some of his own advisers, he suffered the impact of the fallout. Ultimately, he was vindicated, but not every risky venture turns out that way.

Billy would avoid all *unnecessary* risks, as we see with his "Modesto Manifesto," and his constant weighing-in-the-balances of options and appearances. But he was also always taking risks. Every time he appeared on television, held a press conference with reporters who could blindside him, or traveled in troubled countries, he opened himself to all sorts of consequences. Taking risks day after day, year after year, equals some failures. It's simple math. Yet risk is a necessity of leadership.

Sheehy's book *Pathfinders* is based on extensive research plus one-on-one interviews. She contrasts people of "high well-being" who have come up with creative solutions to life's crises with those who flounder. The "pathfinders" responded to failure by recasting the experience in their minds, coming to see it as a useful plus. These pathfinders "turned most often to the same coping devices: work more; depend on friends; see the humor in the situation; pray." Those with low well-being turned to these: "Drink more, eat more, take drugs—indulge; pretend the problem doesn't exist; develop physical symptoms; escape into fantasy."

> Only those who dare to fail miserably can achieve greatly.
> ROBERT F. KENNEDY

"Pathfinders feel the blows—often severely," she writes. "It's just that they do not go down for the count." Her hopeful conclusion from this large study? "Resiliency in failure and the ability to take criticism are not qualities with which one is born; they are acquired strengths."

But to acquire those strengths, one must take wisely calculated risks. "A willingness to risk is the master quality for pathfinding," she says. "It is the linchpin."

Leaders are pathfinders. To lead and thrive, they must deftly secure that linchpin.

Grab the Bull's Tail

Some of us plunge ahead too fast; others hesitate to grab opportunity when we should. Each must lead with lots of self-understanding, wise counsel, and judicious analysis. But for all of us, times come when we have to make that decision: grab the bull by the tail or let it go by.

Grabbing the tail may result in wild, unpredictable things happening. Yet if they do, Mark Twain has a bit of wisdom for us. The great novelist made this wry observation: "A person who has had a bull by the tail once has learned sixty or seventy times as much as a person who hasn't."

If your decision to grab opportunity flings you into the dirt and pain of Roosevelt's "sweaty arena," remember that president's own attitude toward failure; "It is hard to fail," said Theodore Roosevelt, "but it IS worse never to have tried to succeed." And he said what we all realize, even at those moments when we are wondering if we should grab that tail or not: "He who makes no mistakes makes no progress."

Turn Even Unthinkable Failure into Gold

We've all watched leaders who once enjoyed high success and sterling reputations brought low and humiliated. We see spiritual leaders who violated their trust or exploited their constituencies led off to prison. We see CEOs handcuffed, tried, convicted, their careers destroyed, their families devastated.

There are many levels of failures. All of us dread the ones that go beyond mere mistakes, which can be viewed as building blocks of experience. It's inconceivable to most of us that we could experience deep humiliation, but—as the Elephant Man said in the play of that name, "Life is chancy."

Failures come in many ways, some our fault, others not. Taking risks opens us to consequences, and as we lead and take those risks, it doesn't hurt to ask, "What if the very worst happens to me? What if my decisions and bold action result in catastrophes—for me, my family, and those I lead?"

Obviously, the answer starts with how the decision to take action was made, and the hopefully good process and good counsel that led to it. But beyond that, in the "furnace of affliction," the reality is that out of the worst can come remarkable things.

If we think the worst that can happen is either false or true accusation and then imprisonment, we might consider those who experienced profound growth in prison. Solzhenitsyn, who wrote some of his great novels in brutal work camps, once declared "Thank God for prison." Chuck Colson's life was revolutionized by his time in prison and subsequent experience with Christ. John

Bunyan wrote his classic *Pilgrim's Progress* in jail. Jim Bakker, whom the Grahams befriended during and after his prison experience, became a changed and greatly deepened man during his years in prison. Anwar Sadat, Egypt's former president who eventually was assassinated, found such inner peace in prison that he was able to say, remarkably, that his last eight months there were "the happiest period of my life."

Success is never final, and failure is rarely fatal. It's the courage to continue that counts.

WINSTON CHURCHILL

Our decisions and failures as leaders are unlikely to land most of us in jail or in other tragic situations. Yet it is useful in our capricious world to mentally and spiritually prepare for worst-case scenarios. It not only prepares the soul, it also sharpens the mind in the decision process.

We have always been intrigued by Rudyard Kipling's famous advice to treat just the same "those two imposters," success and failure. The results of decisions are in many ways up to God. Leadership is, indeed, forged in the furnace, and failure can extrude the finest of useful and enduring metals.

POINTS TO PONDER

BILLY GRAHAM:

Mountaintops are for views and inspiration,

but fruit is grown in the valleys.

THE BIBLE:

My flesh and my heart may fail, but God is the strength

of my heart and my portion forever.

PSALM 73:26

CHAPTER 12

Experiencing Trauma and Betrayal

Character cannot be developed in ease and
quiet. Only through experience of trial and
suffering can the soul be strengthened, vision
cleared, ambition inspired and success
achieved.
HELEN KELLER

What is the most painful experience you can have as a leader?
Many would say being betrayed by someone you fully trusted,
someone with whom you'd let down your guard and become
fully vulnerable. They would liken it to the shock and bitterness
that often grips a divorced spouse, rejected by the intimate lover
who was supposed to love and protect.

In many ways, leadership is relationships, and if we are effective leaders, generally we need to build close ones. We are wary
at first of trusting anyone too much. We recognize our judgments
about whom we can trust must be accurate, or we can suffer
deeply. Yet sometimes even the most astute leaders get blindsided
by someone good at projecting sincerity and friendship, yet with
a different agenda.

Leaders face this all the time. In a survey of pastors, *Leadership* journal found that about sixty percent had experienced in
their professional lives at least one traumatic event extremely difficult to accept. The vast majority of those said they had felt
betrayed by persons they thought they could trust.

Perhaps you will never experience betrayal. Then again, it's one of the more likely experiences ahead, a time when someone turns on you, opens you to shame and ridicule, or subverts your labors of love, your relationships and aspirations. How you respond when it happens can make the difference between continuing a vigorous leadership or falling as a casualty.

What was the most painful thing Billy Graham experienced in his long years as a leader? What shook him to his core? It was not the betrayal by a close colleague.

According to his wife, Ruth, it was his feeling of being betrayed by Richard Nixon when the Watergate transcripts were made public. Ruth said it was the hardest thing her husband had ever gone through.

Billy had been preparing for his long-awaited international conference in Lausanne, Switzerland. The Watergate scandal became the national obsession, and before leaving for Europe, Billy forced himself to sit down and read the edited transcripts of the Watergate tapes. The recorded voice was unmistakably Nixon's, but Billy did not recognize his good friend. Nixon's filthy language and cold calculation shocked him. Billy retreated to the study at his Montreat home for solitude. The tapes made him physically and emotionally sick: he wept and vomited. Normally an astute judge of character, Billy never saw this devastation coming.

But why such devastation to him personally? He suffered public embarrassment because of his friendship with Nixon, but he had weathered public pain before. How could this sense of having been so wrong have happened, and why did it affect him so deeply?

■ ■ ■

Billy Graham's history with Richard Nixon went far back, and it was a surprisingly close relationship. Today, Nixon may be caricatured in many people's minds, but he was very smart, a brilliant strategist, and an indefatigable worker. Anyone, for instance, who reviews the books Nixon wrote after his presidency must acknowledge the depth of his insights and the breadth of his knowledge. The man who won election to the presidency and opened up China in his historic initiatives was far from a simplistic villain. If he was flawed, this was not clearly discerned by many, and Billy saw his strengths, not his "dark side."

Billy built his friendship with Nixon when he was vice president under Dwight Eisenhower. When Nixon failed to defeat Kennedy in his own bid to become president in 1960, and two years later lost the election for governor of California, he was devastated. Once excruciatingly close to the Oval Office, Nixon sank into depression. It seemed only a few still believed in Nixon—but one who did was his longtime friend, Billy Graham.

"Dick, I believe you'll have another chance at the presidency," Billy told Nixon as they played golf together. "The world situation is getting worse. There'll come a time when the American people will call on you. You have the ability and the training to be president of the United States. Don't give up." Indeed, Billy's respect for Nixon was genuine and deep. He admired his intellectual capabilities and government expertise.

In 1967 Nixon called Billy for advice. The political tide had once again turned. Down and out for five years, Nixon had reclaimed much of his earlier luster. Now he wanted Billy's opinion on making another run for the White House, so he invited Billy to join him in Florida. Although Billy was sick with what he later learned was pneumonia, nothing would come between him and his friend.

During two days in Key Biscayne, Nixon and Billy discussed Scripture and prayed, as they frequently did when together. Shortly before Billy left, they walked along the beach, discussing Nixon's aspirations. Nixon pressed Billy for guidance. "You still haven't told me what to do," he said.

"If you don't run, you will always wonder if you should have," Billy replied. "I will pray for you, that the Lord will give you the wisdom to make the right choice."

Later, Nixon said that Billy, more than any other individual, influenced his decision to run.

On election night, before appearing victoriously to the press, Nixon invited Billy to join his family in the hotel. Billy and T. W. Wilson quickly hopped a cab and headed for Nixon's room. When they arrived, Nixon asked them all to join hands so Billy could offer a prayer.

Such outward manifestations of spirituality impressed Billy. Their many conversations convinced him of Nixon's genuine, if still private, religious belief. Midway through Nixon's first term, Billy wrote his old friend a note: "My expectations were high when you took office nearly two years ago but you have exceeded [them] in every way! You have given moral and spiritual leadership to the nation at a time when we desperately needed it—in addition to courageous political leadership! Thank you!"

Years later, when Nixon fell, Billy's embarrassment stung because the president had betrayed him publicly as a visible ally and privately as a close friend. The association with Nixon tarnished Billy's ministry and legacy, and Billy wondered how he could have been so wrong about him. "Looking back these forty-five years later," Billy wrote in his 1997 autobiography *Just As I Am*, "considering all that has intervened, I wonder whether I might have exaggerated his spirituality in my own mind." He told a biographer, "I just couldn't understand it. I still can't. I thought he was a man of great integrity. I looked upon him as the possibility of leading this country to its greatest and best days. And all those people around him, they seemed to me so clean, family men, so clean-living. Sometimes, when I look back on it all now, it has the aspects of a nightmare."

■ ■ ■

Talk about being refined in the furnace of leadership! The Nixon experience for Billy was the "furnace heated seven times."

He had been disappointed in others before. Early in his career, disillusioned by a leader he had fully respected, he advised others to never put people on a pedestal, nor to expect from them what only God can provide. During his long career, many had failed him. For instance, a colleague of Billy's told us of a teammate who had so greatly failed Billy that he was considered by Billy's associates as "the enemy."

In all cases, whatever his spiritual depth and intensity, Billy still had to deal with his emotions. His response was at the opposite pole of either bitterness or revenge. He turned to the Bible's admonitions to love and to forgive.

In the case of "the enemy" described by his colleague, Billy forgave him and later in life sought him out and invited him to share a meal. And for Richard Nixon, he reached out far "beyond the call of duty." Despite the pain of betrayal, despite the embarrassment, despite the questions of "How?" and "Why?"—Billy never gave up on him.

The night before Nixon resigned, Billy attempted to reach the president by phone, but without success. Even after Nixon left the White House in disgrace, Billy refused to pile on. "I shall always consider him a personal friend," he told reporters. "His personal suffering must be almost unbearable. He deserves the prayers even of those who feel betrayed and let down."

Billy remained pastoral despite being chief among the "betrayed and let down." He tried to visit Nixon in California, but the former president was too sick for visitors. Undeterred, Ruth Graham hired an airplane to fly around Nixon's San Clemente home towing a banner that read, "Nixon. God Loves You and So Do We."

The following spring, Billy finally was able to visit Nixon in California. His daughter, Julie Eisenhower, recalled, "The purpose of the visit was simply to reassure both of my parents of his complete love and faith in them. The lack of hypocrisy and absence of a 'holier than thou' attitude had always impressed me tremendously. Dr. Graham's capacity for friendship and his eagerness to love make him stand apart from other men."

When Nixon died in April 1994, Billy accepted the unenviable responsibility of conducting his funeral. Once again, Billy set aside his private grief to publicly serve his friend. The eyes of the world— not to mention the eyes of Presidents Ford, Carter, Reagan, Bush, and Clinton, and their first ladies—looked to see how Billy would address Nixon's considerable, if severely tarnished, legacy.

In his eulogy, Billy carefully acknowledged the complexity of Nixon's character. He also pointed out his stature, saying, "I think most of us have been staggered at the many things he accomplished during his life. His public service kept him at the center of the events that have shaped our destiny. This week, *Time* magazine says that 'by sheer endurance he rebuilt his standing as the most important figure of the post-war era.'"

Then Billy spoke of the Nixon he had known. "There was another more personal, more intimate and more human side to Richard Nixon—that his family, neighbors, and friends that are gathered here today would know. It was a side many did not see, for Richard Nixon was a private and perhaps even a shy individual whom others sometimes found hard to get to know. There were hundreds of little things that he did for ordinary people that no one would ever know about. He always had a compassion for people who were hurting."

Billy's love for the man who betrayed his trust remained strong. As with many other traumas he had experienced in leading, he did not let natural reactions of self-pity or anger control his responses. Billy, in living through the nightmare had, because of the depth of his faith and commitments, once again been extruded from the furnace as a stronger leader, tempered by the fires.

■ ■ ■

Such tempering has come not only from the deep suffering of the Nixon experience but from the weight of leadership and personal tragedies he's been close to. "When I talk about suffering," he said in his book *Hope for the Troubled Heart*, "I'm no different from you. I would like to live a life free of problems, free of pain, and free of severe personal discipline. However, I'd had extreme pressures in my life to the point where I've wanted to run away from reality."

Note the words "severe" and "extreme." At the Graham retreat center, called the Cove, is a cemetery with designated plots where Billy and Ruth will eventually be buried. Billy has said that sometimes the mental, physical, and spiritual pressures on him have been so great that "I felt like going to the Cove and lying down in the cemetery to see how I fit."

Yet after that wry comment, Billy added, "God has called me to my responsibilities, and I must be faithful." This is no easy mental turnaround, for being faithful has its requirements. Billy also speaks about his being "constantly concerned about being quoted in the press and perhaps saying the wrong thing."

The cost of leadership accentuates sufferings and anxieties, and shallow prescriptions only disappoint. This Billy knows only too well. "I must admit I feel very inadequate at times when talking about God's discipline through pain," he says. "I've been close to those who have lost their children in accidents or lingering illnesses. . . . I have been with leaders whose careers were ruined by their own bad choices. I have been in areas devastated by earthquakes, fires, and bombs. When those I love have suffered, I have wished I could take their pain as my own."

He does not want to be presumptuous when speaking of suffering when he contrasts his with the depths of others' travail. But he does offer hope and turns for personal inspiration to the Bible and examples of believers, without which, he "would be as inadequate to write about suffering as a child would be to explain nuclear physics."

A model for him is the early church's most dynamic and effective leader, the apostle Paul. Billy says that "when it comes to all sorts of suffering, Paul was in the major leagues."

Indeed, he was. Billy quotes Paul's own description of being dishonored, hungry, thirsty, in rags, brutally treated, homeless, cursed, slandered—and considered the scum of the earth. Yet for all Paul's "devastating physical sufferings," it's significant that Billy points out Paul felt even greater pressure as he thought of his responsibilities as a leader.

"If any of you are leaders," Billy wrote, "you know the kind of pressure Paul was describing. Humanly speaking, it can lead to loneliness, depression, and often discouragement. Only God's illimitable grace and peace can carry us through times of trial."

Despite walking in the furnace of leadership all through his career—carrying the weight and pressing the limits under "severe discipline"—Billy has always been the apostle of hope. In betrayal or deep tragedy, he has sought the insights and spiritual resources that enabled him to, in the words of the Bible, "run the race and finish the course."

LEADERSHIP LESSONS | Betrayal

Applying the Principles

As Scott Peck famously wrote as the terse opener of his bestseller, *The Road Less Traveled*, "Life is difficult."

So it is. Resilient leaders recognize that fact early, and they do what they can to endure, to deepen and grow, and to keep leading.

So what can we do to prepare?

Train for the Next Emotional Hit

James E. Loehr, in his book *Toughness Training for Life*, points out, "No matter where you are on the scale of rough times at the moment, sooner or later even rougher times are going to slam into your life. Crises and adversity are deeply woven into the fabric of human existence. . . . Directly, or indirectly, calamities and tragedies touch us all. Sometimes they strike like sledgehammers."

Loehr trains athletes and executives, counseling them to be realistic about future rough spots and to take action in specific ways. "Train every day to get as tough as possible physically and emotionally," he advises, "to elevate your health, boost your productivity, and expand your happiness . . . so that you will suffer less devastation when you absorb your next emotional hit."

It's not pleasant to think an emotional hit is ahead, but it is realistic. Loehr provides a detailed game plan, advising us to get "tough" through physical, mental, and spiritual disciplines. "Tough individuals," he says, "are consistently able to perceive stressful situations as opportunities for growth."

Although Loehr refers to the executives he counsels as "corporate athletes," he's not advising Olympic-level physical training. He advocates consistent discipline in all areas, as an athlete must constantly train to be ready for the next event. This includes physical exercise, eating right, and positive stress-busters, such as a mental oasis of our favorite things.

Apparently Billy has been doing that all along as he's experienced the rigors of international travel. "When I am in yet another hotel room in some city around the world," he said, "I often think of our mountain home, filled with a lifetime of memories and love." He thinks of spring, when Ruth heads for the garden, and the way "she has always kept a home of comfort and beauty for our family."

That's exactly the sort of oasis Loehr advises we visit, to enable our minds and bodies to release the positive chemicals that overcome stress and help us rise to endure the inevitable "hits."

We seldom think of calamities as opportunities for growth, especially when they send us reeling. But of course, they always are. In hindsight, we sometimes see that out of the worst came far deeper understanding of ourselves and of the human condition—a crucial component of effective leadership.

Bitter Medicine in Your Mouth? Check the Directions

Leaders have many occasions to feel bitter. Betrayal by a trusted associate. A competitor's misrepresentation that humiliates the entire team. A bogus lawsuit destroying the company. Life is unfair, so is competition, and like Billy's intense distress about Nixon, we may find ourselves with bitter herbs burning in our mouths.

> *The last of our human freedoms is to choose our attitude in any given circumstance.*
>
> **VICTOR FRANKL**

Like Billy, we have a choice: we can let it fester or we can deal with it. "Bitterness can strangle a human being," Billy has said. "Bitterness is like an abscess."

He turns to the Bible's advice: "See to it that no one misses the grace of God and that no bitter root grows up to cause trouble and defile many." A leader who is bitter certainly will cause trouble, for himself and for many others.

The potency of bitterness is a scary thing. Here's how California pastor John Courson describes it: "This is what bitterness does. It's like taking a bottle of poison, swallowing it, and then waiting for the other person to die."

In other words, *savoring* bitterness is emotionally and spiritually suicidal.

In contrast, Courson quotes the Bible's prescription: "A merry heart does good like a medicine."

"When a person is bitter, angry, caustic, cynical," says Courson, "the chemicals produced in your glands flow through your body. They affect your stomach. They affect your heart. They affect your whole being. Bitterness doesn't pay, even if you have justifiable reason."

To go from anger at outrageous injustice against us to a "merry heart" is a long, almost inconceivable process. But the journey to forgiveness and love, demonstrated by Billy Graham in not only the Nixon tragedy but other experiences, is the way of the effective leader who guards that priceless asset of his or her own physical and spiritual health.

Metamorphosize!

Emily's rejection of Billy as the man to marry was not on the level of a deep catastrophe—yet it had a great deal to do with his metamorphosis. Setbacks and trauma can be catalysts for dramatic changes mentally and spiritually.

J. C. Penney experienced plenty of trauma. In 1898 he established the Golden Rule store, with low prices. He was a "bundle of energy" and "like a person in perpetual motion." He hired men like himself with the highest business and moral standards.

But in 1910 his wife died, and he felt deserted by God.

In 1919 he married again and enjoyed prosperity. But in 1923 his second wife died also. He took refuge in his work.

A third time he married. By 1929 he was worth $40 million. But the great "Crash" came, and he lost his money as well as his excellent reputation.

J. C. Penney ended up in a sanitarium in Battle Creek, broken emotionally and physically. He was near death, not expected to live past morning. Then in his room he heard a familiar hymn from the chapel. In his dying state he asked God to help him, and, in a remarkable transformation, he felt his burden lifted. He was dramatically metamorphosed, soon walking out of the institution on his own steam. He became a man with a deep belief in God.

By the late 1930s he was again prosperous, representing the J. C. Penney Company around the nation. He gave away millions, and for decades vigorously communicated his values and faith. At ninety, he was still going strong.

> *So long as we live in this world, we cannot escape suffering.*
>
> THOMAS À KEMPIS

Sometimes traumas make us desperate. Sometimes they may literally bring us to the edge of emotional or physical death. Not everyone calling out to God in such times experiences a metamorphosis. Such experiences, however, do show the power of turning from overwhelming troubles to the spiritual power that can lead to personal transformation.

Out of the Depths, Communicate Hope

Leaders, of course, must endure not only their own tragedies but those of others as well. When employees are diagnosed with cancer, or cause fatal accidents, or fail morally in ways that stun an organization, a pastoral role is thrust upon the person in charge. Some shrink from it or fear being intrusive. But empathy and wisdom on such occasions become humane building blocks, creating loyalty and trust.

When storms strike individuals or organizations, a leader who responds with genuine concern and calm establishes his or her leadership. We experience our own pain but simultaneously identify with what others feel and think, reaching out to them.

We see this spirit in Billy as he responded to the 1995 Oklahoma City bombing. David Frost observed that although the president and the governor both spoke at the memorial service, it was Billy's words that "offered the most comfort to those who had lost loved ones."

Billy clearly put himself in the place of the bereaved. "Times like this," he said, "will do one of two things: They will either make us hard and bitter and angry at God, or they will make us tender and open and help us to reach out in trust and faith. . . . I pray that you will not let bitterness and poison creep into your souls, but you will turn in faith and trust in God even if we cannot understand."

Staunch Your Wounds, and Drive!

We all experience "emotional hits," and we can't deny them. Even though we may find ourselves hurting badly—very badly—we may still have to lead others.

We love the illustration pastor Ray Pritchard uses to show how sometimes, despite what's happened to us, we need to keep going. "In the movie *Black Hawk Down*," Pritchard says, "a vehicle filled with wounded American soldiers lurches to a stop in the middle of a street where Somali bullets are flying in every direction. The officer in charge tells a soldier to get in and start driving. 'I can't,' the soldier says, 'I'm shot.'"

Sometimes as leaders bullets not only fly but hit us right in the gut, disabling us.

But in *Black Hawk Down*, the officer uses this immortal line after the soldier says he's shot: "We're all shot. Get in and drive!"

The human condition. We're all wounded, but we have to keep going anyway. Sometimes these are words to live by: "We're all shot. Get in and drive!"

POINTS TO PONDER

BILLY GRAHAM:

Comfort and prosperity have never enriched the world

as much as adversity has.

THE BIBLE:

Many will turn away from the faith and will betray and hate

each other. . . . Because of the increase of wickedness, the love of

most will grow cold, but he who stands firm to the end will be saved.

MATTHEW 24:10 – 13

CHAPTER 13

Redeeming the Ego

> Those who stand highest in the esteem of men
> are most exposed to grievous peril.
>
> THOMAS À KEMPIS

Bill Mead, Graham's first executive committee chair, told us about Billy's taking him along on trips to the White House "because he wanted a businessman to come along, someone who knew enough to keep his mouth shut." When President Johnson was terminally ill, Billy called Mead, said that Johnson had invited him to come to the ranch to talk about his funeral, and asked him to come along. "Johnson was sitting on the front porch with his dog on his lap," he recalls, "and then we rode around in his convertible. Lyndon would be telling Billy what he wanted done at his funeral. Two weeks after that, Johnson died. He had felt Billy was from God himself."

Mead, still peppery and engaged in his eighties, added with a sense of wonder, "Billy has that presence and humility. He commands respect from presidents, from Ike, Johnson—all of them!"

We were in Fred Smith's home, interviewing both Smith and Mead, who are friends. Fred said, "Billy was humble but not intimidated."

We wondered how someone could be humble and handle the ego while becoming such close friends with presidents.

"The ego must be redeemed," Fred replied.

"Meaning, you must have a strong ego to lead, but something must happen to it?"

"Absolutely. And you can tell when someone allows God to redeem his ego. I was chair of Billy's Cincinnati campaign and was with him at a breakfast with a reporter who was critical of Billy. He asked him hard questions. However, the published story turned out positive. Billy then told me, with a grin, 'Fred, they don't care if you're a nut so long as you're a sincere nut.' He didn't take himself too seriously."

■ ■ ■

The mix of Mead's words, *presence*, *respect*, and *humility*, seemed oddly juxtaposed. Having the charisma to command respect at the highest levels and the ability to turn hostile reporters into advocates would naturally inflate anyone's ego. Yet it is not only Mead and Smith who reference Billy's humility. As we interviewed many colleagues and friends, his humility became a constant theme.

For instance, when we talked with Lon Allison, director of the Billy Graham Center at Wheaton College, the very first thing he said was, "Have you hit on the humility factor?" He then went on to tell a personal story.

"The first step in my being hired in 1998 was to meet Billy. He was holding a crusade in Ottawa, Canada. Billy always meets with people before he speaks at night, so rooms had been set up for him in the back of the auditorium. As we walked down a hallway with armed guards everywhere, I said out loud, 'This feels like going to the White House or something.' You sensed all the power. Yet when anyone walks into where Billy is, it becomes the absolute opposite. He's Pop. He's Grandpa. He's completely unaffected.

"Sterling Huston introduced us saying, 'You know, Bill, Lon did his doctoral research in evangelistic preaching and communications.' Billy put his hand on my shoulder and said with all seriousness, 'Maybe you could teach me a few things.'

"I just burst out laughing. It was totally unexpected. I said something like, 'Well, since most of my work is based on your life,

I doubt it.' But Billy was totally serious—'Maybe you could teach me a few things.'"

Lon then spoke of Billy's calling him, asking about his family and also sharing concerns about his own family issues. "You simply don't have the sense you're with this world-famous person," said Lon. "If you hear him talk, he always uses the plural pronoun—never I."

■ ■ ■

Redeeming the ego. What did Smith mean? What has transpired in Billy Graham's psyche and spiritual life that has melded him into such a blend of world-class, driving visionary and meek, unassuming student?

One of the many brushstrokes in this picture is the way Billy views himself. We sat in a pancake restaurant in Charlotte with Graeme Keith, treasurer of Billy's organization and a lifelong friend. We had flown there from Wheaton, where the Billy Graham Center with its great white pillars faces the original classic edifice of Billy's alma mater. Before it was built, Billy had talked to us about feeling uncomfortable about the college's naming it for him. About two minutes out of Charlotte's airport, we had turned onto the new Billy Graham Parkway—a major freeway—and passed the seventy prime acres slated for his new headquarters and library. It was hard driving into Charlotte to think of Billy's having external aids to control his ego.

Graeme, who himself comes off humbly despite his being a major force in Charlotte, gets around rather quickly to Billy's natural humility. "I was on an elevator with Billy when another man in the elevator recognized him. He said, 'You're Billy Graham, aren't you?'

"'Yes,' Billy said.

"'Well,' he said, 'you are truly a great man.'

"Billy immediately responded, 'No, I'm not a great man. I just have a great message.'"

We thought of his 1954 tour of Europe when he preached in Mannheim, Germany, where a hostile reporter asked, "What do you know about the suffering of Christ that you preach about so often? You have never suffered. You live well and have the comforts of life."

Billy's response: "When a Western Union messenger boy delivers a death message to a home, he doesn't take part in all the suffering connected with the message. He just delivers the telegram. That's all I am—God's messenger boy."

Graeme went on to tell of the time when he was with Billy in a group setting. A leader in the organization was describing in detail Billy's accomplishments. "He told everyone about all the many things he had done," Graeme said. "But then Billy interrupted him. He said, 'No, that's not right. I didn't do these things. The Lord did.'"

From those who have known him best emerges the picture of Billy's unfeigned belief that he was simply God's ambassador, carrying a message of love to the world. His oft-repeated remark that "my lips would turn to clay if God took his hand from me" gave him a sense that he was, to use Mother Teresa's description of herself, "God's pencil."

At the same time, his driving purpose, like Mother Teresa's, added to the force of his personality and his commanding presence.

Billy titled his autobiography *Just As I Am*. It's the title of the hymn sung during his invitations to receive Christ. Those who have experienced the gentle, soul-searching sounds of thousands of voices singing the invitational hymn know its probing power and abject humility: "Just as I am, without one plea. . . ."

In choosing that title for his own life story, Billy identified himself with every convert walking to the front and confessing sin and weakness. By that title he says that he too is the recipient of grace, and God has done all the work. "Most of all," he says in the book's introduction, "if anything has been accomplished through my life, it has been solely God's doing, not mine, and He—not I—must get the credit."

This is no act. Through the centuries the deepest and most perceptive seekers of God have concluded that those who draw closest to the Almighty have the strongest sense of their own unworthiness. When Billy deflects the glory, it's not an "Aw, shucks" kind of modesty but a sense of being "a brand plucked from the fire by a holy God"—who calls him his beloved.

In a David Frost interview, Billy said that when he preached, "the Holy Spirit is the communicating agent. . . . People are really not listening to me. . . . They're listening to another voice inside, the voice of the Holy Spirit." Billy went on to say to Frost that even when he may preach the message poorly and leave out things he wanted to say, "God knows my motive and he knows my heart, and God uses even that simple presentation that might have been poorly done, and he applies it to the human heart."

Frost then asked, "So there can never be a feeling that 'I've done badly, I've failed tonight'?"

Billy responded, "Oh, I have that feeling quite often. In fact, most of the time I feel I wish I could have represented the gospel better tonight. Really, that's a sincere feeling. Almost every night I say, 'I wish I had done better,' because I'm a representative, really, of Christ. That's a tremendous responsibility."

So we see here his self-perception of being a simple workman with a huge mandate, like an ambassador in wartime carrying gold bullion to people desperately needing it. He's the conveyer of the most important goods in the world, and he believes all is lost or won depending on how he carries the message and how he responds to God's initiatives.

With this perspective, he's not remotely "triumphalistic," a term sometimes used by academics to describe evangelicals who seem so certain of their stance and importance that they come off as arrogant. Yet the perspective drives him to do his very best in the eternal war between good and evil, heaven and hell. He openly admits to struggles with his inadequacy for such a task that is loaded on him as a mere mortal. That's one reason it's painful for him to hear long, adulatory introductions. He feels humble laboring under the magnificence of God. In fact, his feelings can be quite intense. In the groundbreaking ceremonies for his new headquarters, Billy said, "Jesus must increase, and I must decrease. I cringe when I hear my name called in something that has been the work of God through these years."

■ ■ ■

Russ Busby, longtime official photographer for the Graham association, has provided thousands of striking photos documenting Billy's ministry. The hallmark humility natural in Billy's colleagues is clearly evident in Busby. "I don't travel with him," he says. "I show up where I'm supposed to." But he has spent lots of time with Billy and his family. "His ideas and vision are uncanny," Busby says, recognizing the many reasons for Billy to think highly of himself. "But God has always, in God's way—and I don't know 99 percent of it—kept him humble. I don't know what his 'thorn-in-the-flesh' was . . ." Busby stopped with an edge of humor in his voice, "it could have been me. . . ."

Then he explained, "God will do that with each one of us. It's how we react to it that counts. Billy may have a bit of ego for a day or two and be excited about something, but the next time you see him, he's back down to reality with himself, before God. He's one of the few Christian leaders whose attention God can get when he wants it. He's not running so fast or so deeply involved in his own agenda. When God taps him on the shoulder he says, 'Yes, Lord,' rather than 'Just a minute, I have to finish this.' God can quickly get his attention."

God apparently gets Billy's attention quite a bit, and the result is this remarkable phenomenon, not of a placid saint but of broken saintliness—an often tortured soul with a gracious, loving smile, a meekness, yet towering strength.

In our research we've come across vivid metaphors that observers have created to describe this paradoxical Billy Graham. But an image we noticed in a poem by a Franciscan nun, Mary Karr, published in the *Atlantic Monthly*, struck us as perhaps the most fitting. In it, she describes meekness in an arresting way. To understand the Bible's use of the word "meek," she says, we should picture a great stallion at full gallop. At his master's voice, he "seizes up to a stunned but instant halt." Karr then eloquently describes the stallion holding its "great power" in check, listening for the next order.

"Blessed are the meek," said Jesus. When we hear this, we are likely to think of a Caspar Milquetoast and certainly not a magnificent creature racing against the wind with rippling muscles and flying hooves, full of spirit and confidence. But the blessedness and meekness blend in the powerful stallion's response to the master.

In the same way, Billy has power, charisma, a dynamism that has made businessmen say, "He could have been a billionaire," and Hollywood to send contracts to make him a star. But meekness is power under control. As he runs his race, when Billy hears his Master's voice, he listens—and at times "seizes up to a stunned but instant halt."

A parallel image is simply Billy as farm boy, still totally awed by all that has happened to and through him. Over and over we find he expresses total wonder at what has been done through him. He is the boy-become-man who sees far more clearly than most the mixed motives of human souls.

Humility? Billy contrasts the realities of the imperfect human condition with the magnificence of the Creator. He recognizes his is only a small part in a vast creation, having a sense of wonder and awe that he has been chosen.

After we had written this chapter, we came across the same image of the stallion in one of Billy's own writings, published long before the *Atlantic* poem. "Jesus said, 'Blessed are the gentle, for they shall inherit the earth,'" Billy wrote. "Nowhere in Scripture does this word carry with it the idea of being spiritless and timid. It carries the idea of being tamed, like a wild horse that has been brought under control."

Billy was the spirited horse, always listening intently for the whisper of the Spirit.

In his home several years ago, a colleague said to him, after they had looked at some materials about his accomplishments, "Billy, you've always been humble before both God and man." They were walking up some stairs, and Billy was behind him. He called up, "Well, I'll tell you, I'm not as humble as you think I am."

No, Billy is not humble in the simplistic sense, but he has made himself vulnerable to the Spirit to redeem his ego. That is what has made possible the image of the stallion, full of power and vitality, racing against the buffeting wind, but instantly alert to the Spirit's check.

The tensions and pressures of both external and internal forces are not insignificant. As Carl Gustav Jung has said, "Fear of self-sacrifice lurks deep in every ego." If Billy, "mere mortal," can carry such weight and respond so sensitively to the Spirit, so we can at least aspire to sharpen our ears. The process of redeeming the ego is a lifelong one, but absolutely essential to leadership.

LEADERSHIP LESSONS | Ego

Applying the Principles

The word *ego* has at least two definitions: (1) "a regarding of one's self with undue favor," with synonyms of *conceit* or *vanity*, and (2) "a sense of one's own dignity or worth," synonymous with *self-respect*. Redeeming the ego can be described as how effectively our own ego is marked by the second definition rather than the first.

This is captured in the observation by Estelle Smith that "Humility is strong—not bold; quiet—not speechless; sure—not arrogant." Fred Smith puts it this way: "Humility is not denying the power you have. It is realizing that the power comes through you, not from you."

What are the ways that leaders can harness the power of ego so that it doesn't hinder but instead serves the cause?

Be Aware of Mysterious Forces

It does not take long in reading biographical material about General Robert E. Lee to be struck by how committed a Christian he was and how his perceptions and actions were shaped by his reliance on the Scriptures. He viewed living out his religious beliefs as essential, and his intense drive to do so fully was a lot like the spiritual intensity we see in Billy Graham. The two men's worldviews and commitments were largely congruent.

When Lee saw visible results of his own efforts, he would put them into perspective. He believed forces other than his own superb leadership were also at work, forces that were the ultimate arbiters of meaning.

We see this in his perceptions of his failure to lead the South to military victory. After the war, Lee became president of Washington College, seeking to train young men to rebuild the damaged nation. One day Lee called an underachieving sophomore into his office and told the young man that he must apply himself more to his studies, that only hard work would produce success in life. The sophomore somewhat brashly raised the issue of Lee's efforts and the outcome in the recent war: "But, General, you failed."

Lee neither rebuked the student nor conceded his point but said simply, "I hope that you may be more fortunate than I." Lee later elaborated to a friend, "We failed, but in the good providence of God, apparent failure often proves a blessing." As biographer H. W. Crocker points out, Lee's conviction was that "one must do one's duty to the best of one's ability, whatever the cost, whatever the circumstances, and trust that Providence will turn everything, even apparent disaster, to some useful purpose, however dimly perceived, if it can be perceived at all."

> *Humility is to make a right estimate of one's own self.*
> CHARLES H. SPURGEON

Lee's spirit in that regard paralleled Lincoln's remarkable second inaugural address, in which his humility and awareness of Providence are so profoundly expressed and etched in granite in his memorial. How ironic that these men, so spiritually deep and aware, led the terrible struggle against each other in that war. Yet these men were painfully aware of such ironies: that the great forces at work are beyond our facile comprehension, and that awareness of that fact has an enormous impact on the ego.

Such leaders understand that neither success nor failure can be understood immediately, that powers beyond their own are at work. In the David Frost interview cited above, Billy said he recognized his wasn't the most important factor in seeing results, but that "people were listening to another voice inside." The redeemed ego recognizes such mysterious forces and puts all individual efforts into a transcendent context.

In Humiliation, Lead On

None of us anticipates humiliation, and every fiber of our being fights that possibility. Yet leaders often experience, through little or no fault of their own, humiliations that tear at their self-respect. One man, going through deep waters, saw a dog in his yard violently yanking and snapping at an old cloth. He said he felt his reputation was like that shredded cloth.

But in the time of humiliation, leadership is needed all the more, and one's perspective will determine whether the leader folds or steps up to a very different sort of challenge.

One of General Robert E. Lee's most significant moments of leadership was not on a battlefield but on the eve of his surrender. After four years of warfare, during which, except for the final campaign, he had repeatedly outperformed his opponents, he now had to face the reality that he didn't have the men or supplies to continue the war against the well-resourced Union army. His Army of Northern Virginia numbered 15,000, while Union forces under General Grant numbered 80,000. His soldiers weren't ready to quit. Even with their shortages of food and ammunition, they would greet him, "General! General! Say the word, General, and we'll go after them again."

The night before he met with General Grant to discuss an end to the war, his artillery officer, E. P. Alexander, recommended that the Confederate army should "scatter like rabbits and partridges in the woods" and fight a guerilla war.

> I have been driven many times to my knees by the overwhelming conviction that I had nowhere else to go. My wisdom, and that of all about me, seemed insufficient for the day.
>
> ABRAHAM LINCOLN

It had to have been a tempting suggestion. Lee had already lost his home and virtually all his worldly goods, including his savings and investments. Worse, he had grieved the loss of a daughter, a daughter-in-law, two grandchildren, and countless friends and comrades. A patriot devoted to his homeland, he now was deprived of citizenship and liable to be tried for treason. Why shouldn't he give his men permission to continue striking back at those who had carried out the Union's policy of total war, destroying much of the South's countryside?

But Lee looked at Alexander and shook his head. "The men would have no rations, and they would be under no discipline," he said. "They would have to plunder and rob to procure subsistence. The country would be full of lawless bands in every part, and a state of society would ensue from which it would take the country years to recover. Then the enemy's cavalry would pursue . . . and everywhere they went, there would be fresh rapine and destruction." Lee told Alexander that he mustn't think of what surrender would mean in terms of lost honor; they had to do what was best for their country.

Alexander recounted later, "I had not a single word to say in reply. He had answered my suggestion from a plane so far above it that I was ashamed of having made it."

A leader is called to view the situation from a higher plane, to see beyond the immediate situation to the long-term consequences.

Lee's ego was as sensitive as anyone else's. Toward the end he was overheard saying, "How easily I could get rid of all this and be at rest. I have only to ride along the line and all will be over. But it is our duty to live. What will become of the women and children of the South if we are not here to protect them?" As always for Lee, there was a higher responsibility than self.

The Christian tradition has often viewed humiliation as a deepening and purifying process, with Jesus as the primary model of suffering humiliation with extreme grace. That attitude, when seen in a leader facing failure as monumental as Lee's, enables a gritty response to an "ultimate challenge."

The opposite of humiliation, extreme success, calls for the same depth of grace and objectivity. Jerry Jenkins, coauthor of the multi-million seller *Left Behind* series, once quipped, "If I ever act like I deserve this, just punch me in the mouth." His light comment carries heavy truth about how dangerous success can be to our egos.

Think Large; It's Not Egocentric

Missionary statesman Frank Laubach lived with zest and productivity, traveling the globe and writing more than fifty books, creating the "each-one-teach-one method," which pulled millions from illiteracy. He received many honors, and when presented with a Man of the Year Award said, "The Lord will not wish to count my trophies, but my scars."

He had his world-class accomplishments and his ego in perspective.

It's interesting to see in his letters to his father, at age forty-five, when his largest contributions were yet to come, the powerful, spiritual resurgence that caused him to say, "I would find God's will, though every fiber in me said, no." Yet this intensity gave him a freedom. He felt "like one who has had his violin out of tune with the orchestra and at last is in harmony with the universe. . . . Every day is tingling with the joy of a glorious discovery. That thing is eternal. That thing is undefeatable. You and I shall soon blow away from our bodies. Money, praise, poverty, opposition, these make no difference."

And yet, with that perspective—that earthly accomplishment meant little—he prayed, "God, what have you to put into my mind now if only I can be large enough?" He thought a waiting, eager attitude would "give God the chance He needs," and apparently it did. From that time, until he died at age eighty-five,

If you plan to build a house of virtues, you must first lay deep foundations of humility.
AUGUSTINE

Laubach accomplished "large" things far beyond his dreams. Ego, in accomplishing these large things, wasn't an issue, and that was evident in this man who felt "in harmony with the universe."

He expressed interesting ideas about self, saying that "concealment of the best in us is wrong." Laubach saw himself "simply carried along each hour, doing my part in a plan which is far beyond myself."

In *The Secret of Happiness*, Billy quoted Frank Laubach as saying, "Prayer at its highest is a two-way conversation; and for me, the most important part is listening to God's replies."

Avoid Grievous Peril

We started this chapter with a quote from à Kempis about the "grievous peril" of being held in high esteem. Billy was thoroughly aware of that danger. "I feel that people have put me on too high a pedestal," he said in a *New York Times* column. "We do the same with other leaders," Billy explained. "I know, however, that I am not as good as some people think I am. I have seen men in the depths of wickedness and I have thought to myself, 'There I go except by the grace of God.'"

POINTS TO PONDER

BILLY GRAHAM:

God measures people by the small dimensions of humility

and not by the bigness of their achievements

or the size of their capabilities.

THE BIBLE:

If you really keep the royal law found in Scripture,

"Love your neighbor as yourself," you are doing right.

JAMES 2:8

MULTIPLYING
MOMENTUM

A leader: An individual who created an alchemy of
vision that moved people from where they were to
places that they have never been before.

HENRY KISSINGER

When we considered the way Billy's leadership built momentum all the way through his more than sixty years of ministry, we wondered what maintained and multiplied that momentum. As we studied the dynamics, we isolated these four questions:

While many of his colleagues dreamed of filling critical vacuums with new initiatives, like launching a major national magazine, Billy actually went ahead and did it. How did he approach his entrepreneurship so effectively?

How did Billy build all those bridges to leaders of constituencies in many ways the opposite of his own?

We found great numbers of strong leaders throughout the world who consider Billy their mentor, even though most have spent little one-on-one time with him. How did that happen?

Over the years, how did Billy just keep planting all those seeds that bore so many kinds of fruit?

■■■

These four chapters grapple with those questions and attempt to find applications.

CHAPTER 14

Birthing Dreams

> Make no little plans. Make the biggest
> plan you can think of.
> **HARRY TRUMAN**

The entrepreneurial leader is always dreaming of what might be, of what breakthrough device or new publication or ministry could better people's lives. Not all of us are entrepreneurs; many of us who may think like one—and have lots of dreams—find we don't have the combination of opportunity, vision, resources, connections, or persistence to bring to reality what's perking in our heads.

Billy Graham too had many limitations of time, energy, and resources, yet somehow he was continually raising his sights, even as he encouraged other entrepreneurs. For instance, in the early 1950s he traveled to war-devastated Korea with Bob Pierce, endorsing his do-something-now vision for a suffering world. Today the organization Pierce founded, World Vision, is the planet's largest relief agency. Billy became personally engaged with countless ministries, whether established institutions such as the Salvation Army or new ones such as Greater Europe Mission or TransWorld Radio. His multifaceted approach had many results. For instance, according to Dr. Robert Evans, founder of Greater Europe Mission, more than twenty-five evangelical organizations in Europe alone started as the direct or indirect result of Billy's meetings and influence.

Billy also, in a hands-on way, directly spun off or became a primary catalyst for new enterprises. In 1979, even before the televangelists' scandals broke into the nation's consciousness, Billy and his organization took the lead in forming the Evangelical Council for Financial Accountability, which now effectively monitors hundreds of member organizations.

In 1974 Billy helped convene the International Congress on World Evangelization held in Lausanne, Switzerland, to draw attention to the need for world evangelization and to grapple with principles, methods, tools, and strategies. The Congress included over 2,700 representatives from more than 150 nations. The event produced the Lausanne Covenant, which combined an emphasis on evangelism with that of activism against poverty, hunger, racism, and other social ills. That document became a guideline for ministries around the world. Lausanne, and a follow-up event in Manila in 1989 (Lausanne II), helped mobilize Christians to the cause of "calling the Whole Church to take the Whole Gospel to the Whole World."

In addition, Billy's passion to encourage evangelists in developing countries led to three large international gatherings in Amsterdam in 1983, 1986, and 2000. More than 10,000 from 185 countries and territories participated. The Amsterdam Affirmations brought encouragement and clarification to evangelists from many cultures and also resulted in the Biblical Standard for Evangelists, which established guidelines still used today.

■ ■ ■

An enduring and significant example of Billy's entrepreneurial vision and tenacity was the founding of *Christianity Today*. He early grasped the strategic necessity of birthing the publication and concluded that he personally needed to become the driving force to bring this dream into reality. By recruiting and mobilizing, by inspiring and prodding and doing his homework, he built the momentum necessary for a successful launch and long-term survival. The result was the creation of this highly influential, national institution, found in nearly every library, described by journalists and scholars as the nation's most widely read thoughtful religious publication.

What was the entrepreneurial process here? Far from a simple journey between two points, it involved curves, U-turns, and potholes—and years of hard work.

With the celebration of the fiftieth anniversary of *CT*'s founding and well aware of its history and development, we thought it fitting to present a brief case study of Billy's role in launching and sustaining *Christianity Today*.

How did he go about it?

First, *he listened*. Studies of the creative process emphasize that new ideas and solutions do not spring out of a vacuum. First comes the accumulation of facts, impressions, insights, and understanding of needs. Filling the mind with these multiple elements catalyzes breakthrough insights and practical concepts.

During Billy's travels in the early and mid-1950s, he listened to hundreds of pastors and other Christian leaders. "Billy doesn't just meet with people to impress them or convince them," said one colleague. "He listens. Billy listens—because he's always learning." Over and over he sensed a significant vacuum. As he later said to supporters, he found many evangelical leaders "confused, bewildered, divided, and almost defeated in the face of the greatest opportunity," and although he had seen a shift toward orthodox belief, "extreme liberals" were directing some of the major denominations and institutions.

Next, *he applied his full mental powers*. During those years of listening to young pastors and older mentors, professors and business executives, he was letting the input and counsel marinate in his mind. The subconscious is an amazing thing; it is probably no coincidence that Billy awoke in the night with a rush of detailed ideas.

As he wrote in his autobiography: "About two o'clock one night in 1953, an idea raced through my mind, freshly connecting all the things I had seen and pondered about reaching a broader audience. Trying not to disturb Ruth, I slipped out of bed and into my study upstairs to write. A couple of hours later, the concept of a new magazine was complete. I thought its name should be *Christianity Today*. I worked out descriptions of the various departments, editorial policies, even an estimated budget.

I wrote everything I could think of, both about the magazine's organization and about its purpose."

Then, *he drove the process.* What Billy wrote down became the detailed plan he later presented to movers and shakers who could help implement it. But first, he had plenty of preparatory work to do.

He talked first to his father-in-law, L. Nelson Bell, a surgeon but also a lay leader who had started an influential Presbyterian magazine. Bell had been thinking along very similar lines and was enthusiastic about joining him. Billy recruited Harold Ockenga, president of Fuller Seminary and pastor of historic Park Street Church in Boston, along with key businessmen to serve as trustees. Dr. Bell, at the same time, was working on his key contacts.

He sought the money needed. Dreams usually require money, and although throughout his career Billy was extremely reluctant to ask his wealthy friends for donations, he knew the new magazine would require a lot of capital. He wasn't overly optimistic that adequate funds could be raised. When he tried to enlist business leaders, he found them interested but noncommittal. He told J. Howard Pew, head of Sun Oil, that he "was giving more thought to the possibilities of this magazine than to any other single thing in my life." He sensed that if Mr. Pew were to get on board, the dream might become reality.

He and Dr. Bell, who had recently written to Mr. Pew about the magazine, arranged to visit with him. According to Dr. Bell, "On 10 March 1955, we boarded the overnight train from Black Mountain, the station below Montreat, for the definitive discussion with Pew at Philadelphia. They had a two-berth compartment, and as we neared Philadelphia, Billy said, 'Let's pray.' He got down on the floor, not exactly kneeling but almost as if prostrate before the Lord. I'll never forget that morning on the train." Nelson Bell told the staff of *Christianity Today* more than ten years later, "I had never seen a man pray like that before exactly. There was an earnestness about his prayers, that the Lord would lead Mr. Pew, if it was the Lord's will, to do something that would insure the beginning of the magazine."

Clearly the "mundane" task of raising funds was as much a spiritual adventure for Billy as preaching. In Philadelphia, Pew listened to his two friends and agreed to provide significant funding for the first two years. Soon after, Billy wrote him, "We watched great universities that started out to train young ministers for the gospel degenerate into secular, pagan institutions, due to the fact that the founding fathers lost control. Their ideals and original visions were thrown to the wind. I am a relatively young man and I am determined to see this vision, that I believe is from God, carried out and properly controlled. I would suggest that we form a board of trustees immediately."

The most common cause of new magazines failing after their launch is undercapitalization. In its first years, *CT* struggled financially, and Billy continued to urgently solicit from businessmen the needed funds.

He formed a board that was independent. Billy understood positioning and he rejected the most obvious structure. To the majority of his colleagues, the new publication should have become a subsidiary of the BGEA. But Billy saw it differently. He sensed it would dilute the serious publication's credibility to be published by an evangelistic association.

Choosing the more difficult structure not only generated more short-term effectiveness, it provided a long-term structure that enabled continuation of an ever-expanding mission separate from his own organization.

He also decided he should not be named chairman of the board, even though he was the obvious choice. He concluded the magazine would be positioned more strongly to have Harold Ockenga, with academic and theological credentials, serve as chair.

To initiate the process, he called his potential teammates together "for prayer, consultation, advice, and to present concrete proposals." He continued, "I am convinced that we have no rallying point, we have no flag or organization under which we can all gather.... We need a strong, vigorous voice to call us together."

Billy went on to preach his vision and outlined details of editorial, philosophy, news coverage, timing, circulation, and advertising.

Perhaps most important of all, he emphasized that *Christianity Today* should be positive, not divisive, in contrast to many other publications. "This magazine should take the responsibility of leading in love," he declared.

Roughly twenty years later, at a very difficult time in *CT*'s history, trustees met in the Airlie House center in Virginia to evaluate the magazine's future. Reaching deep into his battered, brown briefcase, chairman Harold Ockenga searched for and finally surfaced his copy of Billy's original speech. When he described it, others urged him to read it aloud. Ockenga rose and read the entire text, just as Billy had twenty years before.

As soon as he had finished, one trustee exclaimed, "That's it! That's the mandate!" Said another, "Remarkably prescient. That's still the essential *CT*, and it should continue to be." Agreement rose from the other directors.

Harold Ockenga often said, as board chair, that *CT* was "Billy's magazine," and that he was essentially filling in for him. Billy was not at the Airlie House meeting, but he had laid the foundations so that the original vision continued.

He shared launch concepts with the staff. As editor Carl Henry was preparing the first issues, Billy fed him insights and article ideas. For instance, he was concerned that many assumed that because evangelicals emphasized personal salvation, they ignored poverty. He advocated an article that would show the facts—that evangelicals were very conscious of social needs. He wrote to Henry, "It's easy to sit in ivory towers and talk about social justice; it's quite another thing to get out and actually do it yourself. Dr. Nelson Bell seems to me to be a case in point. While some talk about social justice, he actually went to China and gave twenty-five years of his life to social service in the days before modern medicines, when there was genuine danger for himself and his family."

He celebrated, prodded, and praised. When the first issue of *Christianity Today* came off the press in October 1956, Billy read it thoroughly. He also went to a lot of work reviewing it with others he respected. Then he wrote Carl Henry a lengthy synopsis and evaluation.

Many have expressed amazement at this letter. It was blunt. Reporting on his research with others, Billy wrote, "Almost all have agreed that the content was not strikingly good, considering the terrific roster of editors and correspondents. They all seem to feel that the magazine may be slanted a little too much to the 'egg-head,' and there aren't many egg-heads among ministers. Particularly did I receive almost unanimous criticism of the editorial pages. I, too, would agree that there was not enough ring of joy, strength, and good news."

Concerning book reviews, he reported, "This is where we received probably our greatest criticism. One said, 'Minor League stuff.'"

About the attempts at humor one man wrote him, "Eutychus is terrible." Another said, "A man with no sense of humor trying to be humorous." Yet Billy said he rather liked the humor.

He reported praise for several articles written by theologians.

He was brutally honest about his own article, reporting that one said, "It was a bit too much spinning dust and purple prose." Having criticized his own work he then said that Henry's article was a wonderful idea but that others called it "too verbose." One man used the expression "obscurity reaching for profundity."

But then Billy wrote, "Now, my beloved Carl, do not let any of this discourage you. . . . Personally I was delighted with the magazine." Then Billy went on with pages of practical suggestions and also cautions about being as inclusive as possible without compromise. Henry soon wrote back with appreciation for his insights.

When the second issue was published, Henry received yet another letter, this one brief and congratulatory.

Billy was no mere cheerleader; he was a strategist, a "positioner," a theologian—not in a scholarly sense but in the essentials. Years later one *CT* editor commented, "I don't know how I would have felt if, after editing that first issue, I'd received this letter from Billy Graham. It certainly would have captured my attention—and would have let me know exactly what he was thinking."

Over the years since that first issue was published, Billy, despite sprinting through his own ministry marathon, enabled the *CT* editors and trustees to always "know what Billy was thinking." That is because he consistently stayed true to his principles, and he broke enough time out of his schedule at key junctures to make sure the organization was moving consistently with its founder's mandate. When Harold Ockenga passed away in 1985, Billy finally did accept the trustees' urging that he become chairman of the board. As the organization flourished with additional magazines and related projects, Billy maintained a flow of letters and phone calls filled with optimism, encouragement, and wisdom.

His foundational principles, however—seen throughout this book—were the crucial elements that will continue long beyond the time when he can no longer phone or write. Many times during the past decades when the CTI leadership has faced critical ethical and business decisions, we have asked, "What would Billy do in this situation? What essentials from the mandate he laid down, and the leadership he lived out over the years, would apply to this new fork in the road?" Usually the answers related primarily to moving forward with both love and integrity. Each time the question has been asked, the choice of the road has become clear.

LEADERSHIP LESSONS | Birthing

Applying the Principles

Many of us dream about birthing something new, with our personal stamp on it. Just thinking of making such a dream become reality quickens the pulse and stimulates the mind to create scenarios. Yet we also know the vast majority of such dreams evaporate with the dawn of reality.

Resources. Timing. Contacts. Talents. The list of necessities for birthing dreams is long. But sometimes, with vision and persistence, a dream actually becomes a force in the world.

Trade a Problem for a Dream

Problems come at most of us, often "thick, fast, and furious." We find ourselves enmeshed in them, and any entrepreneurial dreams we have fly by like the months and years we spend solving old problems. That's not all bad. One researcher observed that organizations who addressed and solved one major problem each year were the ones that survived and thrived.

At the same time, Peter Drucker points out that generally, "it is more productive to convert an opportunity into results than to solve a problem." Sometimes we should reprioritize so we can put those dreams front and center.

Drucker also advises that our efforts create the new, not just add an element to

> *Taking a new step, uttering a new word, is what people fear most.*
> **FYODOR DOSTOYEVSKY**

what we are already doing. And, he advises us to think big. "As a rule," he says, "it is just as risky, just as arduous, and just as uncertain to do something small that is new as it is to do something big that is new."

If Drucker is right, that's a huge incentive to break out beyond our ordinary thinking and ordinary tracks. Certainly this is the way Billy approached the launch of *Christianity Today*.

When Billy was seeking wisdom and support among his ministry and business allies, they assumed the new publication would be published by his own organization. Certainly that was the simplest. To create a separate board and separate location and facilities would take lots of additional effort, both short- and long-range. But Billy was convinced the offices should be located in Washington, a strategic city for the launch of a national publication of influence. He wanted a separate board of directors and staff, with leadership from the academic, ministry, and business communities to give it credibility.

He was presciently creating an example of Drucker's later assertion that "in business, the successful companies are not those that work at developing new products for their existing line but those that aim at innovating new products for new businesses." Drucker's words, written forty years ago, have often been validated in corporate experience. Billy's actions, taken fifty years ago, have been validated in that CTI owes much of its success to its structure, carefully conceived to be appropriate to its mission.

Expect Stormy Weather

While we're quoting Drucker, let's add this: "As every executive has learned, nothing new is easy. It always gets into trouble."

Certainly that was true with the launch and first years of *Christianity Today*. Drucker says the only effective means to bail out new endeavors when they run into "heavy weather" is to have "people who have proven their capacity to perform." That's why the new dream can't rely on rookies, no matter how smart or highly motivated. It takes veterans who have been through previous tough times themselves and won't care when thunderheads roll in. Billy knew *CT* was an important project, so he built a critical mass of strong leaders with deep commitments to see the projects through, no matter what squalls threatened to capsize the boat.

In Filling the Bus, Go with Your Gut

The chapter in Jim Collins's *Good to Great* titled "First, Who . . . Then, What" emphasizes the vital importance of getting "the right people on the bus (and the wrong people off the bus)." Collins says that's the first priority, and he documents it well. For instance, he quotes an executive from Circuit City, who was asked to name the top five factors that led from mediocrity to excellence, as saying, "One would be people. Two would be people. Three would be people. Four would be people. And five would be people. A huge part of our transition can be attributed to our discipline in picking the right people."

Collins also echoes Drucker with his "practical discipline" statement: "Put your best people on your biggest opportunities, not your biggest problems."

But in developing the new concept and "putting legs under it," how does one connect, identify, and recruit? In Billy's launching and leading of CTI, he was in a unique position to recruit the right people. His meetings throughout the country put him shoulder-to-shoulder with both lay and pastoral leaders—he and his staff would work with the community's leading Christian business-people and ministers in each city. This gave him up close impressions of how they thought, what they could accomplish, and how committed they were to mutual dreams. Over the years after CTI's launch, he would personally recruit new trustees to achieve the desired mix of business and ministry leadership.

To birth a dream takes lots of recruiting skill, and Billy was always a recruiter, connecting with strong people and thinking about how they might best move the cause forward. It's true that at times he recruited too hastily, carried along with enthusiasm as he saw a person's strengths that hid some weaknesses. But as his associates say, his track record overall had been very, very good.

We see that in his recruitment of Dr. Kenneth Kantzer. In the late 1970s, CTI was in a major transition, and a search had begun for a new magazine editor. Billy had observed Ken's capacities as a theologian and leader and decided he was the man. Ken had largely built Trinity Evangelical Divinity School over a period of years and brought to the table a loving spirit, leadership experience, a quick mind, and a Harvard Ph.D.

When Billy approached Ken, however, the educator politely declined. Kantzer felt he was most effective in academia, and he didn't believe he was equipped to become *CT*'s editor. Yet Billy kept returning to his original premise—that Ken was the man—and was persistent. He contacted Ken again and was again politely refused. But Billy kept after him, and finally, months later, Ken said yes.

In every significant event there has been a bold leader, a shaped vision and, most often, an adversary.

FRED SMITH SR.

The current CTI staff, who went through that time, looks back at that decision as a great day for *Christianity Today*. Dr. Kenneth Kantzer made enormous contributions to the magazine during his years as editor, and after he returned to Trinity, he continued to work with CTI's leaders on many projects, including the Christianity Today Institute, a collaboration of scholars and journalists.

Billy had gone with his gut and brought the right person on the bus.

If You Can't Hover, Connect at Critical Junctures

Leaders positioned to birth dreams know they can't become managers but must hand off those roles. Billy Graham has always worked under lots of pressure, handling demands and opportunities and addressing new challenges. But he casts a continuous eye on events and at pivotal moments has focused on a pressing need.

When CTI went through rough waters in the early 1970s, he personally made sure adequate funding flowed in to ensure its survival. In the late 1970s when the search process for a new editor was stalled, he sought out Ken Kantzer. Always concerned about financial integrity, he insisted an audit committee be appointed from the board. At one point during that same era, he heard some negative buzz from various critics about CTI's new administration. Instead of having others investigate, he requested a personal meeting. The two top leaders flew to Phoenix, where Billy was staying, and explored the issue face-to-face. The meeting clarified crucial understandings and set the tone for the future. Many years later at yet another transition in *CT* magazine's editorial staffing, Billy invited them to Montreat, where he and Ruth hosted them and listened to their new plans. He wanted to know who the additional key players would be and how the structure would function. After making several suggestions, he gave the plans his blessing, and to the staffers, warm encouragement.

Long after the birth of a dream, a founder's personal interest can continue to keep it vital and growing.

Be Realistic

For all the bullish examples included above, we'd be remiss not to include cautions. As Drucker says, new things always get into trouble. A successful birth, when it occurs, is generally preceded by intense and capable preparation. Even then, events may cause stillbirth. As the Bible says, "The race is not to the swift, nor the battle to the strong . . . but time and chance happen to them all."

Since Billy launched *CT* a half-century ago, CTI has launched numerous magazines—some successful, some not. We learned the hard way the survival factors specific to starting magazines: extensive preparation, often several years of it; finding an outstanding champion to make it happen; more capitalization and more effort than originally projected. And, yes, we've had to discontinue some magazines that were not financially viable.

Especially today, wise leaders must know when to pull the plug on a dream that's in trouble. A failed project must not be allowed to drain the future.

We once tried to tell a friend that, but he kept trying to keep his dream magazine alive anyway. He had launched a small publication, but it was dying. Our best people analyzed it for him, but they concluded it simply wasn't viable. Our advice: fold the magazine and move on. We knew from experience it was painful but necessary.

Our friend heard us, but he couldn't let go. For years he struggled on; you could see the suffering in his face. After several years of great financial stress, he had to fold it anyway.

"Cutting bait" can mean moving on to new opportunities. For some additional thoughts on that, you might want to turn to the chapter "Innovating," in part six, where we say a few words about dismounting dead horses and other verities of entrepreneurship.

POINTS TO PONDER

BILLY GRAHAM:

Prayer is not just asking. It is listening for God's orders.

THE BIBLE:

"In the last days," God says, "I will pour out my Spirit on all people. Your sons and daughters will prophesy, your young men will see visions, your old men will dream dreams. Even on my servants, both men and women, I will pour out my Spirit in those days."

ACTS 2:17 – 18

CHAPTER 15

Building Bridges

> A genuine leader is not a searcher for
> consensus but a molder of consensus.
> **MARTIN LUTHER KING JR.**

In leadership literature, a distinction is sometimes made between a leader and a manager. Managers work mostly within an organization while leaders also develop key relationships outside the organization.

By that measure, Billy Graham was clearly a leader. While he led those inside his organization, his primary efforts were directed outward. Throughout his ministry, he built relational bridges with key individuals whose friendship would prove valuable to the cause.

Bridge building is not always a natural inclination. Bridge builders risk upsetting the equilibrium a comfortable distance provides. Yet in today's world that brings us into contact with all kinds of diversity, the need to build bridges to people beyond our own circles is more vital than ever.

Early in his career, Billy Graham had plenty of "natural inclinations" and even prejudices to overcome. After becoming engaged to Ruth, who grew up in the home of Presbyterian missionaries, Billy infuriated her with his stereotypic Baptist suspicion toward establishment denominations. Ruth claims Billy once told her that "Daddy couldn't be in the will of God because he was Presbyterian. I almost gave him his ring back right there."

Billy's marriage to Ruth was just one of many boundary broadening initiatives, and it led to his appreciation and eventual reliance upon the wisdom of Ruth's dad, L. Nelson Bell. Billy later claimed that he "never took a major step without asking his counsel and advice." And, "even though I was a Southern Baptist, I still had an 'independent' streak in me that came from my days at the Florida Bible Institute. Dr. Bell showed me that the strength of my future ministry would be in the church. He actually taught me to be a churchman."

Over the years, Billy's ever-broadening perspective and bridge-building efforts cost him many supporters but won him others. He became a tremendous bridge builder, reaching across denominational, political, racial, and religious boundaries.

Within two years of marrying Ruth, he was attempting to cross denominational divides by changing the name of the church he was pastoring. In 1944, during his eighteen-month stint as pastor, Billy led his congregation, Western Springs Baptist Church, to change its name to the more inclusive Village Church of Western Springs. Why? "There were mainly Lutherans and Congregationalists (but very few Baptists) in the surrounding area," said Billy. Even though he was only a year out of college, his efforts to reach out as broadly as possible had begun.

By the 1990s, many Protestant churches were changing their names to remove denominational labels. It was common for churches, increasingly "seeker sensitive," to remove barriers to skittish outsiders. Names deemed exclusive or off-putting were exchanged for neutral names. So, for instance, Wooddale Baptist Church became simply Wooddale Church. Christ Presbyterian became Christ Church. A Lutheran church in Arizona became Community Church of Joy. A Methodist congregation chose to be known as Spirit Garage.

While such names for churches proliferated in the 1980s and 1990s, this trend didn't start with the sociologically savvy experts of the church growth movement. Billy had intuitively done it in 1944. While still identifying himself as a Baptist, he didn't let his personal preferences in church polity stand in the way of positioning his ministry to reach the broadest possible spectrum. And sixty years later, thousands of congregations have taken that same path toward "mere" Christianity.

■ ■ ■

If bridging to other Protestants was the beginning, it was his reaching out to Catholics that most distinguished his leadership from previous evangelists. He took a bold, almost unprecedented step toward rapprochement with Catholics prior to his 1950 campaign in Boston, a Catholic stronghold. This was an era of suspicion and hostility between Catholics and Protestants. Catholics were forbidden to enter Protestant churches. Conservative Protestant voices called Catholics "papists" or "idolators." The term "mixed marriage" in the 1950s usually referred to the rare Catholic-Protestant marriage, not one across racial lines.

In Boston, Catholics and Protestants had publicly clashed over many issues, including the city's recent sale of a parcel of land to Boston College, a Catholic institution, for one dollar. Prominent Protestant voices called it "a giveaway of the public trust." A Catholic newspaper, in turn, called these critics "enemies of the church."

Into this polarized setting Billy arrived, hoping to gain the support of both Catholics and Protestants for his meetings at Boston Garden.

Despite the advice of some of his supporters, Billy sought out Archbishop Richard Cushing's blessing. He met with Cushing and emphasized the core of his message: justification by faith on the authority of the Bible. Cushing was so impressed with the spirit and conviction of the young evangelist that he wrote an editorial for the diocesan newspaper entitled, "Bravo Billy."

When reporters asked Cushing what he wanted to tell Catholics about the Graham meetings, he said unambiguously, "Go hear Billy."

When Cushing was made a cardinal, and upon his return from Rome, he said to Allan Emery that he had learned three things about his new position: "A cardinal will never starve because of all the events over which he must preside; he would never again be told the whole truth; he would not know for sure who his friends are."

But Billy had somehow earned the trust of Cardinal Cushing.

"Cushing loved Billy," said Allan Emery. "Billy was genuine. He was himself. He didn't hedge. He was clear, direct, and focused on what the Bible said." And Cushing appreciated his spirit and candor.

The bridge built by Billy Graham and Cardinal Cushing led, over the years, to a closer relationship between evangelicals and Catholics.

During the 1964 Graham meetings in Boston, Cushing, recently returned from Vatican II, met with Billy for a forty-five-minute televised conversation. The cardinal, dressed in street clothes rather than the robes of office, assured the evangelist and his supporters that "although we Catholics do not join with them in body, yet in spirit and heart we unite with them in praying God's blessing upon this Christian and Christ-like experience in our community." He encouraged Catholic young people to attend the meetings because Billy's message "is one of Christ crucified, and no Catholic can do anything but become a better Catholic from hearing him. . . . I'm 100 percent for Dr. Graham."

Then Cushing said of the Catholic Church, "I only wish we had half a dozen men of his caliber to go forth and do likewise."

Billy reciprocated. He praised Cushing and Pope John XXVIII and hailed Vatican II as a significant step in clearing the clouds of suspicion and resentment that had divided Catholics and Protestants. Billy professed that he felt "much closer to Roman Catholic traditions than to some of the more liberal Protestants."

While Cushing and Graham were both chided by many in their respective camps for being too cozy with a rival tradition, both men had meant what they said. Observing the rancor that emerged in the 1960 presidential election for John F. Kennedy's being Catholic, Billy observed that from his perspective, "this is sort of a new day." And his bridge building helped usher in that new day.

Historian George Marsden observed that the encounter between Graham and Cushing "stands as a significant marker on the course that Graham steadfastly chose to follow . . . from the narrow confines of the strictest sort of sectarianism to the open ground upon which one is reluctant to deny anyone the right to be called, if not brother, at least neighbor."

In 1981, Billy met Pope John Paul II in the Vatican. Their conversation touched on interchurch relations, moral issues, evangelism, and the emergence of evangelicalism around the world. Immediately afterward, Billy commented publicly about how well they connected on both a personal and a spiritual level.

That spirit would have been hard to find in 1950. But in his lifetime, Billy has seen the climate change from one in which neither Catholics nor Protestants were inclined to seek common ground to one in which Billy could say publicly, "I have found many people in the Roman Catholic Church, both clergy and laity, who I believe are born-again Christians. They may hold different theological views than I hold, but I believe they are in the body of Christ. So I consider them my brothers and sisters."

Billy's bridge-building efforts changed the atmosphere.

Time magazine reporter David Aikman puts it succinctly: "Graham's exemplary warmth toward Catholics, without his giving up any core Protestant beliefs, may have done more to heal the wounds of the great Protestant-Catholic schism of the Reformation than the actions of any other Christian in the last five hundred years."

■ ■ ■

Perhaps an even greater divide was spanned by Billy's efforts to connect with the Jewish community.

Over the years, Billy found many ways to befriend Jews. His 1970 film *His Land* emphasized the common interests Christians and Jews share in the Holy Land. In 1969 Billy was awarded the Torch of Liberty Plaque by the Anti-Defamation League of

B'nai Brith. Billy developed a friendship with Rabbi Marc Tanenbaum of the American Jewish Committee, the two of them inviting each other to speak in various venues. In 1977, Billy received the first American Jewish Committee's National Inter-religious Award for his efforts to strengthen "mutual respect and understanding between evangelicals and Jewish communities." As the late Rabbi Tanenbaum said, "The evangelical community is the largest and fastest-growing bloc of pro-Jewish sentiment in this country," and "most of the progress of Protestant-Jewish relations over the past quarter century was due to Billy Graham."

It helped that Billy's daughter, Gigi, lived for a while on a kibbutz. It helped that on his trips to the Soviet Union that Billy met with persecuted Soviet Jews and pressed their case privately with Soviet officials, urging the Soviets to allow Jews to emigrate and to relax restrictions on rabbinic training and language instruction in Hebrew. Billy said his goal was not to convert these Jews but to rescue them from their oppression and bring them to lands of freedom. It helped that Golda Meir, the late prime minister of Israel, hailed Billy as "a great human being and outstanding spokesman for peace and rich brotherhood."

When some conservative Christians were quoted as saying, "God Almighty does not hear the prayers of a Jew," Billy distanced himself from such remarks.

When his own Southern Baptist Convention singled out Jews to be targets of conversion efforts, Billy disassociated himself. While he confirmed his intent to present the message of Jesus to everyone, he said, "I believe God has always had a special relationship with the Jewish people. . . . In my evangelistic efforts, I have never felt called to single out Jews as Jews. . . . Just as Judaism frowns on proselytizing that is coercive, or that seeks to commit men against their will, so do I."

Billy's relationship with Jews took a major hit when, in early 2002, the National Archives released the tape of a ninety-minute conversation recorded in the Oval Office in 1972 between President Nixon and Billy Graham. In an unguarded discussion, Billy

226

made strongly negative comments about Jewish control of media "and what they are doing to this country."

The Jewish community was furious. Even Graham biographer William Martin, who studied the entire transcript, wrote in an online commentary of his reaction: "I shuddered, and still wince, at hearing and reading those words, but I think it quite likely [his statement] 'how I really feel' refers to the liberal political and social convictions of the particular Jews in question, not to their status as Jews."

When the tapes were made public, Billy quickly apologized. "My remarks did not reflect my love for the Jewish people," he said. "I humbly ask the Jewish people to reflect on my actions on behalf of Jews over the years that contradict my words in the Oval Office that day."

You never know when the strength of a bridge is going to be tested. While some Jewish leaders continued to express disappointment and anger, their reactions were mostly tempered by Billy's record. Over the years, he had reinforced his bridge to the Jewish community. Now, that bridge proved strong enough to carry the weight of his careless remarks with Nixon.

Yes, some Jewish leaders continued to grouse about "the insensitive way he prays at public gatherings." Rabbi Samuel Stahl said, "In his prayers at presidential inaugurations in 1993, 1997, and 2001, he concluded his words in the name of Jesus and to the Trinity. Christian prayers in Christian settings with Christian congregations are perfectly appropriate. However, I do not approve of offering sectarian prayers at public functions."

But in the end, Billy's lifelong pattern was to be clearly and distinctly Christian, yet one that built bridges of friendship, understanding, and support to the Jewish community.

■ ■ ■

Billy built bridges not only across denominational and ethnic divides, but also across the gulf between the academic and activist worlds. Billy freely acknowledged that he was no intellectual, and many intellectuals made it clear they had no sympathy for Billy. Yet he sought out several of the most prominent theologians who had publicly criticized his message and methods.

One summer he met the renowned German theologian Karl Barth and his son, Markus, and together they went hiking in the Swiss Alps. Barth was publicly skeptical of the value of mass evangelism. As they hiked, Billy mentioned that he would be holding an outdoor meeting in the nearby city of Basel.

"Don't be disappointed if few people come," said Barth kindly. He also warned Billy that in Switzerland, no one would respond to his invitation to come forward to receive Christ.

As Billy describes it, "When I did hold the meeting in Basel, Karl Barth showed up, in spite of the pouring rain. I recognized him huddled under an umbrella."

Some 15,000 others also attended that rainy event, and Billy preached from the gospel of John, chapter 3: "You must be born again." When he gave the invitation, hundreds streamed forward.

Afterward Billy greeted Barth and asked him what he thought of the message.

"I agreed largely with your sermon," said Barth, "but I did not like that word *must*. I wish you could change that."

"It's a scriptural word, isn't it?" asked Billy.

Barth agreed it was, but he felt that a preacher should not give an invitation. Instead he should simply declare that God had already acted.

Billy summed up the conversation: "I heard him out and then said I would stick to Scripture. In spite of our theological differences, we remained good friends."

Later, in Zurich, Billy sought out Emil Brunner. Though a more liberal theologian than Barth, when Billy raised the issues that he and Barth had disagreed on, Brunner said, "Pay no attention to him. Always put that word *must* in. A man *must* be born again." And he supported Billy's use of the invitation.

By personal connections like these, Billy was able to see the larger picture and the various streams of thinking within it. He learned from these giants even as he helped them understand his purpose.

In 1963 when Billy was holding meetings in Los Angeles, he invited Helmut Thielicke to sit with him on the platform. Thielicke, a prominent pastor in Berlin after World War II, had earned enormous influence through his preaching, lectures, and books. He shared the common European suspicions of the American "show-business" approach to faith.

Despite his reservations about identifying with Billy, he accepted the invitation to sit on the platform, but Thielicke wrote later, "I kept my eyes wide open critically."

The atmosphere at the meetings, however, and his correspondence afterward with Billy, built a bridge the skeptical German hadn't anticipated. Prepared to dislike what he feared might be an overly flamboyant faith, Thielicke said, "As the people came forward in their thousands to confess their faith, however, I was aware only of calm meditation on the part of his crew and detected no expression of triumph. His message was solid stuff."

After the event, Thielicke wrote Billy a letter in which he admitted his own change of heart. "I confessed that whenever I had previously been asked for my opinion of him, I had said that I felt that many essential elements were lacking in his proclamation of the gospel," and that he felt Billy offered an "individualistic doctrine of salvation."

Billy's response to this letter built yet another span onto the bridge.

"I found the answer he gave me extremely significant," said Thielicke. "I was, he said, completely right in my criticism. What he was doing was certainly the most dubious form of evangelization. But what other alternative did he have if the flocks that had no shepherds would not otherwise be served? This answer gave him credibility in my eyes and convinced me of his spiritual substance."

At times, however, Billy's efforts at bridge building were rebuffed. In the 1950s one of the sharpest critics of his ministry was the theological titan and leading spokesperson for mainline Protestant Christianity, Reinhold Niebuhr. The esteemed vice president of New York's Union Theological Seminary deemed

Billy's gospel simplistic and insufficient, and his critiques were prominently published in national magazines.

When the Protestant Council of the City of New York announced it was inviting Billy Graham to hold evangelistic meetings in Madison Square Garden, *Newsweek* reported Niebuhr's anger, quoting him as saying, "We dread the prospect."

In July of 1957, right in the middle of the campaign, Niebuhr wrote in the hugely popular *Life* magazine that "Graham's message promises a new life, not through painful religious experience but by merely signing a decision card. Thus, a miracle of regeneration is promised at a painless price by an obviously sincere evangelist. It is a bargain."

For months, in the influential magazine the *Christian Century*, Niebuhr had been attacking Billy's approach. "Revivalism," charged Niebuhr, "requires the oversimplification of moral issues and their individualization for the sake of inducing an emotional crisis. Collective sins are therefore not within the range of a revival." And "Graham still thinks . . . the problem of the atom bomb could be solved by converting the people to Christ, which means he does not recognize the serious perplexities of guilt and responsibility."

Regarding racism, Niebuhr conceded that "Graham does not condone racial prejudice. But neither does he incorporate the demand of love transcending racial boundaries into his evangelistic appeal."

What was Billy to do? Most leaders are tempted to avoid critics, to shield themselves from the pain of a well-positioned adversary. Though the prospect of meeting face-to-face with such an entrenched and well-equipped intellectual foe was intimidating, Billy was determined to try. Perhaps even this chasm could be spanned.

One of Billy's associates called Niebuhr to see if he would agree to a meeting, but he declined. Not one to give up easily, Billy worked though the chairman of the Union Theological Seminary board, a prominent banker, who confidently said there would be no difficulty in arranging a meeting.

But he came back "with his tail between his legs," recalled Billy. "Niebuhr simply refused to see me."

He never did succeed in meeting with Niebuhr. But despite the occasional failure, Billy continually worked to bridge all sorts of divides. It's what effective leaders do.

LEADERSHIP LESSONS | **Bridges**

Applying the Principles

As a boy, Billy took a cat and shut it in the doghouse with the family collie overnight. The next day, the cat and dog came out friends forever. Billy joked, in his autobiography, that the incident may have sown the seeds of his vision for ecumenical relationships and his own bridge-building tendencies.

If leadership effectiveness is largely a function of how well you can get dogs and cats to get along, or at least how well you can mobilize disparate groups to work with people different from themselves, then what are the ways to do this? How do you begin to build those connections to people and groups not naturally inclined to work with you? Billy's approach reveals several key principles.

Show Interest; Admit Limitations

Bridge building sounds good, but it's almost always humbling. One of the best ways to build bridges is to admit our peculiarities and limitations up front. After all, in most cases they're readily apparent to others anyway.

"Always try to associate yourself closely with those who know more than you," said Dwight Eisenhower, "who do better than you, who see more clearly than you do. Don't be afraid to reach upward . . . such associations will make you a better person."

When Billy Graham went to Britain in 1946 just after the war, he carried some American cultural baggage. For years he had lived the Youth for Christ motto: "Geared to the Times,

Anchored to the Rock." And his natural inclination was to dismiss the British clergy as neither geared to the times nor anchored to the Rock.

But his time in war-ravaged England convinced him that if revival was going to come, it would have to come through the mainstream denominations. As John Pollock comments: "The Southerner who had scarcely met an Episcopalian began to grasp the peculiar significance of the Church of England." His bridge-building efforts, begun in 1946, later paid off in significant ways in the success of his campaigns in 1954.

While other Americans were viewed as blasé or "know it all," Billy endeared himself to his hosts with his courtesy and eagerness to soak up the British scene.

Even his occasional faux pas was forgiven. Jerry Beavan, one of Billy's aides in those years, told us, "I remember the time he was invited to Queen Elizabeth and Prince Philip's royal estate up in Sandringham. When he went in, the butler put his hand out, and Billy shook hands with him. What the butler was asking for was Billy's hat! Billy literally was, as he frequently says, a farm boy from North Carolina. And suddenly he's thrust into these situations. But he had the charisma to pull it off, to fit into those situations."

Billy put it this way: "Learning was an insatiable desire with me. I burned to learn, and I felt my limitations of schooling and background so terribly that I determined to do all I could through conversations, picking up everything I could from everybody."

Find Common Ground

How could Billy connect with people in India, Hong Kong, and South Africa? What allowed him to work with Catholics, Jews, conservative Protestants, and intellectuals? He found ways to emphasize their common ground.

When he met with three Iraqi religious leaders in 1999—a Shi'ite Ayatollah, a Sunni leader, and a Patriarch of the Chaldean Church, Billy began by discussing humanitarian aid. Though there are significant differences between Christianity and Islam, Billy pointed out "that God wants us to have compassion on those who are suffering and do what we can to help."

J. I. Packer, a British theologian who teaches in Vancouver, told us, "Billy comes to people not as a visitor from outer space but as a fellow human being. He doesn't come primarily as a Baptist or an American; he comes as a full-grown messenger of the gospel. He has something precious, a message he'd like to share with them."

His approach is not from a position of superiority. He boasts in neither his qualifications nor his methods. He focuses on the fact that he's utterly ordinary.

"Billy acquaints himself with what's going on in the country he's visiting," says Packer, "and then he has the great gift of talking to people as if they are simply human beings, just folks, not products of a particular culture. That's why he's able to communicate in a transcultural way: '*You* have a mind, *you* have a heart, and *you* have a family.' He has a gift for sticking to the main things that apply to all human beings."

As leaders, it's easy to unconsciously draw attention to our own peculiarities and preferences—our "unique selling point." But in establishing a connection with a different sphere, the starting place is not my uniqueness but our common ground.

Creatively Reframe Differences

Almost inevitably, as a bridge-building relationship develops, opposition and disagreements arise. Bridge building succeeds only if both sides want to use the linkage.

Sometimes this means explaining things in innovative says. Cliff Barrows told us about Billy's ability ("I think it was divinely imparted to him," said Cliff) to reframe divisive issues in a positive way, especially in press conferences. For instance, when he went to Israel for the first time, the Israeli press had not been favorable, suggesting Billy was coming only to "proselytize."

"The Israeli officials refused to allow us to use the stadium," said Cliff. "They had indicated we could use it if we didn't talk about Jesus Christ but just gave a lecture. That, of course, was totally unacceptable.

"I remember the day our press conference took place in the King David Hotel," Cliff continued. "One government official asked to see Billy. Billy asked me to join him, so we had a cup of tea with this man. Concerned about Billy's reaction to being refused the use of the stadium, he was visibly relieved when Billy assured him, 'Don't worry. I will not say anything that will be an embarrassment to your country or to your leadership.'

Look out for the good things, not the faults. It takes a good deal bigger-sized brain to find out what is not wrong with people and things than to find out what is wrong.

R. L. SHARPE

"Well, when the press conference began, the room was jammed. Billy had an opening statement: 'I want to tell you why I've come to Jerusalem. First, I've come to see the places that are holy and sacred to our Christian faith and to Christians around the world.' The audience nodded at this implied support of tourism. 'Second, I've come because God has called me as an evangelist to preach, to go into all the world to preach the gospel. I've been almost every place, but here's one major place I haven't had a chance yet to speak.' That too was acceptable. 'Third, there are several thousand Christians in this country who have been praying for us, for our meetings here and in other places, and I've come to report to them what God has done in answer to their prayers. Fourth, I've come to thank you and the Jewish nation for proselytizing me as a Gentile to follow a man who was a Jew and who claimed to be the Son of God.'

"The reporters just about bit the erasers off their pencils. But they were writing it down. Then he told them the story of how, as a student under the preaching of Mordecai Ham in Charlotte, he had to decide whether Jesus was who he claimed to be—the Son of God—or whether he was a liar and imposter who didn't deserve a moment of anyone's time. Bill said, 'The only way I could prove it was to just commit my life to him as he asked me to. And I did. So, I thank you for this Jewish man, who also was the Son of God, who changed my life.'

"You could have heard a pin drop. The next day in the press, the reports were overwhelmingly positive, emphasizing that Billy had been touched by God, and he was welcome in Israel. Now that was a stellar case of divine wisdom given him. But I saw that happen in Africa, India, Nagaland—other places where they were ready to run us out, but God blessed and honored him as he explained why he was reaching out to them."

Build Camaraderie

Differences don't have to mean the destruction of the bridge. Every relationship is going to face some seemingly enormous conflicts—different goals, different values, different ways to do things.

Presidential adviser David Gergen observed this about his boss. "From his days as governor, Ronald Reagan understood the importance of floating coalitions. Someone who fought you today might be your best friend tomorrow, so you kept your relationship up."

Gergen confesses, "Years ago, I didn't realize that camaraderie mattered much to leadership. I now think that a leader can barely survive without it. To Reagan, as to other presidents like Eisenhower, Johnson, and Ford, relationships with others were the oil that kept friction down and allowed their initiatives to move more smoothly through the system."

Bridge building means acknowledging the difficulties and, at the same time, reaffirming your desire not to let them end your relationship.

Cliff Barrows also remembers how Billy bridged even potentially tense political chasms. "In Budapest during the Cold War, we were sitting across the table from a sharp and intense young man who wanted to tell us how he was converted to communism and why he was motivated by it. Billy said, 'I'd like to hear that, and then I want to tell you how I was converted to Jesus Christ.' The conversation was wonderful. The young man said, 'Well, I'd like to convert you to communism.' And Billy said, 'Thank you. I want to convert you to Jesus Christ.' They shared openly with each other. It was great."

Bridges aren't built by hiding our foundations and intentions but by admitting where we are, respecting those on the other side, and affirming the worth of the connection.

Bring People Together

Bridge building also means emphasizing ways that people can work together, not just work independently.

Rick Marshall, reflecting on the lasting effects of a Graham campaign points to the cooperation between the various churches in a community as perhaps its most significant accomplishment. "Building this cooperation was so important to Billy's strategy that a team of six to ten of his people would work for a year or more to mobilize the local churches, which spanned the breadth of Christianity.

"We adapted our plans to local needs and opportunities," said Marshall, "and this development of the mission was very unifying, very cross-denominational. At the end of that yearlong process, Billy would come in. The public event itself we viewed as the tip of the iceberg.

"We see the impact of a campaign as 45 percent preparation, 45 percent preservation, and 10 percent proclamation," Marshall continued. "The big public meetings [the 'proclamation'] get the most visibility, but the real heart of a mission is largely unseen by the public and takes place primarily in the local churches."

Building bridges among a wide spectrum of churches led to long-lasting effects. For many of us in leadership, the relationships bridge building produces may turn out to be the most significant thing we accomplish.

Building Bridges

POINTS TO PONDER

BILLY GRAHAM:

Tears shed for self are tears of weakness,

but tears shed for others are a sign of strength.

THE BIBLE:

Learn to do right! Seek justice, encourage the oppressed.

Defend the cause of the fatherless, plead the case of the widow.

"Come now, let us reason together," says the LORD. "Though your

sins are like scarlet, they shall be as white as snow."

ISAIAH 1:17 – 18

CHAPTER 16

Igniting Other Leaders

> Every generation is strategic.
>
> **BILLY GRAHAM**

"I have spent my life in the wake of Billy Graham, like a small boat following his great ship."

This assessment comes from Jay Kesler, a "small boat" of significant achievement. Longtime president of Youth for Christ, he went on to lead Taylor University as its president for many innovative years, and all through his career he pastored churches on the side. Now in retirement, he's again pastoring, serving on various boards, including CTI, and addressing audiences in multiple venues, from distinguished lectureships to college graduations and student gatherings.

A few years after Kesler became YFC president, Billy was holding a crusade in Rio de Janeiro and YFC was also meeting there. Billy and Jay were in the same hotel, so when Billy went up to the roof to get some sun, he asked Jay to join him. "While he was resting and recuperating, we talked for a couple of hours about the challenges of youth ministry," Jay remembers. "He's a good listener, and I felt affirmed. He encouraged us to stay focused on evangelism and avoid the secondary issues: eschatology, various denominational differences, modes of baptism, and all the political things."

One of the most profound effects of Billy's leadership has been his stoking the fires of other leaders beyond his own organization. He wasn't building his own empire, he was building something bigger. He did so through hundreds of connections like his contacts with Kesler, and in worldwide meetings such as his conferences in Amsterdam, in which thousands of evangelists came to draw inspiration and direction. It was his idea to launch this great enterprise and his driving-force leadership that made it happen.

His vision was large, indeed, and it inspired the 10,000 leaders from 180 countries who were there. Here is what he told those assembled. "We are the first generation that has the awesome capacity to destroy mankind from the face of this planet because of the development in incredible weapons of mass destruction. But we also have within our hands the technological breakthroughs in communications that make it possible to reach every corner of the earth with the gospel in this decade. Let us therefore ask God to give us fresh vision. It may be painful for us to face the failures of our lives honestly and confess them to God, but may God break through the barriers in our hearts and minds to strengthen our hands, to enlarge our vision, to be used of God for his Glory and his joy."

Billy wasn't only an encourager. He read every draft of the document developed in Amsterdam that gave guidance to these thousands of Christian emissaries. He was determined that the best theology and strategy would inform them as they carried the good news to their own nations.

"He opened up the territory for the rest of us," Kesler says, "and we looked to him for many directional cues."

What sort of cues? For one, Kesler remembers decades ago YFC trying to chart a course on the race issue. "His example was so important to us. Up until then, in the conservative Christian worlds, we believed that to deny the gospel was a sin, but to deny the social justice issues was just kind of a mistake. Watching Billy, we saw that we needed to put them both in the same category, that one without the other was truncated. One could be as deeply disobedient to Christ over social issues as one could be over theological issues. That's what made us 'new evangelicals.'

"He integrated his campaigns and brought into his organization associate evangelists who were black," Kesler said. "We saw what Billy did, and we too in the 1960s platformed black leaders such as Bill Pannell and Tom Skinner. On the cover of our teen magazine, *Campus Life*, we ran a photo of white and black teenagers riding in the same convertible. We had hundreds of magazines sent back from groups that would not distribute it in the South. But we were committed to this, and Billy's example confirmed for us that this was the right direction."

Jay is quick to say his contacts with Billy were limited, and that's an important point. Many of those heavily influenced by Billy spend little one-on-one time with him. Jay says that despite relatively few in-person meetings, "Billy has been huge for me. He embodied what we wanted to emulate." Jay, a voracious reader of thoughtful books, and a brilliant communicator, has very different capacities from Billy. Yet like many leaders with the same core commitments, he saw in Billy integrity, wisdom, and a flag he could follow.

Jay also points out it was not just Billy. "The whole Graham organization and all their people were tremendously encouraging to me," he says. Jay searched for the best way to express this, finally landing on, "The best metaphor is King Arthur. The Knights of the Round Table had deep affection for and loyalty to Arthur. Billy is the combination of about ten people who gave over their whole lives and careers to reach the world for Christ. I've never been around a Billy Graham insider who spoke with anger or envy or disillusionment about their involvement in the Association. They're not fawners or sycophants or courtiers, they simply have a shared vision."

Starting in his earliest days of ministry, Billy had this broad and lasting impact on leaders, both clergy and lay. For instance, after his meetings in England in 1954, the makeup of the clergy of Great Britain was significantly altered. British scholar J. I. Packer estimates that in 1944 only 5 percent of British clergy could be considered conservative and evangelical; by 2004 more than 30 percent of Church of England clergy are some type of evangelical, a change that Packer says can be traced to Graham's impact in 1954.

The 1957 New York City campaign provides another example among many. A year after its conclusion, a united rally was held in Madison Square Garden, and when converts from the meetings were asked to stand, thousands rose. Perhaps the greatest long-term impact was on New York's pastoral leadership. Although Billy had not been present for nearly a year, one minister told him that it was impossible to adequately express how much the campaign had boosted morale, confidence, and motivation among the ministers of New York.

■ ■ ■

As the twenty-first century dawned, Rick Warren was being hailed as "America's most influential pastor." Not only had he planted a church twenty years earlier that had grown to 21,000 attendees each weekend, but he had just authored *The Purpose-Driven Life*, a book selling over twenty million copies in its first two years, perhaps an all-time record for any book.

An earlier book, *The Purpose-Driven Church*, while not reaching the stratospheric sales levels of the second book, was hugely influential among church leaders, and it sold well enough to allow Warren to invest significantly in *pastors.com*, a website that offers inspiration and resources for those in ministry.

We had worked with Rick over the years on articles in *Christianity Today* and *Leadership*, and when we emailed him to ask if he had observations about the leadership of Billy Graham, he responded immediately: "I'd do anything to honor him; he's had such a profound impact on my life behind the scenes."

We asked him to explain.

"Billy has been a personal mentor for me for a long time," Rick wrote back. "In fact, I just got back from spending an afternoon at Billy and Ruth's home. Neither he nor Ruth is doing very well healthwise, so I flew out just to cheer them up and encourage them. We had a precious time when Billy had me lay hands on him and pray for his health. I love them both so much, and Billy's fingerprints of influence are all over my ministry."

While we knew both Billy and Rick had Southern Baptist roots, we hadn't realized the personal and pastoral relationship between them. "How has Billy influenced you as a leader?" we emailed back.

"We've pretty much kept our relationship out of the limelight, but he's taught me so much about being a Christian leader and statesman who can cross denominational and international boundaries and serve everybody. My personal goal is to finish the ministry God assigns me in the twenty-first century with the same level of integrity and humility that Billy modeled in the twentieth century."

We were intrigued. We hadn't realized the significant way that Billy had shaped Rick's ministry.

We knew Rick's *The Purpose-Driven Life* had spawned "40 Days of Purpose," a program of spiritual emphasis that more than 40,000 churches of all denominations across North America had used. We hadn't realized his vision for a cross-denominational effort had been inspired by watching Billy Graham. But it made sense. Like Rick, Billy had never been ashamed to admit his particular Southern Baptist roots and affiliation, but he never allowed it to confine his relationships. He embraced a wider circle. He thought about "the whole world all the time."

But Billy's breadth of vision and his personal integrity aren't the only leadership lessons that Rick learned from Billy. One of the most profound influences, we discovered, was the model of Billy's approach to a leadership team. Rick consciously sought a similar team relationship at Saddleback Church.

"Billy and his team have been the model of teamwork for our leadership team at Saddleback. We intentionally modeled after them," Rick wrote. "Billy's top team—George Wilson, T. W. Wilson, Cliff Barrows, Grady Wilson, George Beverly Shea, Tedd Smith, Sterling Huston—they've been together forever. The advantage of this is that you become best friends, and there are no egos or internal politics involved. They all just love each other as dear friends. There have been times when I've sat on stage and watched Cliff Barrows watch Billy during a portion of the crusade, and I knew that Cliff knew *exactly* what Billy was thinking at that moment. It was like they could read each other's minds and make adjustments without even having to talk about it.

"The team even wanted to live near each other. Both T.W. and Bev Shea built houses on the same mountain road as Billy's home.

"A few years ago, Billy invited me to attend the ceremony in the Capitol Rotunda where he received the Congressional Gold Medal. One of the things that struck me about that event was that when Billy received that reward, he said, 'This medal really belongs to my team'—and he listed each of the names of his dear friends who served with him all these years. It was very touching."

We asked how he applied the lesson of that kind of teamwork at Saddleback.

"When I began Saddleback—which I had made a commitment to pastor for the rest of my entire life (I was twenty-five)—I intentionally followed Billy's model of teamwork in selecting guys who would also dedicate the rest of their lives to serving this one church. All of our senior leadership are 'lifers.' We've been together twenty-plus years and have committed to growing old together.

"Much of the growth of Saddleback can be attributed to this team of one mind, one spirit, identical values, close friendship, and personal commitment to each other for life. I get the privilege of serving Christ with my best friends. That's why we never have to deal with internal politics at that level.

"Billy taught us the value of teamwork."

■ ■ ■

Ravi Zacharias was a young professor on the faculty of Alliance Theological Seminary in Nyack, New York, up the Hudson River north of New York City. In the early 1980s, Leighton Ford had heard tapes of Ravi's presentations, and he forwarded those tapes to Billy Graham. Billy listened to them and subsequently invited Ravi to speak on "The Lostness of Man" as a plenary speaker at the international gathering of itinerant evangelists in Amsterdam in 1983.

We called Ravi, a native of India, to ask about Billy's influence on his life. What impression did he have meeting Billy for the first time?

"We met in Amsterdam; my wife was with me. I remember the first thing he said to me was 'I have already read the text of your message, Ravi. It is powerful. With your permission, I would like to preach it sometime.' That told me the humility of the man. As a younger evangelist, you're already nervous to meet him for the first time, but he sets you at such ease.

"Then, when I sat down after preaching, he leaned over and said, 'I really don't need to get up and preach now.' He and Cliff Barrows exchanged some words about how God had moved in that meeting. Once again, a mark of the man's humility. He then stood up and preached a powerful message, but he was very self-effacing.

"That's what he did throughout the conference in Amsterdam: he kept reaffirming that the evangelists there were powerful instruments of God's work in the world."

We asked Ravi about Billy's influence on these grassroots evangelists from virtually every nation in the world.

"There was no one else in the world," said Ravi, "who could have brought about a conference like that, raising the resources for it, and elevating the work of the evangelists of the world. He didn't need it, but we did. If you ask anyone who attended, even if they don't remember any of the messages, they remember the people they met and the networks they established.

"And the role of these more than 10,000 evangelists was ennobled and honored. They returned to their nations encouraged and equipped to make a difference."

What difference did the Amsterdam conference make on his own leadership?

"It opened up so much of the world to me," Ravi responded. "My whole ministry took a dramatic turn after that. Invitations to speak poured in from many parts of the world. But in addition, two other things happened at the conference.

"First, I was made aware that a vast majority of evangelism was being done to reach 'the unhappy pagan,' the person whose life is falling apart and who is ready to grasp the gospel because it offers hope for their painful situation. I realized there are large numbers of people who are not unhappy, who find their lives fulfilling, at least apparently so, and I sensed the need for someone, maybe me, to speak to 'the happy pagan.' From Amsterdam, my wife and I went to India, where we saw the great need of pastors there, and I told my wife, 'I would love to be an evangelist to the skeptic, to the honest intellectual who has intellectual objections to faith. I'd like to develop that kind of Christian apologetic ministry.'

"Second, I remember Billy Graham saying, 'You have never evangelized a person until you have told them about the cross.' Billy told of a difficult moment when he preached and had no response whatsoever. Then one of his colleagues put his arm around him and said, 'Billy, you ought not be surprised. There was no cross in your sermon tonight.'

"Later, when I told Leighton Ford about these reflections, he said, 'Billy has always maintained that it's fine to reach the intellect, but if you lose the simplicity of the gospel, you will not accomplish the task. I knew that was the way to go. I'd seen God take Billy, an honest man with integrity and a simple trust in the profound power of the gospel, and I said, 'That's what I want to be.' The Lord used Billy Graham and the Amsterdam conferences to light a fire way beyond what he ever imagined."

Ravi Zacharias went on to launch a ministry to skeptical intellectuals that has offices in Atlanta, Toronto, Oxford, Singapore, India, and Abu Dhabi.

■ ■ ■

John Huffman's awareness of Billy began when he was just six years old. John's father, a pastor and YFC leader, had in 1946 brought Billy to Boston for the first time, and while there, the evangelist took his small son for a walk along the beach.

"Just this month, Billy brought up his memories of meeting me when I was a little boy in Boston," John told us, referring to the recent visit he and his wife, Anne, had with Billy and Ruth in their home. John described how all through his career, Billy had kept up contact.

As a young man, Huffman was studying at Princeton Seminary when Billy spoke there and reconnected with him, asking him to write an article for *Decision* magazine. "During the Los Angeles crusade of 1963, he invited me to bring a date to the Actors' Guild Benefit Fund Dinner at the Beverly Hilton." At that event, John was impressed with Billy's ability to consistently communicate, no matter what the audience. "In front of some of the most powerful people in Hollywood, he gave as gracious, as loving, and as faithful a presentation of the gospel as he had done the previous day at the concluding meeting of 130,000 people at the Los Angeles Coliseum."

Billy's approach to effectively staying on message, as well as his respect for scholarship and his large vision, formed an essential model for Huffman. He continued throughout his career to pursue his studies, pastored major Presbyterian churches in Pittsburgh, Miami, and Newport Beach. He currently serves on the boards of Gordon-Conwell Seminary, CTI, and World Vision, which he chaired for many years.

As we talked with John after a CTI committee meeting, he pointed out the way Billy initiated engagement with multiple generations. His ability to learn from, lock arms with, and inspire leaders who were older or younger or his peers, reveals a fascinating rhythm of leadership effectiveness—starting with Billy's emergence as a young man with much to learn.

First of all, Billy learned from the generation ahead of him: L. Nelson Bell, Wheaton College president V. Raymond Edman, as well as President Eisenhower and Senator Frank Carlson. Second, he maintained vital connections with those in his own generation: ministry leaders like Robert Evans of Greater Europe Mission, as well as those in the national spotlight like Mark Hatfield, and George H. W. Bush. In addition he was, in John's words, "concerned about the children of his peers," people like John who would ultimately carry on the mission. "What surprised me," John said, "was how through the years he would invite me to play a round of golf, or call me up at almost any time of the night or day with some question or insight he had, or even asking for help on a message he was preparing—treating me not as a person twenty years younger, but graciously and humbly asking for my counsel. He never came across as someone who had all the answers and was dispensing them to the next generation; but in the process, he was both a voice of wisdom and a mentor."

John mentioned that Garth Rosell, who matriculated at Princeton with John, had a similar experience. Garth's father, Merv, had been a major figure in early YFC days and was a friend of Billy's.

We contacted Garth at Gordon-Conwell Seminary, where he serves as a professor of history. Garth, who has a special interest in the study of revival and reform, agreed that Billy had grown under both older mentors and with his generational peers. "Billy seems to have given significant attention to the raising up of leaders who could carry the work once he was gone."

Although Garth's contacts with Billy were infrequent, "they were exceedingly important in the shaping of my life and work. At several strategic points in my life, a letter, a note, or a phone call would arrive to provide exactly the kind of gentle encouragement I needed. Perhaps because of his friendship with my dad, I always sensed that he took a special interest in me and what I was doing."

Frank Thielman, son of the Grahams' pastor in Montreat, tells of the time he was wrestling with his decision about either staying at King College as a professor or accepting an invitation to join the newly formed Beeson Divinity School. He was torn. "Dr. Graham called," Frank told us. "He said, 'Your dad tells me you're really struggling with this decision.'

"I said, 'Yes, I really am.' And we talked about it, and he helped me work it through. He didn't tell me what to do, he just helped me through the pros and cons."

Billy, well-connected, knew the president of King College very well and used his broad base of knowledge and networking the territory. "He was supportive of King College, and he wanted me to be real careful about moving from there. At the same time, he understood the Southern Baptist scene, and he knew I did not, because I was a Presbyterian and didn't have a clue. It was an amazing thing for him to call and help me understand. It wasn't going to help him in any way."

We asked Frank how Billy processed this with him.

"He asked questions about the schools. He was basically being a pastor to me, calling someone with no way of repaying the favor. He assured me that whatever decision I made was good with him. His friendship didn't depend on which choice I made."

Another time, Billy learned Frank was writing a commentary on Philippians and asked for a copy of the manuscript. "He read it and offered a little commendatory blurb for it. This was when he was ill—but he reaches out to people and seeks to help them. Talk about a purpose-driven life!"

The list of names of such younger leaders in all fields, from business to politics to academics, is remarkably long. Some are names we don't recognize; others are known mostly in their own circles.

As John Huffman observed, Billy's leadership dynamically interfaced with many generations, igniting and enriching in two-way streets of "touch" and communication. And as influential pastor Leith Anderson told us, "Billy's willingness to allow others to succeed may be his greatest lasting impact. Through the success of others, he brought evangelicalism to a high-water mark of size and influence."

■ ■ ■

Gordon MacDonald is currently editor at large for the journal *Leadership* and chair of World Relief. As pastor of Grace Chapel in Lexington, Massachusetts, he was involved in Billy's New England crusades. As a speaker with InterVarsity Christian Fellowship,

Gordon had opportunity to interact with Billy at the organization's conference for university students. We've selected Gordon's story to conclude this chapter.

"It was mid-evening, and my wife, Gail, and I were getting settled in our hotel room on the campus of the University of Illinois, where the triennial Urbana Missionary Conference would begin the next day. The year was 1979. There was a knock on the door of our room. Opening the door, I found Billy Graham standing there with a small paper bag in his hand. Handing it to me, he said, 'Here's the medicine I told you about. I went down to a drugstore and got it for you.'

"An hour before, Gail and I had sat at dinner with Billy and others who were to be speakers at the convention. For some reason, I had mentioned that I'd had the flu and that my stomach was still having difficulty digesting food. Billy overheard this and suggested a remedy that could be purchased over the counter at any drugstore. Gail and I made a mental note to look for it the next day.

"Now, an hour later, here's Billy Graham standing at our door with the medicine. I was speechless. All I could finally blurt out was something silly. 'Billy, I can't use that medicine. I'm going to encapsulate it in plastic as a monument to your kindness.'

"I had met Billy Graham on a few previous occasions, but apart from the privilege of shaking his hand, I could hardly claim to know him. Yet here he was, serving the need of a young and somewhat obscure pastor.

"Years later Billy would stand in the pulpit at Grace Chapel, where I was pastor, and call an audience of Christian leaders in New England to prayer at the beginning of his six-state, 1982 New England Crusade. On several occasions during those weeks, he invited Gail and me to drive with him to various crusades. He liked, he said, the way the two of us prayed for him, and that we were not reluctant to pray for him and the upcoming meeting, even while the car was in motion.

"He would phone us at home to ask if I had any suggestions for sermon topics, or did I have any particular quotes or stories that would be useful for the sermon he was preparing. His conversation was always marked with a humility and a passion to see the outpouring of God's Spirit upon our part of the world.

"Then, a few years later came the most terrible moment of my life. Everything in my life (and Gail's) came to a halt because of my personal failure. On a Friday morning in May of 1987, I told the board of the organization I was leading that I would immediately step down as its president. As soon as I had done this, Gail and I went to our home with the intention to withdraw from public life for an indefinite period of time. It was the darkest hour either of us has ever known.

"We were hardly in the door of our home that morning when the phone began to ring. I would have ignored it, except that it kept ringing and ringing. When I finally answered, there was the familiar voice of Billy Graham. 'Gordon, this is Billy. I've been trying to call you all morning.' I could hardly speak. He went on, 'I want you to know that you've already been forgiven by God, and that I forgive you.'

"As far as I can remember, this was the first word of forgiveness spoken by anyone except Gail. I wept. How had this man heard of my situation so quickly, and why would he take the time to call and offer this hopeful word?

"After several more minutes of conversation, he concluded the call saying, 'Why don't you move down here to Montreat for a year or so and help me write sermons?' I could not imagine this happening, but the very fact that Billy would say this brought a ray of sunlight into that darkness. What a creative way to say that there just might be a tomorrow.

"Each time Billy Graham has walked into my life he has marked it. He gave me a sense of the high standard of genuine godliness in a man who can preach to millions, engage with presidents, and yet never become so aloof that he could not bring a bottle of medicine or a word of grace to a flawed man in need of kindness."

LEADERSHIP LESSONS | **Igniting Leaders**

Applying the Principles

To develop this application section, we turned to Leighton Ford. Why? Two reasons:

First, Leighton was mentored by Billy, starting when he was in high school. His local YFC group hosted the young evangelist. "I'd seen him preach," Leighton says, "and we were all rather in awe of his unusual gift. We had all kinds of expectations."

Although seven hundred people showed up at the meeting, only one responded by coming forward. "I'm sure Billy could see I was disappointed. He came over and put his arm around me, gave me a big hug, and said, 'Leighton, I see you have a concern to win people to Christ. I believe if you stay humble, God will bless you. I'm going to pray for you.' He really encouraged me, and I've never forgotten that arm around the shoulder."

For decades thereafter, many of them ministering at the heart of Billy's organization, Leighton thrived under Billy's steady encouragement and door opening.

The second reason to turn to Leighton for this chapter is his personal focus on mentoring young leaders. It's his central ministry. "When our son, Sandy, died at age twenty-one," he told us, "God gave me a desire to help other sons and daughters. There was a sense of extending what Billy had meant to me with that arm around the shoulder."

In the early 1980s, Leighton saw "a whole new generation of leaders under forty emerging all over the world." He decided to start a new organization. "At the time of Hurricane Hugo, which came through Charlotte, we held a strategic planning meeting. Then I went up to the lake for a little retreat, and it was as if God said to me, 'You won't make a difference by multiplying programs but by investing in people.' I thought about how Jesus had preached to multitudes but also poured his life into a dozen people. I felt very much led to bring together a dozen young men and women whom I knew. They became what we call our 'point group.' Now they're all about fifty years old—I've been working with them every year for fifteen years—and they, in turn, are influencing younger people."

In our interviews, we quickly sensed Leighton's unique effectiveness in empowering and mentoring younger leaders with high potential. He spills out a steady flow of practical and thoughtful insights; here are a few of them:

Choose Wisely; Share Openly

We can attempt to encourage many, and in life's ordinary flow, the small gesture and the caring word can raise sights and empower. But if we invest more heavily in a few, as Leighton has, we face what he calls "the challenge of selection."

"It's a matter of prayerful discernment and spiritual chemistry," he says. "Who are the people I'm drawn to who are drawn to me? Then it's saying, How can we listen together to what you're hearing? It's not my agenda, but what is God saying to you?"

Leighton counsels mentors to learn to be open. "We need to share our lives. I do more of that than I would have thirty or forty years ago, sharing experiences, including pitfalls and mistakes.

"Long-term tracking of people is very important. Someone says a 'spiritual director' is someone who remembers your song when you've forgotten it. When you've been with someone over ten years, you see the ups and downs and can help them stay in tune."

In his writings on leadership, Leighton has emphasized ways Jesus led his followers "past their selfish and narrow horizons." How can mentors do that?

"In a sense, Billy did that for me by allowing me to sit in on some private conversations. Exposure to different people in diverse situations expands our horizons."

> The final test of a leader is that he leaves behind in others the conviction and the will to carry on.
>
> **WALTER LIPPMANN**

Leighton described how this had worked with a longtime friend, Ken Shigamatsu, now the pastor of a vibrant, multigenerational church in Vancouver. He had met Ken at the first Amsterdam conference when Ken was a Wheaton College student. Now he's become a trustee of Gordon-Conwell Seminary.

"I was asked to go to Singapore to speak," Leighton said, "so I asked Ken and another Chinese American named Tim Lee to go with me. Each day in Singapore, as I sat down with the leaders there to prepare my message for that night, I'd say, 'Here's what I'm planning. How does this relate to people in Singapore? Give me some illustrations. Some idioms.' I'd have Ken and Tim sit with me, listening in.

"To expose leaders to a different setting, to a different culture, lets them see these broader horizons."

Entrust the Trustworthy

After Leighton had completed seminary, Billy invited him and his wife, Jean (Billy's sister), to England and Scotland, where he was having crusades. He opened doors for Leighton to do some preaching there. In 1956, when Leighton was only twenty-three, Billy asked him to move to New York and take charge of church relations for his meetings. "That meant going all over New York and meeting pastors and enlisting their involvement. That was the biggest crusade Billy had ever had. I look back at that and think, *If it had been me, and that was the biggest thing I'd ever been involved in, would I have invited a twenty-three-year-old?* He took a chance."

At the same time, Leighton was a very promising seminary grad. "He knew me. He'd observed me. He knew I had some gifts and qualifications, that I was theologically trained and intellectually aware, but he really took a chance."

Entrusting someone with large responsibilities always includes taking a chance, and especially with young aspirants who have no track record. Well might Leighton wonder if he would have done what Billy did. Yet the principle is clear: to grow and be stretched, the leaders of tomorrow must be given significant responsibilities today.

Look Down the Road

Emerging leaders don't stay static; they need to be empowered in changing dynamics, and this necessitates fresh thinking. Leighton remembers that after eight years of working with Billy, he called him up to Montreat one day and said, "Leighton, I've been thinking and praying about this. I think you ought to develop your own team and go to Canada, your native country, and evangelize across Canada. We'll support you if you want to start your own organization, or you can be part of our organization."

Leighton bought into the idea and said he'd prefer staying with the BGEA. "I put together a little team. Billy encouraged that, but he didn't tell me how to do it." Leighton developed a strategy to minister coast-to-coast across Canada, which they did the next half decade with Billy's full support. "But we developed it in our own way, in our own style."

Why this initiative from Billy?

"He saw at that point, I think, that I shouldn't just stay 'under his wing' but to move out on my own. He encouraged me to do that, and it was a very major thing."

We pushed Leighton to share a little more about that.

"Perhaps he saw I had potential to be more than an assistant to him; maybe it was for both my sake and to avoid possible conflict down the years—if I grew impatient with a lack of scope. It was a lot of foresight on his part."

> Leadership is stirring people so they are moved from inside themselves.
>
> FREDERICK R. KAPPEL

Empowering and mentoring happen in a flowing stream of emerging opportunities that change strategies.

Broaden, but Keep the Sharp Edge

Leighton once was asked at Duke Divinity School how he had seen Billy Graham change over the years. The question was new to him. He made a few stabs at it, then this image came to mind, and he said, "Billy Graham has been like an arrowhead. An arrow has a very sharp point. He has the sharp point of the gospel. He's kept that sharp edge. But then, like the base of an arrow, he's grown in understanding how the gospel affects every area of life. He transcended his roots of a rural, segregated upbringing to a much broader understanding of the kingdom of God. Racial justice, poverty, nuclear warfare, unity among Christians—all of these things he's seen in the light of Christ. So while he's grown broader, like the shaft of an arrow, he's grown deeper into prayer and Bible study and into his life with the Lord.

"Some leaders as they age get broader but lose that cutting edge. They become dull, without a sharp point. The best leaders keep that cutting edge, go broad, and go deep. Billy is one very wonderful example of that."

POINTS TO PONDER

BILLY GRAHAM:

The men who followed Jesus were unique in their generation.
They turned the world upside down because their hearts
had been turned right side up.

THE BIBLE:

Command them to do good, to be rich in good deeds,
and to be generous and willing to share. In this way they will lay up
treasure for themselves as a firm foundation for the coming age,
so that they may take hold of the life that is truly life.

1 TIMOTHY 6:18 – 19

CHAPTER 17

Sowing Seeds in All Seasons

> Life is not just a few years to spend in self-
> indulgence and career advancement. It is a
> privilege, a responsibility, a stewardship to be
> lived according to a much higher calling.
>
> **ELIZABETH DOLE**

Leaders cannot avoid it. For good or ill, they are sowing seeds everywhere they go, in everything they do. A kind word, a clear insight, a visit to the hospital, a bold stance on a murky issue. A leader's every action has consequences both intended and unintended. People are like plowed ground; seeds find the soil of minds and emotions, sprouting powerful changes. Who knows the results? Tiny seeds can produce sturdy trees or nourishing grains or delicate flowers.

We all know, however, that sowing good seed is often hard, tedious work. It means being consistent, maintaining at all times our integrity, our focus, our faith. Sometimes we're tempted to drop a few burr and thistle seeds—a curt response, an avoidance, a lapse into just a bit of self-indulgence, or to go "off-message." We may long to escape the necessity of always being "on," of day after day, year after year following through on all our commitments to those who look at our every word and action.

At times, we simply want to escape.

However, there's a far better solution—*recovery*. The Bible says we should "not be weary in well doing," but that does not mean we should become work drudges. We are invited to serve with energy and joy, and that means a rhythm of hard work, yes, but also the laughter of friends and the recharging from solitude, and, most of all, the empowering of consistently being true to our deepest values and commitments.

Such empowerment was Billy Graham's greatest source of recovery from the need to always be "Billy Graham." He would refresh himself in his hotel room with his Bible, and he would interact with colleagues who would strengthen, deepen, and encourage him. But he would also don a baseball cap and sunglasses and mix with the crowds, not as Billy Graham but as an interested observer, taking the pulse in youth settings or city events. He also knew how to relax, spending vacations with his wife, Ruth, and close friends like Johnny and June Carter Cash. The pressures on him aggravated many physical problems, so he often visited Mayo Clinic and tried to keep in shape by jogging.

So, during his many decades of struggling with the weight of his fame, he kept working at what people today call self-management. And he kept sowing seeds consistently, on vacation or off, in settings both formal and casual, taking action and speaking to others in ways resonant with his convictions. The apostle Paul said that he was prepared "in season and out of season." So was Billy.

One day during a break at a CTI board meeting, Billy and some other trustees stepped into a hotel hallway. A long ways down the dim corridor was a cleaning lady who looked toward them and smiled. Then she motioned with her hand in a timid hello.

Billy broke from the other trustees and walked down the hall to talk to her. She had watched him on television; she had been to a crusade; she appreciated his ministry.

Billy graciously talked with her for several minutes before rejoining the group, but both the woman and the trustees had been affected by his simple action of breaking from the press of issues and reaching out in simple, gracious friendship.

Sowing good seeds all the time results in serendipities—the surprises that may astound the sower. Seeds take root and grow into unexpected new realities.

■ ■ ■

The number of serendipities Billy initiated as a result of all those thousands and thousands of seeds sown would fill many volumes. Here are just three:

■ ■ ■

"As a new Christian working at a hotel," says Mark Driscoll, "I once had the privilege of chatting for about ten minutes with Billy Graham, who was staying there as a guest. He was sitting in the restaurant by himself, wearing a Minnesota Twins baseball cap, reading the paper and eating breakfast when I approached him to introduce myself. He asked if I knew the Lord, and I explained that I was a new Christian and that God had called me into ministry. His words were very encouraging, and he kindly promised to pray for me.

"After our informal conversation ended, other people seated around him in the restaurant recognized who he was. Rather than rushing off to avoid being bothered, Dr. Graham graciously stayed in the restaurant to visit with people, share the gospel, and pray over the children who came to sit upon his lap and have their picture taken with him as if he were Santa Claus. His gracious spirit and humble approachability made a great impression upon many of the non-Christians I worked with. To this day I sincerely thank God for working through Billy Graham in such a wonderfully faithful manner, both in and out of the pulpit."

Mark Driscoll went on to plant Mars Hill Church in Seattle and to form an entire church-planting network, Acts 29, which by 2004 had launched more than a hundred churches.

■ ■ ■

Casual interaction in a family and a gracious giving of his time to a different young man had larger ramifications than anyone would have thought at the time. In the summer of 1985, the family of then Vice President Bush invited Billy Graham to be their weekend guest in Kennebunkport, Maine. He preached at the small church, St. Ann's by the Sea, that the Bush clan attends.

Afterward, back at the house, George H. W. Bush gathered the younger Bushes around the fireplace with Billy and suggested they should talk about spiritual issues and ask questions. The younger George Bush had been struggling with his drinking problem, which was lowering his energy and competing for his "time and affection." His being together with Billy was to have a profound effect.

"What he said sparked a change in my heart," George W. Bush has explained. "I don't remember the exact words. It was more the power of his example. The Lord was so clearly reflected in his gentle and loving demeanor. The next day we walked and talked at Walker's Point, and I knew I was in the presence of a great man. He was like a magnet; I felt drawn to seek something different. He didn't lecture or admonish; he shared warmth and concern. Billy Graham didn't make you feel guilty; he made you feel loved."

During that conversation Billy turned to Bush and said, "Are you right with God?"

"No," Bush replied, "but I want to be."

That encounter, while not producing instantaneous change, did nevertheless have a lingering effect.

"Over the course of that weekend," said Bush, "Billy Graham planted a mustard seed in my soul, a seed that grew over the next year. He led me to the path, and I began walking. It was the beginning of a change in my life. I had always been a 'religious' person, had regularly attended church, but that weekend my faith took on a new meaning. It was the beginning of a new walk where I would commit my heart to Jesus Christ."

Over the next year he began reading the Bible regularly, using a one-year Bible that his friend Don Evans gave him, and he tried to stop drinking—but without success.

Then came his fortieth birthday party in Colorado Springs. The morning after, as Bush went jogging around the scenic Broadmoor Hotel, the view was spectacular, but he was feeling miserable. His head was throbbing, and he feared he wouldn't be able to complete his usual three miles.

"About halfway through, I decided I would drink no more," Bush later wrote. "I came back to the hotel and told Laura . . . 'I'm quitting drinking.' I'm not sure she believed me at first." And the decision stuck. Indeed, as he has stated publicly many times, he has not touched alcohol since.

That moment in 1986 has proven to be significant. Bill Minutaglio, whose biography *First Son* chronicles how Bush often felt he fell short—from his average grades in the Ivy League to his enlistment in the Texas Air National Guard, to his bad luck in the oil business—writes, "It's pretty clear that stopping drinking was a real turning point for Bush, because it gave him the energy to study politics at the highest level, and it alerted him to his own political possibilities. It changed him. He realized that if he straightened up, the sky was the limit."

Years later, when he had ascended to the presidency, Bush asked some religious leaders to pray for him by saying, "You know, I had a drinking problem. Right now I should be in a bar in Texas, not the Oval Office. There is only one reason that I am in the Oval Office and not in a bar. I found faith. I found God. I am here because of the power of prayer."

■ ■ ■

Planting seeds also includes sticking to one's guns and maintaining integrity in the face of conflicting pressures. Who knows who will be watching and who will represent soil on which good seed might fall?

In 1959, Billy was planning meetings in Little Rock, Arkansas. The timing couldn't have been more volatile. Less than a year earlier, voters in Little Rock had voted 19,470 to 7,561 "against racial integration in all schools in the district." The vote meant the city's four high schools could not open as public institutions with any blacks in attendance. The school board attempted to lease the schools to a private corporation to permit segregated classes to continue. The U.S. Supreme Court then issued a ruling that forbid "evasive schemes for segregation." The schools were forced to accept black students. But the protests weren't over.

Just two weeks before the event, two unidentified women threw two tear-gas bombs inside the front door of the school administration building while the board was meeting on the second floor. The next week, dynamite blasts destroyed a city-owned station wagon and an office in the school administration building. Members of the community requested that Billy hold segregated meetings to avoid inflaming the situation further.

This had to be a difficult moment. No one would have blamed him, considering the violence, for backing off his stance of integrating his meetings. After all, this was 1959!

Billy refused, however. To come under those conditions, he explained, would violate the gospel that he stood for. He insisted on integrated meetings, and the meetings were conducted that way—open to people of any race. On September 13, with Governor Orval Faubus and 30,000 others in attendance, Billy Graham preached in War Memorial Stadium. He referred to the desegregation crisis stating "only Christ can heal these scars and wounds." When he offered an invitation to accept Jesus, six hundred people came forward. Billy then asked the news media to "carry this story of hundreds of people of both races standing at the foot of the cross to receive Christ."

The stand "really touched me," said former president Bill Clinton, because his grandparents were among the few white people he knew who supported integration. "And at the most intense time in the modern history of my state, everybody caved," Clinton remembers. "And blacks and whites together poured into the football stadium. And when the invitation was given, they poured down together, down the aisles, and they forgot that they were supposed to be mad at each other, that one was supposed to consider the other somehow less equal.

"And he never preached a word about integrating the schools," Clinton said. "He preached the Word of God. And he lived it by the power of his example."

■ ■ ■

Sowing seeds effectively also means doing so in multiple and varied contexts. Senator Mark Hatfield pointed out to us how Billy demonstrated this to him in 1957 when he was Oregon's secretary of state, and they came into contact in New York.

"Billy was having his famous meetings in Madison Square Garden," Mark told us. "They closed off a number of streets and had the big session in Times Square. As those streets angled off, Billy was standing in the center, and they had the platform and microphone with a PA system down those streets. It was a mass of people in every direction, all funneled into the center of the square.

"What impressed me was how Billy used the theater marquees. He took *Love from a Stranger* and other movie titles blinking in bright lights and built his simple gospel message out of the environment of those marquees."

Mark realized that Billy was adapting his message to the culture in the same way the apostle Paul had. "They listened to Billy because he put it in a familiar context," Mark said. "It reminded me of Saint Paul when he started his missionary work and was first in Lystra. He said, 'I've come to tell you about the God who makes the rain to fall and the grass to grow.' He was speaking with relevance to his particular audience. Then in his next place he was talking to a Jewish congregation, and he said, 'I've come to tell you about what the prophets in our history have told us, the coming of the Messiah.' So Paul put the gospel into that context. Later he talked to the Greeks, and he said, 'I've come to tell you about the unknown God that you've erected an altar to.'

"To me, it was such a dynamic parallel of Billy's message being couched in everyday language with pertinence to familiar things and symbols that the people could recognize. He used to say that he had only one message, just different verses. He never veered from his message, but it was always relevant, and it was relevant to the listeners of that day and that place and time."

Mark saw in his long association with Billy the evangelist's consistent ability to lead in many contexts.

"To me that was one of his great demonstrations of leadership," Mark said. "He could give the message in London, through interpreters throughout Asia. It was worldwide, phenomenal—not just the crowds and numbers of people he preached to, but he was able to communicate with each of those cultures through those interpreted languages."

The context principle is not just for communicating the message to large crowds or for intercultural connection. It's at the core of leadership: every follower is an individual with a set of perceptions, every group is part of a culture, every challenge has a context. First, one must understand, then communicate with empathy and creativity.

Sowing seeds means carefully planting them so that they have the best chance to take root and grow.

LEADERSHIP LESSONS | Sowing

Applying the Principle

As leaders, some of us have many gifts, others, few. Sometimes we may feel our particular gifts are ordinary seeds with little potential for significant fruit. Yet as we refine our skills and grow as leaders, each of us might be amazed at how our uniqueness unexpectedly teaches and inspires others.

Apply Your Giftedness with Great Expectation

We asked Mark Hatfield about his use of what he had seen in Billy Graham's leadership.

Mark responded, "Billy never found an inappropriate place or audience from which he felt any restriction of sharing the gospel. It was just a part of him. I learned that lesson from Billy Graham: there's no inappropriate audience or organization that you cannot share your philosophy of life. You can give them a straightforward and simple answer."

He then added, "Also, Billy's reaching out to all cultures, all languages, all kinds of humanity to show his compassion, his desire to share the good news with them, his concern about their poverty and their plight."

In 1957 in New York, Billy Graham was unaware of how Mark Hatfield was taking all those mental notes. He was also unaware that Mark would go on to become a national leader. Civic leaders must daily contextualize their messages, and the future senator adapted applications of what he had seen in Billy and used them for a lifetime.

The seeds a leader scatters will often take root and bear fruit in unexpected ways.

Having "great expectations" about multiple effects of our leadership is not unrealistic. In fact, expectations are often a major factor in serendipitous results. It was often said about Billy Graham that he had "great expectations." He, in turn, was often amazed at the many unanticipated results of his efforts and prayers.

Prioritize Self-Management

Sowing seeds in all seasons is a tall order. Bill Hybels, who has led a pioneering, burgeoning ministry for decades, has learned that what's required is not just skills and focus but attention to the heart and soul of the sower.

In his book *Courageous Leadership*, he tells this story: "I'll never forget the day three wise advisors came to me on behalf of the church. They said, 'Bill, there were two eras during the first twenty years of Willow Creek's history when, by your own admission, you were not at your leadership best: once in the late 1970s and again in the early 1990s. The data shows that Willow Creek paid dearly for your leadership fumble. It cost all of us more than you'll ever know.'

"Then they said the words I'll never forget: 'The best gift you can give the people you lead here at Willow is a healthy, energized, fully surrendered, and focused self. And no one can make that happen in your life except you. It's up to you to make the right choices so you can be at your best.' While they were talking, the Holy Spirit was saying, 'They're right, Bill. They're right.'"

Hybels shares this story not to beat on himself but to emphasize a vital, often-neglected necessity. We knew Bill reads management and leadership books voraciously, so we perked up when he admitted that an article he read "seriously messed with my mind." He read that leadership expert Dee Hock recommends that "management of self should occupy 50 percent of leaders' time and abilities." Bill said he was stunned by that idea. "His suggested percentages bothered me so much," Bill said, "I couldn't finish the article. I tucked it away in my desk drawer to give his ideas a few hours to simmer in my mind."

By chance, Bill read an article by Daniel Goleman, the author of *Emotional Intelligence*. "Goleman has spent much of his time," Bill said, "analyzing why a small percentage of leaders develop to their fullest potential while most leaders hit a plateau far beneath what one might expect from them. His conclusion? The difference has to do with (you guessed it) self-leadership. He calls it 'emotional self-control.' According to Goleman, this form of self-control is exhibited by leaders when they persevere in leadership despite overwhelming opposition or discouragement; when they refuse to give up during times of crisis; when they manage to hold ego at bay; and when they stay focused on their mission rather than being distracted by other peoples' agendas."

You cannot suddenly fabricate foundations of strength; you must have been building them all along.

PHILIP YANCEY

Bill thought long and hard about Goleman's corroborating data and concluded: *Maybe Dee Hock's percentages aren't all that absurd.*

Hybels, Goleman, and Hock are likely on to something. We can't sow seeds for a lifetime without strongly intentional self-management and continual plugging into "voltage," as explored in the chapter on that topic. We may object that it's self-centered to spend all that time on ourselves. However, it's essential we prioritize our own physical, psychological, and spiritual vitality, and we can do that in many interactive and productive ways.

Don't Step on a Green Shoot

Sometimes a negative example goads us best. Years ago we invited a pastor to fly to Chicago and spend some time talking about articles he had written for *Leadership*. We were impressed with his contributions and wanted to encourage him to develop more.

During our time at lunch, we complimented him on his work; he grew sober. "Before these *Leadership* articles, I hadn't written anything for many, many years," he said.

"Why?"

"I felt I had nothing whatever to offer."

We said that was clearly not the case, and he told us his story. As a young man he had written something and, with great anticipation, had sent it to a well-known pastor and writer. When he found a reply in his mail, he eagerly opened it. Instead of encouragement, however, he read a curt reply saying he had no talent and should not waste his time writing.

"I was stunned and for all these years haven't written another thing."

We were stunned too. Perhaps his youthful, initial efforts were shallow, but that didn't justify squelching a hopeful young man. With an impatient, quick note, this erudite but at times "crusty" theologian blew a chance to, if not encourage, help him put his efforts into perspective.

When we are "established," we sometimes don't realize the power we have, and the impact of our smallest action.

Harry Truman didn't make that mistake. He understood the weight of his words. Once, as he took questions from an audience, he had to respond negatively to a high school boy. After the meeting was over, he had the Secret Service bring the boy to him to reassure him. Truman said he hadn't wanted that boy to go through his life with the reputation that he had been put down by the president of the United States.

> When we are out of sympathy with the young, then I think our work in this world is over.
>
> **GEORGE MACDONALD**

Truman understood that his feet could be like giant boots crushing green shoots. We, in turn, may not be president, but each of our boots may seem large, indeed, to many of those we lead.

Just as Truman was sensitive to the boy, so Billy Graham has always realized the impact of his words. He knew that even in the most casual moments, his actions affected others, especially the young.

Frank Thielman, who cherishes the times Billy mentored him as an adult, also recalls the days as a boy when he was often in the Graham house.

"I was good friends with Ned Graham. He's about my age," Frank told us. "I was up at their house many times, playing with Ned. I can remember Dr. Graham fixing us grilled cheese sand-wiches and tomato soup when lunchtime rolled around.

"They sometimes had a penny hunt. Mrs. Graham would hide pennies in the cracks all around the house, which is a log cabin, and there are all sorts of cracks in the wood everywhere. And then there would be a contest to see who could find the most pennies.

"One time when Dr. Graham was there, he sensed that it might make somebody feel bad who hadn't found as many pen-nies as somebody else, so he said, 'I want everybody to bring their pennies to me, and I'm going to give everyone a dollar no matter how many pennies you have.' So he did. Everybody came up to him with their little bags of pennies, and he cashed them out and gave each of us a dollar or two."

Frank's recollections are that Billy "just enjoyed us." Pre-sumably he did, and also in the "pennies" story we see his empathy. He had no idea his son's friend was drinking all this in and would apply that spirit in his leadership roles himself. Billy was just naturally sowing the seeds of his spiritual and personal commitments.

Thielman said to us, "The Grahams are very much in private what they claim to be in public. Dr. Graham is an integrated per-son. He doesn't speak beyond his own experience, beyond his own commitments and convictions." One of Billy's commitments, clearly, is to encourage and boost the young and impressionable.

Touch Others—With Awe at Your Powers

When we have good seed to sow, its germination is an awesome thing. Jesus spoke of the tiny mustard seed becoming a great tree.

When we lead others, we have powers that should fill us with awe and a sense of deep responsibility. The touch of a leader radiates power, for good or for ill.

Years ago a woman was at a retreat where Billy greeted participants. With his usual graciousness, he recognized her and her husband and gave them each a hug. Twenty years later, the woman still says, "I was hugged by Billy Graham." As leaders, we touch, correct, hug. We may not be Truman or Graham, but we're usually unaware of the power we possess. It may be a power that affects very few, but to those few, a touch can be decisive.

It may help to think of the power of a mother. It was Freud who said that the one who wins the heart of his mother can accomplish anything. A mother may not affect many, but to her child, she empowers—or the opposite.

A leader's touch—the cautions, discourse, hugs—radiates out in circles from family to colleagues to the crowds. Sowing seeds in all seasons is more than planting words or concepts or driving a corporate process. It's consistently sowing with a sense of great responsibility and of great possibilities.

POINTS TO PONDER

BILLY GRAHAM:

The most eloquent prayer is the prayer
through hands that heal and bless.

THE BIBLE:

Be prepared in season and out of season; correct,
rebuke and encourage—with great patience
and careful instruction.

2 TIMOTHY 4:2

PART
SIX

DEEPENING
IN EVERY DECADE

It is the child-spirit that finds life's golden gates,
and that finds them all ajar.

JOHN HENRY JOWETT

Some leaders as they age draw back and start to calcify. Others keep growing and maintain their power. These last four chapters explore how, starting at the beginning of his ministry, Billy kept developing, not only as a person but as a leader in a dramatically changing world. He

- Leveraged weaknesses
- Plugged into voltage
- Innovated
- Led with love

Throughout the decades, Billy maintained his spirit of facing fresh challenges with fresh ideas, but always with his commitment to make love the driving force.

His friend Joni Eareckson Tada once said, "Love is extravagant in the price it is willing to pay, the time it is willing to give, the hardships it is willing to endure, and the strength it is willing to spend."

In this section, we look at how Billy fleshed that out, especially in the final chapter, which starts with the question we asked in our very first interview for this book: "What would you say is the bottom line distinctive of Billy Graham's leadership?"

CHAPTER 18

Learning—and
Leveraging Weaknesses

> In times of change, learners inherit the
> earth, while the learned find themselves
> beautifully equipped, to deal with a world
> that no longer exists.
>
> ERIC HOFFER

Great strengths are usually accompanied by significant weaknesses. The visionary may ignore vital details; the driving-force leader may not notice those driven under.

Effective leaders, to say nothing of great leaders, accept their weaknesses and leverage them. First they admit them, then adapt, delegate, and constantly learn.

In many ways, it's advantageous to realize that no one human being knows all that much. After all, it's a very large and complicated world, and no one can claim more than a modest slice of knowledge and insight.

As we researched and interviewed, we were profoundly impressed by Billy's deep sense of his own limitations. But we were equally impressed at how his awareness of them was turned into a mighty lever.

Billy Graham, despite his preaching to millions, has often professed he wasn't a great preacher. It's true that others were more eloquent. Yet this drove him to concentrate on the essentials and to depend not on his own skills, but the Spirit. He insisted he was no scholar or intellectual, and he was right. Yet he was very savvy.

He had not only innate intuitions but understood that others had insights to share. He knew how much he needed those insights, and he knew how getting them would connect him with others. Therefore, he consistently set himself to learn from everyone.

During a discussion in the CTI offices, Billy once told us, "I am thinking about the whole world all the time." That statement amazed us. With a burden like that, how could he feel anything less than a great range of limitations, including cultural divides? From language idioms to mind-sets, the challenges to the communicator are legion.

We asked Rick Marshall, one of the team, about this. He described his reactions the first time he went to Billy's hotel room. "It was strewn with newspapers and magazines," he said. "I was very impressed by that. Here was someone not resting on his laurels but reading the papers—not just one, but several."

Rick told us that Billy's staff would prepare a profile of each community and connect him with key leaders. "It was Billy's openness that won them," Rick said. "You know the root meaning of the word *disciple* simply means "a learner." You stop learning, you stop growing. He was a learner."

Rick emphasized that Billy worked hard at cross-cultural understanding. "In Britain in '84, we were in six cities that summer," he explained. "The former chairman of the British Bible Society and John Stott and others fed him anecdotal and illustrative material. He was reading the papers and watching television every day, listening to the BBC. So, he communicated in ways current and appropriate for the culture. If Billy did bomb, he had someone like Grady Wilson who would tell him, or Ruth. In other words, he had a group of confidants who weren't afraid to be critical.

"The same year Billy was to minister in Helsinki, Finland, he met Dr. Arthur Grimstead, a professor at Concordia Seminary in Moorhead, Minnesota. He was so impressed with Art's grasp of Lutheran tradition that he had him travel to Helsinki to be at his side to help interpret for him Lutheran theology. It showed up in his messages."

■ ■ ■

All this listening and learning on Billy's part, which continued throughout his lifetime of ministry, started very early. We talked about that with Billy's younger brother, Melvin Graham, shortly before he passed away.

When Billy had left the farm, Melvin had stayed on—back when plowing was done with mules, their first tractor not purchased until 1939 when Billy was twenty. Now, nearly eighty, Melvin was still active in land development.

"Billy comes to Charlotte just to get away," he told us. "Last month he called from the Park Hotel and asked me to come up and talk to him." He described driving Billy around Charlotte and answering his questions. "Why didn't you go to college?" Billy asked.

"Well," Melvin responded with a smile, "I was milking cows, Billy Frank."

We asked, "Where do you think Billy's growth came from?"

"Billy Frank would interact with just about anybody," he said. "It didn't matter who they were, kings or paupers. He studied a lot. He prayed a lot. He'd get on his knees and flatten out on the ground and call on the Lord. I've seen him."

Melvin had mentioned Christian leaders who had influenced Billy, and we asked about that. He suddenly pulled up his chin and said, "Tell you what—it just now came to my mind! There was a fella named Bill Henderson, had a little grocery store in the black section of Charlotte—just a run-down little dump of a place. He was a tiny fella. He had long sleeves that came way down, and he wore a tie that would hang down below his waist. But I tell you, that little old man, he knew the Bible!

"This was probably the late forties," Melvin explained, "and Billy had been around a lot of places."

We nodded, remembering this was when Billy was United Airlines' top traveler and had preached in many European cities.

Melvin wagged his head in wonder. "Henderson barely made a living. It was a place the black people would come to get chewing tobacco and stuff like that. Most black people loved him, but that little man got beat up on many times, got his store robbed time and time again, but he just loved the Lord. I mean, he just *loved* God. Billy loved to hear Bill Henderson tell him about the Scriptures. He lived them; it wasn't weekend Christianity. And he could pray. He'd pray for Billy and his young ministry. And he witnessed all the time."

"Did this influence Billy's focus on evangelism?"

"Absolutely," replied Melvin. "In the afternoons Billy would go there and just sit and talk to him. He'd sit on an old crate—I don't think they had a chair in the place—and let Bill teach him."

Melvin's word picture is instructive: the young Billy Graham, fresh from air travel all over the country to address large audiences, taking time to sit on a crate to learn from a humble, authentic witness in the trenches. The image blends with his constant learning from executives, professors, pastors, presidents—and his candid, well-read wife. We heard over and over again, "He was always learning, always teachable."

■ ■ ■

Billy himself said of his early ministry, "Learning was an insatiable desire with me. I burned to learn, and I felt my limitations of schooling and background so terribly that I determined to do all I could through conversations, picking up everything I could from everybody." Near the end of his ministry, in his mid-eighties, he said, "I am a man still in process."

Billy Graham has been a passionate student ever since his conversion. A recent study revealed how high achievers very often have the capacity to identify, attract, and bond with high-quality mentors. Billy was a master at doing this.

He especially resonated with those who were both spiritual and intellectual; when these two traits came in the same package, the attraction was irresistible. In Oxford in 1947, Edwin Orr was writing his doctoral dissertation on the Second Great Awakening. In that academic atmosphere, he and Billy talked of Wesley and

Whitefield and the marks of true revival, praying together for another Great Awakening.

Yet Billy was also ready to learn from intellectuals who differed from him. Billy never flinched at connecting with scholars but positioned himself as a learner with deep appreciation for scholarship and its role—and was always candid about his own limitations.

On a pragmatic basis, he studied his predecessors: Dwight Moody, Charles Finney, Billy Sunday. For instance, he cribbed all sorts of publicity, church mobilization, and programming ideas from the game plans of Moody and Sunday. Billy was always quick to learn from anyone with a better idea or a better method.

He also learned from his critics. One writer castigated him for a statement that was seen as insensitive to the poor. Graham wrote him an apology and urged him to "kick me in the pants" when necessary—and thereafter he watched what he said.

Billy listened to those close to him, including, perhaps first of all, his intelligent and perceptive wife, Ruth. Interviewees often told us Ruth was crucial to Billy's success, and her advice was often pungent. For instance, in the 1950s when she heard that Billy had speculated he might be elected president if he ran on the right platform, Ruth called him and said she "didn't think the American people would vote for a divorced president, and if he left the ministry, he would certainly have a divorce on his hands." It was the same sort of response her father, L. Nelson Bell, had given him about entering politics, and Billy had listened. With a multitude of such counselors, he kept his focus.

The sources of advice were broad. When Melvin was telling us about Bill Henderson, who was Brethren, we asked about denominational influences. His response was to tell a humorous story about Billy's colleague, T. W. Wilson.

"Old TW said someone had asked him, 'TW, if you wasn't a Baptist, what would you be?' And TW said, 'I'd be ashamed.'"

Melvin had smiled as he told that, and we could all envision TW, tongue in cheek, delivering the punch line. Melvin then added, "That's the way Ruth was about Presbyterianism. If she wasn't a Presbyterian, she'd be ashamed."

We see here—in the humor and ease yet also the strong positions—that the breadth of influence from many streams of Christendom stretched and informed Billy. But the wisdom did not come without strongly differing positions, emphases, and beliefs. Sometimes he had to wrestle through what became crucibles of faith or strategy.

Learning from others was not just a matter of picking up skills and insights. What if others challenged the basic assumptions on which he had staked his life?

■ ■ ■

A major crisis of belief was precipitated by his early colleague, Chuck Templeton. They had ministered together in Youth for Christ, and Billy had considered Chuck more gifted in many ways than he. Templeton went on to Princeton Seminary, where he began to doubt significant tenets of the faith. Billy would meet with him in New York, where Templeton would pose questions about the Bible and theology that Billy could not answer. It became a painful crucible, indeed, for Billy understood the stakes. If he had significant doubts about the Scriptures and felt he was being intellectually dishonest, he would lose the call and the power that fueled his ministry. It rocked him to the core.

Through discussions with both Templeton and conservative scholars and colleagues, and through long and agonizing periods of reflection and prayer, he broke through to a certitude that he could rely on the Scriptures and the essentials of Christian faith. Billy had carefully weighed all the contrasting input from others, mixing it with prayers and tears and laying it all before God. As Melvin and so many others have said, in times of great challenges, Billy would call on the Lord with great fervor. Allan Emery observed that the difference he has seen in Billy—contrasted with so many other leaders—is that when confronted with a crisis, he would spend literally an entire night in prayer seeking God's direction and empowerment.

Although in the Templeton experience he drove belief stakes into the ground that would anchor his ministry, issues of strategy presented different sorts of crucibles. He would have to weigh advice against advice, friend against friend, faction against faction.

For instance, in trying to decide whether or not to go to the Soviet Union in 1982, the pressure was intense. Likewise, passionate calls for him to start a Christian university were so strong that he purchased land in North Carolina and began the process, then eventually backed off. Years later, proponents of the university concept were still deeply disappointed.

Some would say Billy listened to too many people and wrestled with decisions too long and made too many U-turns. But the bottom line is, he wrestled and prayed them through. Looking at his lifetime of zigs, zags, and straight lines, it all adds up to remarkably focused leadership.

■ ■ ■

Sterling Huston handled Billy's campaigns for twenty-eight years, and, on meeting with him, it's easy to see why he did so well at it. Warm, impeccable, organized, confident yet low-key, he epitomizes the best-of-the-breed leaders who go into cities to make the Graham meetings happen.

"Billy had a great sense of conviction that what he was doing was the will of God," Sterling told us.

We asked, "So he listened to everybody, but his ultimate learning was from listening to God?"

"Yes, and the signal he received was not full of static."

We were sitting around an oval table at CTI, on which Sterling had laid his papers. Trained as an engineer and always well prepared, he had studied the materials we had sent and now drummed a finger on our outline, saying the principles being explored were sound, including the emphases in *Good to Great*.

"How did he listen to you, Sterling?" we asked. "As he chose cities to go to, how did he sort out the many voices?"

Sterling leaned forward. "I always began the process of exploring crusade cities by asking, 'Billy, what are some cities on your heart?' Some he mentioned I would think to myself, *I know the religious makeup there; it would take two years to meet with all the leadership. That city is not united, and I don't know of any prayer movement there.* Many time my observations were correct, but sometimes I'd go there and find God had been at work preparing the leadership of the city to work together. Billy had that spiritually intuitive sense of where God was working. I would report my findings back to him, giving reasons why we should or should not go to a particular city. He listened carefully to my recommendations, but he always made the final decision only after praying about it."

We nodded. "You said that his friends would sometimes try to persuade him to go to a city that probably wasn't ready. We often hear he's known for changing his mind. Yet you spoke of his commitment once his decision was made. How does a readily changed mind and strong commitment fit together?"

Sterling smiled. "In my twenty-eight years of directing Billy's crusades, it was very rare that his friends might have unduly influenced his decisions. I can only think of two cities where this might have happened. Sometimes he would delay making a decision on crusade cities for several months while he prayed and consulted others, but when he finally had peace of heart about a city, we could move ahead with confidence that his decision was firm. His eventual commitment and the process he went through to make the decision assured and energized the people who worked for him. His track record was awfully good about being in the right place at the right time, which was ultimately confirmed by the blessing of God on the meetings."

We concluded that even Billy's "weakness" of waffling on certain difficult decisions because he didn't want to say no, and his not wanting to fire anyone, was leveraged into strength—because he was ever the humble learner, giving strong colleagues their freedom and passionately driving toward the best win-win approach. For instance, he knew that if you don't feel called to play the role of "bad cop," you have to find someone who could.

As Jack Modesett, CTI's chairman, observed about Billy's reluctance to fire employees, "Churchill wouldn't fire people either! Yet what a leader he was."

Billy accepted his weaknesses, leveraging them and keeping his eyes on the goal.

■ ■ ■

Joni Eareckson Tada, who was paralyzed from a diving accident when she was a teenager, has been an outstanding leader herself, despite her dramatic limitations. She founded and leads her organization, Joni and Friends, which encourages and equips those with disabilities, has written outstanding books, and has often appeared with Billy. We found her insights about leveraging weaknesses especially insightful as she told us about her experience at Graham's Moscow crusade in the early 1990s: "My translator was Oleg, a young Russian man who was severely visually impaired. He commented while we were on the platform, 'Joni, isn't it wonderful that God is using me, a blind boy, and you, a paralyzed woman to reach the people in my nation of eleven time zones?' I got a lump in my throat, just thinking of his point: that God delights in choosing weak people to accomplish his work. I was about to respond to Oleg when I saw Billy Graham slowly rise (with a little help) from his seat to walk to the platform. It was around the time he had received an initial diagnosis of perhaps Parkinson's disease. As I watched Mr. Graham steady himself to step up to the pulpit, I said to Oleg, 'Friend, God is using not only a blind boy and a paralyzed woman but an elderly man on shaky legs to reach your people!'"

How did Billy react when she shared those thoughts with him? "He wasn't embarrassed. This is what has inspired me most about this extraordinary leader. Not only does he keep moving ahead, despite his physical challenges, he seems to boast in them."

Joni then pointed us to God's words in 2 Corinthians 12:9 — "My grace is sufficient for you, for my power is made perfect in weakness."

"Mr. Graham is keenly aware that God's power always shows up best in weakness," said Joni. "This is why he inspires me with my own disability of thirty-seven years. His example of perseverance under pressure speaks volumes to me and to many others. It's probably why the BGEA, with every crusade, systematically in the spirit of Luke 14:21 goes out 'into the streets and alleys' to 'bring in the poor, the crippled, the blind and the lame.' This tells me Mr. Graham knows God's heart when it comes to the lowly and needy. He reflects this through his own humility, and he lives it daily."

■ ■ ■

Journalist David Aikman includes Billy Graham as one of six "great souls who changed the century." He says Billy made mistakes of judgment at different points in his career, but he "never stopped admitting his own faults and weaknesses."

Aikman summed up this way: "To remain humble, teachable, and gracious amid success and in the face of sometimes bitter opposition and criticism is the mark of true virtue. And to remain relentlessly loyal to God's call while exposed as consistently as Graham has been to all the world's power and glory, well, 'tis the mark of a Great Soul."

LEADERSHIP LESSONS | Leveraging Weakness

Applying the Principles

In a world that's constantly changing, no fixed set of knowledge is sufficient. As John Naisbitt observed, "No one subject or set of subjects will serve you for the foreseeable future, let alone for the rest of your life. The most important skill to acquire now is learning how to learn."

The situation is akin to that of Meriwether Lewis making plans for his journey to explore the great Louisiana Purchase in 1803. He didn't know exactly where he was going, other than following the Missouri River to its source and proceeding from there to the Pacific Ocean. The land he would be traveling was unknown to him. How do you pack for a trip that is literally "beyond the map"?

While he brought as many supplies as he could, his approach was to recruit men—starting with Captain William Clark—who could live off the land and adapt to unexpected situations. These men were prepared to learn and improvise as they went along. And as it turned out, it was their good fortune to meet knowledgeable guides and mentors, including the teenager Sacagawea, who provided the resources they needed.

Likewise, today's leaders, entering a rapidly changing world, are also exploring "beyond the map." The ability to learn as we go and leverage weaknesses may be tomorrow's most important leadership skill.

Compensate, and Dodge Disaster

Billy Graham is a positive person, but not because he believes in himself. He is positive because he has faith that God is going to work, and he is constantly aware of his own human limitations.

John Akers, for decades the point person for Billy's high-level, international initiatives, told us, "Billy was wholly afraid that he would bring about disrepute to the gospel. He realized the potential there is for disaster."

As a result of remaining conscious of his own weaknesses and the potential for failure, Billy continually sought to compensate for his own shortcomings.

Interestingly, the most effective way to do that is not to bemoan our own limitations. It's just the opposite: it's to eagerly and happily glean from the strengths that others offer.

In the book *Geeks and Geezers*, Warren Bennis and Robert Thomas reflect on "how era, values, and defining moments shape leaders" of two very different generations—the geeks (those aged twenty-one to thirty-five) and the geezers (those over seventy). One key finding is that among the geezers, every person who was able to continue to play a leadership role retained the qualities of curiosity, playfulness, eagerness, fearlessness, warmth, and energy.

Instead of despairing over their age, they were "open, willing to take risks, hungry for knowledge and experience, courageous, eager to see what the new day brings."

Listen Intently

"I remind myself every morning: nothing I say this day will teach me anything. So if I'm going to learn, I must do it by listening," said Larry King, the famous interviewer and a close friend of Billy Graham.

Billy certainly shared that trait with his friend. When we interviewed Graham biographer William Martin, he told us that listening was one of Billy's great strengths. "He never hardened into the place where he assumed, 'Here I am. I'm Billy Graham, and you and your ideas can bounce up against me.' No, he was always willing to grow, like a ripple that is constantly moving outward in an ever-growing circle. He showed that in his willingness to cooperate with more and more different groups."

Learning is not attained by chance. It must be sought for with ardor.

ABIGAIL ADAMS

"Billy wants to learn," said Martin. "He has the ability to give you his full attention when you're talking to him and is generous in his response to people. That's very appealing."

Jay Kesler told us, "The great issue of our day for leaders is how to lead in a postmodern, pluralistic, multicultural environment. How does one maintain convictions with civility? Billy Graham has done that. This is to me the largest leadership quality needed in the modern world."

"Anyone who stops learning is old, whether at twenty or eighty," said Henry Ford. "Anyone who keeps learning stays young."

Learn from Unlikely Sources

Roald Amundsen was a national hero in his native Norway. He gained worldwide acclaim as an explorer in being the first person to reach the South Pole and the first to touch both poles in a single lifetime.

According to a profile in *U.S. News & World Report*, Amundsen's great gift "was a willingness to learn from those around him." In this, he was much like Billy Graham. In 1903, Amundsen was on the way to becoming the first person to navigate the Northwest Passage between the Canadian mainland and its Arctic Islands. He became fascinated with the Netsilik, an isolated group of Eskimos, and he lived as they lived: "He careened down hills in the dog sleds, slept in their igloos, and adopted their reindeer-fur dress."

> I like to listen. I have learned a great deal from listening carefully. Most people never listen.
>
> ERNEST HEMINGWAY

What he learned from these unlikely educators eventually proved strategic in Amundsen's ultimately successful attempt to reach the South Pole. His choice of dogs and his use of reindeer fur helped him survive the brutal conditions of Antarctica, while his rival, Sir Robert Falcon Scott of England, perished making the same attempt with more traditional equipment. Learning from unlikely sources made the difference between success and failure, life and death.

Repristinate!

Sometimes a leader is charged with protecting a certain asset—whether an endowment, a tradition, or an institution. But even the task of preservation demands learning and growth.

In his book on leadership, *Certain Trumpets*, Garry Wills points out that in order for a tradition to be worth passing on to another generation, you must repristinate it, make it pristine again—"restore it to its original state or condition."

He quotes G. K. Chesterton: "Conservativism is based upon the idea that if you leave things alone, you leave them as they are. But you do not. If you leave a thing alone, you leave it to a torrent of changes. If you leave a white [fence] post alone, it will soon be a black post. If you particularly want it to be white, you must be always painting it again. Briefly, if you want the old white post, you must have a new white post."

What people celebrate as tradition is usually a thing that's been changed by time. "All things that resist change are changed by that resistance in ways undesired and undesirable," says Wills. "The tradition must be repristinated if it is to be worth following."

What this means for leaders is that even preservation requires growth, learning, and continual renovation. Graham board member Bill Pollard said, "Everything—including relationships—tends to deteriorate with time unless the new, the improved, the changed is added."

This is what Billy Graham was doing by his habit of asking people to teach him. He was repristinating his relationships and his understanding.

POINTS TO PONDER

BILLY GRAHAM:

In God's economy, a person must go down into the
valley of grief before he or she can scale the heights of
spiritual glory. . . . One must come to the end of "self"
before one can really begin to live.

THE BIBLE:

God chose the foolish things of the world
to shame the wise;
God chose the weak things of the world
to shame the strong.

1 CORINTHIANS 1:27

CHAPTER 19

Plugging into Continuous Voltage

When we come to the end of ourselves,
we come to the beginning of God.
BILLY GRAHAM

Billy's colleagues often speak of the constant pressure Billy has always felt. It's easy to see why.

Imagine the pressure of conducting the funeral for the disgraced former President Richard Nixon while the nation skeptically watched and listened for every nuance. Imagine the emotional demands on him when he conducted the memorial service after the Oklahoma City bombing.

The service at the National Cathedral right after the 9/11 attacks on the World Trade Center and the Pentagon presented perhaps the greatest pressure of all. The nation was in deep shock; the entire world would be watching on television. Billy's words and tone, both for Americans and for people of all other nations, had to be just right. That would be challenge enough to step up to at the height of your powers. But it was a frail octogenarian with serious health problems who mounted the steps to the platform with steady purpose and told the nation, "God is our refuge and strength; an ever-present help in trouble. Therefore we will not fear, though the earth give way, and the mountains fall into the heart of the sea."

With internal strength, Billy declared, "You may be angry at God. I want to assure you that God understands these feelings you have. But God can be trusted, even when life seems at its darkest. From the cross, God declares, 'I love you. I know the heartaches and the sorrows and the pains you feel, but I love you.'

"This has been a terrible week with many tears. But also it's been a week of great faith. . . . And [remember] the words of that familiar hymn that Andrew Young quoted, 'Fear not, I am with thee. Oh, be not dismayed, for I am thy God and will still give thee aid.'"

Despite his frailty, Billy's presence, poise, and message touched the sorrows and fears and brought hope and a deeply Christian response to his nation and to the world. He found the inner resources to rise to that momentous occasion.

More than twenty years before that service, we sat in a restaurant with a close friend of Billy's who had gone to college with him. In his 60s, this Christian leader had just retired. "Billy should hang it up now," he told us. "He should shift to a role of senior statesman and retire from all the pressure of carrying the weight of his organization." He said this in loving concern for Billy, and, indeed, we thought it likely that with all the health problems Billy was already experiencing that he would change his pace and get off the leadership point and out of the spotlight's glare.

Instead, Billy continued for another quarter century of holding meetings all over the world; continued in the nitty-gritty of leading his organization; continued to sweat over the funding of bringing ten thousand evangelists to Amsterdam three different times; continued to appear on news shows to represent the gospel; continued to minister to every U.S. president of his era and participate in their inaugurations; continued making countless public appearances while keeping up private connections with soul mates. In the phrase voiced by President George W. Bush when Billy was hospitalized and unable to attend the funeral of Ronald Reagan, Billy was "the nation's pastor"—but he was also the leader of an organization and of a vast movement.

How could he maintain the strength and sense of commitment to do all that, not only in his last decades but throughout the unrelenting pressure of the leadership sprint/marathon he has run for sixty years?

■ ■ ■

Billy has not been impervious to the pressures; his body and psyche have paid a steep price. But he has taken his own advice, so often expressed in various ways in his newspaper columns, books, and articles. He has continually plugged himself into the spiritual and psychological voltage that has made this half-century saga possible.

From the beginning, his spiritual power has come from prayer and the Bible. His colleague, T. W. Wilson, called him "the most completely disciplined person I have ever known." The discipline started around 7:00 a.m. each day, when he would read five psalms and one chapter of Proverbs. He started there because, as he often said, the psalms showed him how to relate to God, while Proverbs taught him how to relate to people. After breakfast he would pray and study more Scripture. Even under the pressure of travel schedules moving him from city to city, from hotel to hotel, often through many time zones, he strove to study and pray each morning.

Some close to Billy describe him as more adaptive to circumstances in fitting in study and prayer, but all emphasize his spending large amounts of time connecting with his source of wisdom, cleansing, and power.

Even in the early days of youthful vigor, the demands on him made him intensely aware of his need for that power. When the 1957 New York campaign was so effective that the pastors asked him to stay for another month of meetings, he told Grady Wilson he didn't think he could make it even one more day. "All of my strength has departed from me. I've preached all the material I can lay my hands on. Yet God wants me here." In all, he wound up preaching virtually every night there for over three months, making additional public appearances and speaking at many of them during the day.

Grady Wilson believed it was "the prayers of people all over the world" that gave Billy the needed stamina for the task. Yet he also believed that the grueling time in New York drew down his reserves. "Since that time, I don't believe he's ever regained all his strength."

Cliff Barrows agrees. "Bill was so weary in the latter few weeks, he felt he just couldn't go another day, but the Lord kept giving him strength. But at the end of the meetings, something left him, something came out of him physically that has never been replaced."

Despite the recurring sense of being drained and empty, Billy didn't quit. As Grady observed, "When he mounts the platform, though, it seems the Holy Spirit gives him a resurgence of vitality and power."

Pastor Warren Wiersbe offered us similar testimony. "When Billy stood up to speak one night, I thought, *This guy is not going to make it.* You could tell he was not at his best physically; he just didn't look like he was up to it. And then something happened, like you plugged in a computer—that power was there. The minute he stepped into that pulpit and opened his Bible, something happened. I've heard him say that when he gets up to preach, he feels like electricity is going through him."

This is the picture so often described by his colleagues: weakness drawing on the Spirit. And it wasn't simply physical fatigue but a wrestling with the realities of the human condition and his own shortcomings. "All of us are awfully human," observed Grady. "Billy is painfully aware of his humanity." He noted, for instance, that "Billy has a temper, but he keeps it in check." How? "He stays close to his Lord and spiritual discipline and prayer."

Rick Marshall, in his first meeting with Billy, was amazed at his being so open about his fatigue and by his humble prayers. "I remember thinking to myself, *This is Billy Graham?* It was such a contrast to the persona I had watched filling the stadium with his booming voice and authority. But when I was actually with the man, I was overwhelmed by the humility, the raw honesty before God about his own inability and physical limitations. That was the way I viewed him for the next twenty-three years. It kept me willing to stay within an organization that placed a lot of demands on me."

Rick quoted the apostle Paul's statement, "When I am weak, then I am strong," as setting the basis for this strange mixture of strength through weakness. Like Paul, Billy leaned into his weaknesses.

"Now think about it," Rick said. "If anyone could have been confident, it would have been Billy. But I never saw that. I saw only humility and a bowed head. In fact, I made a point for the last twenty campaigns to bring a team of pastors to pray with him every night before he went into the pulpit. That, I think, became for him one of the most important moments. It was his way, too, of saying, 'I don't do this in my own strength.'"

■ ■ ■

It has often been said, "No man is a hero to his butler." Well, how about to his photographer?

Russ Busby has been the eyes and memory of Billy Graham ministries since the earliest days—he was one of the organization's first employees. We caught up with him by phone at his Southern California home, following his commute that day from the Graham offices in Charlotte. When asked about Billy's success, Russ immediately emphasized the same core dynamic. "It's his personal time he spends with the Word. He listens for what God says to him; so when Billy says something, it comes out of his own experience."

As we explored various aspects of Billy's leadership, Russ always came back to Billy's spiritual disciplines and the Bible. "His ideas are uncanny. God has given him the most unusual vision in almost every area of sharing the good news. It *has* to be a gift from God!" When we asked Russ how all that study of ancient Scriptures connected with Billy staying relevant, he described Billy's connecting the Bible's timeless principles with ever-changing realities. "Let's go back to what Jesus said. If you want to be the greatest, you must be the servant of all. Not the leader, the servant. Billy is a servant of all, including his team. It's 'What can I do for you? What do you need? Where are you coming from?' You are back to Bible principles. That's where he learned it all."

T.W., Grady, Rick, Cliff, Warren, Russ, and literally thousands of other colleagues and leaders have been up close and personal enough to experience the humility and authenticity of Billy's study and prayers. What does this have to do with leadership principles? Billy's sincere prayers with them made them part of something more than meetings and machinery. They sensed his heart and opened their own hearts to the mission.

They also knew that Billy struggled mightily in prayer, and that it was not merely a river of balm and energy he simply accessed. He was open about his own struggles.

In one of his books he writes that he prayed "long and earnestly when I was going through a dark period, but there was no answer. I felt as though God was indifferent, and that I was all alone with my problem. It was what some would call 'a dark night of the soul.'" In this case, Billy shared his feelings with his mother, who urged him to "reach up by faith in the fog and you will find His hand will be there." He took her advice and "experienced an overwhelming sense of God's presence."

But such affirmation was no permanent victory. Instead, it was a constant return to the Source. "Every time I give an invitation, I am in an attitude of prayer," he says. "I feel emotionally, physically, and spiritually drained. It becomes a spiritual battle of such proportions that sometimes I feel faint. There is an inward groaning and agonizing in prayer that I cannot possibly put into words."

This intensity in prayer was at the beginnings of his ministry. William Martin tells the story from Roy Gustafson, one of Billy's groomsmen and a close colleague. Roy, Billy, and two other men were walking out in the hills, talking about an important decision. They agreed to pray. Billy said, "Let's get down on our knees."

Roy was wearing his only good suit, so he got his handkerchief out, laid it down carefully, and knelt on it. As they prayed, Billy's voice sounded muffled to him. Roy opened his eyes and saw that while three of them were gingerly kneeling, Billy was flung out prostrate on the ground, praying fervently, oblivious to the dirt.

■ ■ ■

Billy's prayer connection was not only unusually fervent, it was also as natural to him as breathing. Perhaps most of the time his prayer life was not overt and conscious but more like a computer application that runs in the background—fully functioning but not seen on the screen.

A. Larry Ross, who served as Billy's director of media and public relations for more than twenty-three years, told us the story about his initial discovery of this side of Billy's prayer connection. "The very first time I set up a network interview for Mr. Graham was with NBC's *Today* show in 1982. I went in the day before to meet with the producers and ensure everything was set. I assumed Mr. Graham would want to have a time of prayer before he went on national television, so I secured a private room. After we arrived at the studio the following morning, I pulled T. W. Wilson aside and said, 'Just so you know, I have a room down the hall where we can go to have a word of prayer before he goes on TV.'

"T.W. smiled at me and said, 'You know, Larry, Mr. Graham started praying when he got up this morning, he prayed while he was eating his breakfast, he prayed on the way over here in the car they sent for us, and he'll probably be praying all through the interview. Let's just say that Mr. Graham likes to stay "prayed up" all the time.'

"We didn't need to use that room," Ross added. "That was a great lesson for me to learn as a young man."

■ ■ ■

"The great things happen to those who pray, and we learn to pray best in suffering." Helmut Thielicke quoted these words of philosopher Peter Wust, and he had good reason to know their reality firsthand. A faithful pastor persecuted by the Nazis, Thielicke would preach week after week to his suffering parishioners, communicating the gospel of hope when there seemed no hope, for Allied bombs were destroying their church and country. After the war, his powerful messages of love and courage drew thousands; one of the sermon series became a remarkable book on the Lord's Prayer, titled *Our Heavenly Father*.

"The great things happen to those who pray." Yet prayer is not only the source of grace and joy but also of striving and pain. The source of great things, but not without great engagement. Leadership is, indeed, forged in the furnace.

Billy realized that he stood on the shoulders of giants like Thielicke, Luther, and Wesley. Martin Luther, who knew a thing or two about leadership, famously said he was so extremely busy that he could not get it all done without spending four hours each day in prayer. And John Wesley, who also established a worldwide movement, said flatly, "God does everything by prayer, and nothing without it."

Billy was quick to identify prayer as the vital ingredient in his first Boston meetings. He would tell the story of a day when he walked by Harold Ockenga's office and saw a remarkable sight. The distinguished clergyman, always fastidious in dress and manners, was literally under a rug, praying fervently. Billy was greatly moved by seeing him so mightily wrestling with the Lord, and later attributed much of the spiritual fruit of those New England meetings to Harold Ockenga's prayers.

But there is more to the story. Allan Emery, who was on the point leadership with Graham and Ockenga for those Boston events, tells with love and appreciation just what his friend was praying about under the rug.

Dr. Ockenga had been in the forefront of inviting Billy to hold the New England meetings and worked energetically to bring them about. Yet the limelight on the evangelist caused him feelings of envy. Billy was doing in New England what Ockenga had not been able to do. Ockenga was under the rug that day, pouring out those feelings to God.

Envy can block effectiveness and wither the soul. Harold Ockenga understood that, and he refused to give in to it. Instead of coddling himself with self-pity, he poured out to God his feelings and his concerns for the burgeoning initiatives. Perhaps he had to be as persistent as the widow in Jesus' story, who had to keep petitioning the judge. Whatever the level of intensity and stubbornness of his emotions, he ended up under the rug over them, and that made a crucial difference. He came to God confessing his total weakness, for who can on his own eradicate envy or desire for power? And the answers came, according to Emery, "in great and mighty ways."

Many decades after the incident—a few years before Ockenga's death—we interviewed him in Boston. When we asked Ockenga how he handled the pressures of serving as president of Fuller Seminary in California and simultaneously as pastor of Park Street Church in Boston, three thousand miles away, and later as president of Gordon-Conwell Seminary and chair of CTI, his response was, "I've always been very busy, but there's a secret to that." His eyes twinkled as he pulled out some papers and told us that for forty-one years he'd kept a prayer list. "When I go over it, I'm reminded by the Lord if I haven't tried to solve a problem. If I have enemies I'm praying for, something may come to mind that I can do about that."

It's significant that he prayed for "enemies." Did prayer release anxieties about his responsibilities? "Yes, that's right," he said. "I never worry about them."

As a result of the intensity and longevity of both men's prayers, all sorts of things were made possible, including the highly fruitful partnership of Ockenga the intellectual and Graham the "simple" communicator. They made a remarkable team for decades, complementing each other's strengths and weaknesses. They led not only through their own institutions but through related ones like *Christianity Today* and the National Association of Evangelicals.

Billy has written, "Tennyson's well-known words, 'More things are wrought by prayer than this world dreams of,' are no mere cliché. They state a sober truth."

Again, Peter Wust: "The great things happen to those who pray." Billy believed and personified that, and it made possible his ability to lead others in those great endeavors.

LEADERSHIP LESSONS | Continuous Voltage

Applying the Principles

When you purchase a computer, you get an owner's manual and usually a troubleshooting guide. Almost invariably, the first instruction is, "Make sure the computer is plugged into the power source."

It's an obvious necessity, but in life and leadership, that elementary step is often overlooked. Leaders must be aware of what fuels them. Sometimes they become so focused on their objectives, so driven to accomplish, that they don't notice a power outage.

Gordon MacDonald, in *Ordering Your Private World*, describes this situation: "A driven person is usually caught in the uncontrolled pursuit of expansion. Driven people like to be a part of something that is getting bigger and more successful. . . . They rarely have any time to appreciate the achievements to date. . . . Driven people are usually abnormally busy. They are too busy for the pursuit of ordinary relationships in marriage, family, or friendship . . . not to speak of one with God."

Jesus said, "What good is it for a man to gain the whole world, yet forfeit his soul?" (Mark 8:36). Most leaders know the all-consuming demands that come with leadership. Yet without attention to our souls, our greatest human efforts eventually sputter out.

Recognize That Spiritual Health Isn't Automatic

Mindy Caliguire worked for several years in a marketing firm; now she helps leaders with "spiritual formation." She understands that keeping spiritually healthy amid the demands of leadership isn't easy. Here's how she communicated that to a group of leaders. "What tends to emerge in the life of a person who neglects their soul?" she asked them. "What symptoms creep in?" She explained that leaders face ever-increasing loads that can yield ever-diminishing returns with an ever-elusive inner life. "So, what are the signs of soul neglect?" she asked.

"At first the room was silent," Mindy said. "Then somebody ventured, *'anxiety,'* and I knew they 'got it' (not every group does). Once started, I couldn't write their answers on the flipchart fast enough. They called out *self-absorption, shame, apathy, toxic anger, chronic fatigue, lack of confidence, isolation, no compassion, self-oriented, drivenness, loss of vision.* Minutes later, every square inch of the page was crammed with words describing soul neglect. A sad feeling hovered over the room as many of these leaders, 'weary of well-doing,' saw themselves in the mirror.

> Prayer is a summit meeting in the very throne room of the universe. There is no higher level.
>
> **RALPH HERRING**

"Then, with much relief, we turned the page and I asked the opposite: 'What emerges in your life when your soul is healthy? When you're connected with God?'

"This page also filled up quickly: *love, joy, compassion, generosity of spirit, peace, ability to trust, discernment.* These words, too, got crammed into every inch of white paper. Heads nodded in acknowledgment as individuals recalled seasons of life when this was their experience. *Boundlessness, creativity, vision, balance, focus.* All in all, a pretty desirable list.

"Then I brought it to a vote. Holding up the Soul Neglect list, I asked, 'Who votes for this?' Everyone laughed! No one in their right mind would choose to live this way."

Then Mindy pointed out that every day, each of us is voting for one or the other of these two lists.

Deepen a Dry Well

Bill Leslie was an inner-city pastor and community organizer. We talked to him shortly before his sudden and unexpected death several years ago. We asked him about the spiritual power needed to be a community leader in a tough neighborhood in Chicago.

He told us that over the years, he felt continuously worn down in his efforts to alleviate suffering, fight poverty, and persevere despite the crime and violence that permeated his neighborhood. One day when discouragement and conflict caused him to hit bottom, he made an appointment with a nun, Ann Wilder, who had been recommended to him as a wise counselor and spiritual director.

"Bill, I want you to come up with a word that characterizes how you feel right now," she said. "What's the first word that comes into your mind?"

"I feel raped," said Bill.

"Who has raped you?"

Bill told us later, "The first word that came to mind was *God*." But he said to Ann, "I know theologically that God doesn't rape anybody, but I feel raped by God."

"Who else has raped you?"

"The church. Everybody comes to me for something, but no one takes care of me. I can ask for anything for somebody else, but I never can ask for anything for myself. I feel like an orange: the church has squeezed every bit of juice out of me."

"Anybody else?"

"Yeah, the community has raped me. Everybody depends on my networks. Any organization in the community that wants money asks me to write their proposals."

All the good from the Saviour of the world is communicated through this book. All things desirable to man are contained in the Bible.

ABRAHAM LINCOLN

Bill smiled as he recalled the conversation. "Finally she wisely said—and I've learned to do this with others, 'Would you mind if I change your image? Let's change the image from that of rape to that of a farm pump. Let's say that everybody who comes by grabs the handle and pumps.' And I nodded, 'They sure do.'"

Ann pressed on. "Have you read those passages in the Bible about being a servant?"

"Yes," said Bill. "Those are the ones that got me into this trouble."

"Do you believe them?" Ann asked.

"Yeah," Bill said, "I believe them, but it doesn't feel good."

"The real problem is your pipe isn't deep enough," Ann said. "You're pumping surface water, so by 10:30 in the morning, they've pumped you dry. Deep down there are underground streams. If you can get your pipe down there, there's so much water that no matter how much anyone pumps out of you, they'll have a hard time lowering the level of the water even one inch.

"That water is always cool. Even though the pump is used a lot, the water goes up through the pump, and the pump is refreshed. Have you ever heard that passage in John 7, 'Out of your innermost being shall flow rivers of living water'? That's what I'm talking about."

Ann winked and added, "I guess what I'm really saying to you, Bill, is that you need a personal relationship with Jesus Christ."

Bill laughed, because as an evangelical Christian, he figured he was the one who was supposed to be saying that to the nun. He told us, "She knew I had a relationship with Jesus but was trying to say, 'Way down deep, you're shallow!'" Bill chuckled at the irony of that phrase. "The problem was, I didn't know anyone who had anything deeper than I did."

"If you're serious about this," Ann suggested, "I think we can help you get your pipe down deep where the people can pump. You may get tired every now and then, but you'll stay refreshed and energized."

Bill followed her direction. And between Ann's regularly pointing him back to his spiritual source, his paying attention to his physical health, and the developing of some key friendships, Bill was able to continue to effectively lead without consuming himself.

Trust the Power Given

Because Billy realized the power didn't come *from* him but came *through* him, he didn't feel obligated to overreach with his methods.

Jack Hayford, himself a powerful preacher, observed, "Billy Graham reveals a remarkable absence of the superficial, of hype, or of pandering to the crowd. . . . His communication consistently avoided exaggeration or 'slick' remarks. There's never been anything cutesy or clever about his style. There are no grandiose claims or stunts employed to attract attention. Graham merely bows in prayer while seekers come forward—moved by God, not a manipulative appeal."

That confidence in the power of the message frees the leader from having to work over-hard on presentation techniques to convince the hearers. When a basketball player is not in a position to take a shot but puts it up anyway, coaches call it "forcing the shot." Forced shots are usually ineffective. Coaches will tell players to wait until they're in a good position, then the shot has a better chance of success. Likewise, people can sense that efforts are forced when a leader isn't convinced his message is sound.

Because Billy was well connected to his continuous voltage, he knew where the power came from. He simply made himself available to receive it.

■ ■ ■

Energy and power come in different ways to different leaders. Bill Leslie was exhausted by the inner-city needs around him. Yet Danny Morris, a leader in the United Methodist Church, was stretched and energized by engaging with such needs. "A positive tension that indicates spiritual health," Danny told us, "is being able to walk in God's presence, enjoy him for ourselves, yet still feel the world's hurts. Recently it struck me that most of my friends are fairly well-off and well educated. My friendships were causing me to miss seeing the world through the eyes of the broken, lonely, and downtrodden."

So Danny went to night court, where people who had been arrested were brought in before a magistrate.

"As I watched the parade of people, suddenly I realized the people I usually ran around with were not typical. I saw drunkenness and poverty. I saw victims of fighting and cutting, the rawest kind of life you can imagine. I discovered I was completely out of touch with these kinds of hurts."

Spiritual voltage can be generated by the tension of seeing deep needs, getting beyond our own troubles, and becoming part of solutions.

Develop Voltage-Producing Friendships

John Wesley used the term *conferencing* to describe the kinds of thoughtful reflection and interaction with others that can deepen and keep current our spiritual lives.

We talked to Robert Cooley about Billy's influence on him in this regard. Billy, as a founder of Gordon-Conwell Seminary, spoke at Bob's inauguration as its president. "I remember his admonitions to me," Bob told us. "In the casual conversations that surrounded that event, he emphasized strongly the importance of a life of prayer and spiritual formation in leading the seminary. He kept saying, 'I know how much you're going to have to depend upon this.' That struck me right at the beginning, because coming out of the university, I didn't have anyone who would take that message to me. But he kept emphasizing this."

We asked Bob how that had played out during his many years as the seminary's leader.

"I immediately established the discipline of daily prayer in the president's office. I invited everyone and anyone who would join me for prayer. My day began with prayer. I had one professor, J. Christy Wilson, who never missed a day during his time at the seminary in joining me. It was the discipline of committing to prayer, sharing needs, concerns, and praise. Those were essential disciplines that I tried to not just model but to make integral to my daily life."

"Did all of that empower your leadership?" we asked.

"It did in a number of ways," Bob said. "It created more joy within. You can easily get entrapped in the wake of the day's programs and concerns leading an organization—no wonder the word *burden* comes to mind. The weight of the issues can rob you of your joy. But prayer teaches you that rejoicing becomes an activity. It's more than a feeling. It's a discipline. It's a daily thing."

POINTS TO PONDER

BILLY GRAHAM:

Unless the soul is fed and exercised daily,

it becomes weak and shriveled.

It remains discontented, confused, restless.

THE BIBLE:

Create in me a pure heart, O God, and renew a steadfast spirit

within me. Do not cast me from your presence or take your

Holy Spirit from me. Restore to me the joy of your salvation

and grant me a willing spirit, to sustain me.

PSALM 51:10 – 12

CHAPTER 20

Innovating

> You can judge your age by the amount of
> pain you feel when you come into contact
> with a new idea.
>
> JOHN NUVEEN

Continual change is the reality of our era. Global competition and rapidly shifting consumer demands force businesses to "innovate or die." Social norms and expectations keep shifting. Peter Drucker reminds us, "Reality never stands still very long."

Authors Arnold Brown and Edith Weiner captured our entrepreneurial march into the future: "In a time of rapid, turbulent, and confusing change, you must fall away from a past that prevents you from seeing the potential ahead."

Effective leaders must blend history and precedent with wisdom from the past, applying them to emerging realities. Billy Graham launched his ministry in an era when many religious leaders warned that Christianity would survive only by "modernizing" its message. Yet he stubbornly preached historical, biblical Christianity. At the same time, he communicated this message innovatively. Billy may have drawn from the organizing genius of Dwight Moody and the preaching dynamics of Billy Sunday, but he used communication tools as they emerged, keeping the message the same but adapting to the delivery systems. "We used every modern means to catch attention," Graham said, in describing his early days with Youth for Christ. This spirit continued throughout his career.

■ ■ ■

In the quest to increase effective communication, Billy constantly pursued new avenues. During a 1954 crusade that packed London's Harringay Arena for twelve weeks, Billy experimented with landline relays, which carried his voice to overflow venues across the British Isles. Organizers set up speakers in 430 churches and auditoriums in 175 cities. Surprisingly, Billy's gospel invitation spurred an even greater response in many of these remote locations than it did in Harringay, because the listeners could focus more intently without the distractions of arena seating.

More than four decades later, Billy was still employing the latest technologies. In March of 1995, Graham stood in a pulpit in Puerto Rico delivering a series of messages heard by as many as one billion people. How? His distinct Southern intonation was beamed toward thirty satellites, which redirected the signal to receiving dishes in more than 185 countries. The sermons were then translated into 116 languages. "It is time," he said, "for the church to use technology to make a statement that in the midst of chaos, emptiness, and despair, there is hope in the person of Jesus Christ."

Why the strong motivation to innovate? Billy's associates insist his drive to innovate was rooted in his calling to reach out to others with God's love. What else, they ask, could motivate him in the 1960s to don sunglasses, shabby clothes, and a baseball cap to mingle in New York City among protesters of Students for a Democratic Society? Why else would he walk into a music store, load up on rock albums, and then sit down at his Montreat home to hear an unfamiliar generation's coming-of-age anthems? Graham left his generational comfort zone because he believed in his message and loved those who needed to hear it.

This confidence and compassion endeared him to peculiar audiences. During his 1971 meetings at McCormick Place in Chicago, Billy endured periodic boos and hisses from some three hundred hippies and Yippies who gathered to taunt the evangelist. During the invitation hymn, this group elbowed their way forward to further disrupt Billy's efforts. Then a group of thirty "Jesus People"—a dynamic, Christian splinter movement from the youth counterculture—linked hands and confronted the protesters, chanting "Jesus" and encouraging them to submit their lives to Christ. The protest faded, and the "Jesus People" passed along a message that eventually reached Billy on the podium: "Tell Billy Graham: 'The Jesus People love him.'"

Billy—for many a symbol of the "establishment"—was beloved by many in the counterculture. How was this possible? Among many factors, they appreciated his efforts to humbly reach out on their terms rather than force them to "clean up" and meet in environments comfortable to him. Historian Larry Eskridge has noted the significant impact of Billy's innovative leadership. Had Billy taken issue with hair length and music styles, perhaps evangelicalism would have developed a debilitating generation gap.

Eskridge wrote, "Without the welcoming arms of Billy Graham and other evangelical leaders, there would have been no bridge 'back' for thousands of refugees from the counterculture—just another disillusioning hassle and prolonged battle with another facet of the Establishment."

■ ■ ■

Generational changes often catch leaders unaware, and Billy's sensitivities did not ensure against that. Rick Marshall noticed in the late 1980s a developing generational disconnect. As director of Billy's campaigns, he relied on the support of local ministers, who began hinting to Marshall that evangelism meetings had run their course. Even Billy's biggest supporters were concerned. Marshall remembers their saying, "If you're younger than fifty and don't watch *Larry King Live*, you may never have heard of Billy Graham!"

Marshall knew the campaign programming had become dated, so imagine his concern when the cochairmen of Billy's 1994 Cleveland campaign—businessman Gordon Heffern and former Cleveland Indians all-star Andre Thornton—asked him how the BGEA would help them reach Ohio's youth. "I was stunned. Privately I thought, *I don't think we can do that because I've been watching over the last several years, and the kids aren't coming.* We have youth nights Monday, Thursday, and Sunday, but there's no reason for the kids to come."

Spurred on by Heffern and Thornton's challenge, Marshall brainstormed ways to encourage youth to come hear Billy. He created plans for flashy visual presentations and edgy rock music. This initiative was so new and, for the Graham team, unusual that a few program technicians created T-shirts that read "The Billy Graham 'It-Seemed-Like-a-Good-Idea-at-the-Time' Tour." When Rick brought up the concept with Cliff Barrows, Billy's partner and longtime music and program director who normally made programming decisions, Cliff said "Rick, this is too hot to handle. You have to talk to Bill."

So Marshall took his plan straight to the CEO. "I got Mr. Graham on the phone and shared with him the vision. You know what he said? 'That's nothing. Let me tell you about what we used to do.' And he went all the way back into the 1940s and told me about the Youth for Christ rallies: horses on the stage tapping out answers to Bible questions; a hundred pianos in the middle of football fields; crazy, wild clothing and ties with bright lights hooked up to battery packs."

YFC's motto, "Geared to the times, anchored to the Rock," had meant innovation. As YFC's first full-time employee, Billy had used every cutting-edge ploy to communicate. Marshall said, "Billy, we don't need horses or flashy ties, but we need the same willingness to take a risk."

And Billy responded, "Let's do it."

Many employees, however, did not salute the decision. Lon Allison said of that time, "In the whole organization, Rick didn't have an advocate anywhere on his flanks, except for one person." After all, the BGEA had pioneered a highly successful strategy for stadium evangelism that flourished for decades with only minor tweaks. They invented mass evangelism's dominant paradigm.

With Billy's blessing, however, Marshall booked two of the

most prominent Christian music acts—dc Talk and Michael W. Smith—and developed a youth-focused advertising campaign to broadcast on rock radio and local television stations. At 4:00 p.m., before the debut of Billy's reinvented youth night, 35,000 kids eagerly waited for the stadium gates to open. When the festivities finally began at 7:00 p.m., 65,000 youth first screamed for their favorite musicians, then listened intently to Billy.

Marshall told us, "We didn't have a clue what we were doing that first concert. I had two old men ushering, holding yellow ropes and standing in front of 5,000 kids, trying to keep them back from the stage. After that, we learned we needed to provide crash barriers and let the kids come up front to experience the intensity of a real concert.

"The superintendent of police, who'd been at Cleveland Stadium for thirty-three years of Browns games, told me that while the official attendance was 65,000, we had closer to 80,000. He had never been in a building with more kids or seen youth stay completely silent for a longer period of time than they did when Billy preached. That night we touched the next generation," Marshall said.

Inspired by the Cleveland response, the BGEA dubbed youth nights "Concert for the Next Generation" and planned similar events for upcoming meetings. Of the twenty-three cities that hosted Graham "concerts," thirteen broke stadium attendance records, including San Diego's Qualcomm Stadium with 72,000 people in 2003. The octogenarian evangelist was breaking stadium records all over America on youth nights.

Indeed, the results validated Billy's risk. He had listened to wise counsel and remained relevant. Of the younger generation's musical tastes Billy said, "I don't really understand what they're saying, and I don't like the music. But I like them. They like it."

Ruth Graham, typically, described the approach with a vivid image: "Groups like dc Talk fill the pond, and Billy gets to fish."

Rick Marshall reflected, "By the time Billy reached his eighties, I figured he was probably speaking to four or five generations in those meetings.

"I learned something about change," he continued. "While there's a lot of discussion about change and the necessity of it, I discovered through my dialogue with Billy that change is not about the head—it's about the heart. When the heart is soft, the mind is open to change at any age."

LEADERSHIP LESSONS | Innovating

Applying the Principles

In the early 1960s the book *The Dynamics of Change* made a startling assertion. Not only would change continue, it would continually accelerate, expanding geometrically. We who decades ago first read the book's assertion questioned it, saying, "Everything's already changing so fast that it can't go even faster!" But it has, with the drumbeat of change building more and more momentum with jarring acceleration.

Globalization. Breakthrough technologies. Economic volatility. Generational chasms. Religious upheavals. The need for innovation today goes far beyond thinking up new gadgets or even adapting to new cultural norms. So much is happening and will continue to happen that even the nature of needed innovations will shift on us before predictions come true. Henri Nouwen wryly observed that he felt "at a loss when people asked me about next month, let alone future years." The immediate cacophony of explanations and forecasts deliver fragments of truth, but as forces plunge us faster and faster into yet more change, we must recognize innovation will require more creativity, quickness, and depth than ever before.

In one sense, this is nothing new. Every leader has always had to innovate. Even in "stable conditions" people change or die, resources expand or dry up, someone gets an idea that catches fire and changes the chemistry. Adapting to new realities and bringing experience to bear is what leadership is all about.

So in dramatic moments of change, or in dealing with the change inherent in people and organizations, the necessity is a balanced, innovative mind-set.

Keep Progress in Perspective

Wherever we find ourselves on the spectrum, from early adapters to wary troglodytes, we do well to adjust our personal enthusiasms or cautions to the realities at hand. Doing that takes broad perspective beyond our personal experiences.

The more we know, the more we can apply. For instance, we are always impressed by the way Peter Drucker handles questions about current dilemmas. Before giving a practical application, he'll tell a story about some twelfth-century monk or the early development of General Motors or Japanese manufacturing experiences. Having depth of knowledge and multiple reference points enable us to see the big picture and thereby refine our applications. Although today's global seismic shifts are changing everything, in many ways principles are ageless, and we see their applications best in multiple contexts.

Broad knowledge also helps us put innovation itself in perspective. How much of it is progress is hotly debated. In fact, some make the case that scientific and technological advances, which fuel all this information overload, are hurtling us toward disaster.

Innovation is a "mixed blessing," but the truth is that any team, any organization must grow and innovate.

Ten years ago when CTI's chairman Jack Modesett was a new trustee, we flew to his office in Houston for a creative session. "You need a frontier mentality," he challenged us. "Expand your horizons, but also prepare for failures." He advised that success comes with "running scared" while realizing that time and events can catch you if you don't stay ahead of the curve.

Find Innovators

The particular challenge before us may require simply our own wisdom—or if large and complex, a team of those capable of fresh thinking.

To innovate takes innovators—people who have open minds, creativity, and drive. The *Economist* magazine once ran a lengthy article on innovation that repeatedly emphasized this point. It contrasted countries "wide awake and innovating aggressively" with those "dozing off." The difference? The innovative countries had plenty of talent. "Countries that sustain lots of competitive and innovative firms," said the *Economist*, "were better at churning out well-trained young people with all the skills their industries needed. An abundance of talent is essential to success."

In any field a leader pressing for innovation needs an abundance of talent: people who have the ability to adapt and seek new solutions. First, they must be identified. Then, if not already on board, they must be recruited and constantly nurtured.

Obviously, it helps in the nurturing if the leader has innovative capacities personally, but attitude can make up for lack of endowment. Creating an environment of innovation and creativity is a matter of insight, determination, and communication.

What sort of environment? The old clichés still work in this future in which we have already landed. For instance, "Employ the cutting edge of technology, not the bleeding edge." (In other words, don't be *too* early an adapter.) "Think outside of the box"—constantly stretching our imaginations and using Drucker-like breadth of information. "Dismount dead horses." This one sounds so easy—who keeps riding a dead horse? But when you've invested money and passion into something and people are producing it regularly, it's very hard to declare it dead and get out of the saddle.

But declaring it dead gives us the opportunity to saddle a new horse.

Be Quick—But Realistic

In this age of hyperacceleration and the need to produce results instantly, the pressure mounts to push people beyond their limits and to equate urgency with results.

Tom Watson Jr., even before he took over from his father as president of IBM, recognized the need for innovative talent. He concluded "the smart way to protect our future would be to have electronics engineers—large numbers of electronics engineers." Years later, however, as IBM was working flat out on its breakthrough Capitalist System 360, he "learned the hard way one of the great secrets of computer engineering: throwing people at a software project is not the way to speed it up." He quoted a droll engineer who had written him, "The bearing of a child takes nine months, no matter how many women are assigned."

What an apt metaphor for any process of innovation! Every adaptive step forward involves not just the bright idea but its refinement, buy-in by others, and its development and application. Fit the pace and the process to the project.

We see this in Billy's early use of new technology to speak to much of the globe simultaneously. Like all his meetings and international conferences, talented leaders researched in depth the multiplicity of factors, evaluating everything from time frames to technology. They refined scenarios, worked with partners around the world, then rolled out a successful initiative that reached a billion people at one time. Careful planning, careful execution.

This is not to say all this was easy or flawless. Innovation by its nature is messy. So is working with people. That's why realism about pace and progress are crucial.

Lighten Up with Mongol Chiefs

The acceleration of change makes especially relevant this ancient Chinese curse: "May you be a leader in a time of transition."

Think about that.

An old adage says, "The pioneers are the guys with the arrows in their backs." Having a thick hide helps when pioneering, especially considering that the Chinese curse so trenchantly applies today. To be an innovative leader means drawing on all this book explores, like courage and inner resourcing as well as building a loyal team. Injecting a light touch can put it all in perspective. For instance, Harry Truman insisted on honest government and realistic adaptation. On meeting resistance to some of his initiatives, he had a humorous response. At that time, the

Floogie Bird was a toy made to fly only backwards. He made it famous by seizing on this fact and dubbing his critics "Floogie Birds." He puckishly described them as resisting progress, wanting to fly only backwards.

Floogie Birds abound; it's counterproductive to demean them. In fact, we will likely learn something from listening carefully for valid points. But even as we take criticisms in stride, looking through a lens of humor can help. For instance, in one loosely structured organization, regional leaders with internal political power would come to the outfit's summit meetings voicing resistance to new plans. The organization's leader, preparing his team, described these men as Mongol chiefs mounted on war horses, riding up over the ridge to confront them. This image drew a lot of knowing smiles, helping those who had to meet the Mongols to relax a little.

The Graham team, as noted, was well known for appropriate humor. Like condiments, a light touch often makes experiences more palatable.

Unabashedly Grope

The innovative process is far from straightforward business analysis, audience research, application, and rollout. Over the decades at CTI, we've often used the word *grope* to describe it—a process like groping in a dark room for a door handle. The word has various meanings, including the sexual one, but as we've reflected on the process of finding solutions to "unsolvable problems," we kept coming back to it. Sometimes a solution was so simple that we asked, "Why couldn't we have come up with this four meetings ago? Why did we need to grope through all this analysis and dialogue?"

That's why we were glad recently to come across this statement by Albert Einstein: "How do I do my work? I grope."

The innovations most of us try to develop fall far short of breakthroughs in nuclear physics. But the commonality of digging deeply, even when we don't see the immediate application to the problem, is universal.

A man was commissioned to write a slogan for a soap commercial. He read everything he could about the product, where the rare materials originated, how it was manufactured, its unique qualities. He visited the factory; he talked with employees; he thought long and hard. The owner handed him a check for $10,000 in payment but complained that it seemed like a lot of money for very few words. The writer's apt retort? "You're not paying me for those few words. You're paying me for the thousands I've rejected."

A whole lot of groping!

For years IBM's slogan was, "Think." It became synonymous in people's minds with the company. It's often been said about Billy Graham that he has the capacity to "think big." Where others saw limitations, he saw possibilities. His business manager, George Wilson, once said he came up with "programs that just don't seem feasible," yet "you know that whatever program he is going to project, the Lord has led him to it in the hours of the night."

From his earliest days, Billy was good at identifying the core issues. Bill Martin told us that at a time when many conservative Christians didn't believe in going to movies, "Billy showed movies in churches. A lot of people thought movies were wrong, and Billy Graham said, 'It's not the fact that it's on the screen or moving, it's the content that's important.' Which, of course, makes perfect sense—but you have to remember he was a pioneer in that."

Billy kept his entrepreneurial attitude. For instance, unable to attend and chair a CTI board meeting in the mid-1980s, he sent a telegram typical of this spirit, "This is a new day," he challenged the trustees, "calling for new means of effective communication." A couple of decades later, Billy encouraged Sterling Huston to take the point on partnering with many organizations, such as CTI, to develop Internet evangelism initiatives.

Whatever our age, blending the spiritual and creative and paying the price of long and intense "imagining" can result in breakthroughs that previously seemed unrealistic.

POINTS TO PONDER

BILLY GRAHAM:

I am selling the greatest product in the world.

Why shouldn't it be promoted as well as soap?

THE BIBLE:

Do not dwell on the past. See, I am doing a new thing!

Now it springs up; do you not perceive it? I am making a way

in the desert and streams in the wasteland.

ISAIAH 43:18 – 19

CHAPTER 21

Leading with Love

Whom you would change,
you must first love.

MARTIN LUTHER KING JR.

Our first interview for this book was with John Corts, a key employee of Billy's organization for thirty-five years, ten of them as its president. After a dinner conversation that ranged over the decades, we asked, "John, what would you say is the bottom line distinctive of Billy's leadership?"

John paused a long while. Finally he said, emphatically, "Love. The difference between him and so many other leaders is that whatever the circumstances, Billy always led with love."

As we continued interviewing and researching, John's assertion has been confirmed throughout the process. Billy led with love.

Yet some would ask: What's love got to do with it? Aren't the essential requirements of leadership to be results oriented and to personify authenticity and employ a variety of techniques and emphases?

Not according to Hudson Armerding, former president of Wheaton College. In his book on leadership he says, "When the characteristics of leaders are enumerated, love is not usually included. Yet this quality is central."

Billy Graham often quoted the Bible's familiar words, "For God so loved the world that he gave his only Son," as well as Scripture's profound assertion, "God is love." Yet how did this belief permeate his leadership and actually impact people? How did he balance this off with the leader's necessity to face brutal facts and take action on them, and to deal with life's rugged realities? After all, the Bible also speaks of God's wrath and judgment, which Billy warned about. Some religious leaders are viewed as emphasizing lots of wrath and little love, lots of anger and little compassion.

Somehow, in the most difficult situations, Billy has communicated a heart full of love for others. People sense it. His internalizing love has deepened through the years as he has listened intently to the Spirit, whose first fruit the Bible says is love. In a *Christian Century* article, Billy explained what had been happening to him after a decade of international ministry.

> I am now aware that the family of God contains people of various ethnological, cultural, class, and denominational differences. . . . Within the true church there is a mysterious unity that overrides all divisive factors. In groups which in my ignorant piousness I formerly "frowned upon," I have found men so dedicated to Christ and so in love with the truth that I have felt unworthy to be in their presence. I have learned that although Christians do not always agree, they can disagree agreeably, and that what is most needed in the church today is for us to show an unbelieving world that we love one another.

In his meetings, Billy has often asserted, "God is saying to you, 'I love you. I love you. I love you.'" His love has been obvious to others and has radiated to his colleagues and those he leads, as well as to the watching world.

■ ■ ■

Two years after 9/11 with its destruction of the World Trade Center, Billy was holding meetings in Dallas. Some Americans felt all Muslims were suspect. Billy's colleague, Rick Marshall, told us, "It surprised me to learn that one of the largest U.S. populations of Muslims is in central Texas. We were at Texas Stadium in October, right between Dallas and Fort Worth. Billy did an interview with the *Dallas Morning News*, and one of the questions the writer put to him was, 'Dr. Graham, do you have a message for the Muslims of Texas?' He answered without hesitation.

"The next day the headline on the front page, bottom section was 'Billy Graham has a message for Muslims: "God loves them, and I love them."'

"It was a powerful statement. Talk about cutting right to the heart of the gospel! Everyone was talking about it, because it defused so much anger and so much criticism. It brought to the table the hallmark of Billy's ministry."

We asked Rick about Billy's handling of religious and other differences. "To me," he said, "Christians have often been too strident and legalistic. Billy has always been theologically rooted in grace. The imperative for him was evangelism—the evangelist sees the heart. If it's Muslims or Hindus or anyone else, his focus is to love them and to share with them the love of Christ."

Billy's emphasis of love spans the entire spectrum of cultural divisions. An issue that has wrenchingly divided both culture and the church is the "gay agenda." As with his stance toward other religions, he has clear theological parameters. But his message to gays is not judgmental.

When Hugh Downs interviewed him on the *20/20* television program, the subject turned to homosexuality. Hugh looked directly at Billy and asked, "If you had a homosexual child, would you love him?"

Billy didn't miss a beat. He answered gently, "Why, I would love that one even more."

The emphasis on love does not brush away the terrible realities of Muslim-Christian conflict or tensions stirred by polar-opposite beliefs about homosexual behavior or other chasms between antipathies. Billy is painfully aware of them. He realizes that people will have their differences and not every dispute can be resolved.

Once he was asked a question about "the secret of love," in light of his long marriage to Ruth. His response was telling: "Ruth and I are happily incompatible."

Happily incompatible! A paradox. He doesn't sugarcoat life's painful realities but affirms that despite them, two dramatically different people can live as man and wife. Love doesn't smooth the road, according to the old proverb, but it puts springs in the wagon. Or in the words of the Bible, love "covers a multitude of sins."

His colleagues sense the authenticity of his love, and it bonds them to him. Graeme Keith emphasized to us that Billy always wanted to communicate his message in love. "If you look at his sermons, you see the emphasis of love, and he projects this love to all around him."

We looked up a just-published Billy Graham sermon and, sure enough, there it was: "The Bible teaches that God is love, and if you don't remember anything else, remember this: God loves you! He loves you so much that he gave his Son to die and to take your judgment on the cross. The cross is your judgment; but he took it for you because he loves you."

The love Billy expresses is cognizant of tragic realities, especially human pride and self-centeredness. For him, the ultimate reality is God's human creation needing redemption through the exquisite suffering of Jesus.

■ ■ ■

Billy's decision to emphasize love started early. He did not react in kind to the bitter criticisms of those fundamentalists who were outraged by his having Catholics and "liberals" on his platform. He responded with silence and with love.

At the founding of *Christianity Today*, surveying the personal attacks and divisiveness among conservative Christians, he wrote that the magazine should set as its goal "to lead and love rather than vilify, criticize, and beat. Fundamentalism has failed miserably with the big stick approach; now it is time to take the big love approach."

In answering his critics, Billy said in a very early issue of *CT*, "The one badge of Christian discipleship is not orthodoxy but love." Editor Carl Henry, whom he had hired, said much the same, criticizing not the theology of fundamentalism but its "harsh temperament" and its "spirit of lovelessness and strife."

Billy's friend Francis Schaeffer would later expand on this in his book *The Mark of the Christian*. In it, Schaeffer asserts that the authentic work of a follower of Jesus is love. He quotes the "last commands" of Jesus to his followers as he was about to leave them: "I will be with you only a little longer. A new commandment I give you: love one another. As I have loved you, so you must love one another."

Billy has taken this command from his Leader very seriously. To many ears, the fact that Billy would call employees like Sherwood Wirt "beloved" sounds strangely foreign. But the word not only comes from the Bible, it was what Billy felt toward his fellow disciples and what he determined to make central in his life.

It is a fascinating footnote that Mordecai Ham, at whose meetings Billy was converted, later noted with remorse that he wished he could restart his ministry and "love people" as Billy did. Perhaps Mordecai got the message too late, but Billy's example shaped thousands of leaders in orthodox Christian activism, centering their emphasis.

* * *

How far should love extend? Jesus said we must love our enemies, which when put against specifics may seem naive and even absurd. Love the brutal competitor or the person who slips in the verbal knife, wrecking a business or a marriage or a life?

To genuinely love a vicious enemy would take supernatural power. The Bible's original Greek uses *agape* to describe exactly that—supernatural love that transcends human capacities. Martin Luther King Jr., in leading the Civil Rights Movement, advocated "persuasion, not coercion" and the transforming power of love. He said, "Love must be our regulating ideal. Once again we must hear the words of Jesus echoing across the centuries: 'Love your enemies, bless them that curse you, and pray for them that despitefully use you.'"

King explained what the Bible's word means when facing rough realities: "*Agape* is disinterested love. . . . *Agape* does not begin by discriminating between worthy and unworthy people, or any qualities people possess. It begins by loving others *for their sakes* . . . therefore *agape* makes no distinction between friend and enemy; it is directed toward both."

So Billy showed love, even to his most savage critics and to those who had hurt him the most. He was moved by compassion for those who suffer or have no hope, his love extending to Christian, Muslim, Hindu, agnostic, or atheist. That's what *agape* required of him.

Billy believed education and legislation were important but inadequate. In light of the world's atrocities, he wrote in *The Secret of Happiness*, "Government and civil laws are like the cages in a zoo—they can restrain evil, but they cannot change the basic nature of the human heart. Art and education may refine the taste, but they cannot purify the heart. The Holocaust was carried out by educated people, some brilliantly so."

When he and Ruth visited the Nazi death camp of Auschwitz, they were deeply moved. "We saw the barbed wire, the instruments of torture, the airless punishment cells, the gas chambers and crematorium. Every square foot of that terrible place was a stark and vivid witness to man's inhumanity to man. We laid a memorial wreath and then knelt to pray at a wall in the midst of the camp where 20,000 people had been shot. When I got up and turned around to say a few remarks to those who had gathered with us, my eyes blurred with tears and I almost could not speak. How could such a terrible thing happen—planned and carried out by people who were often highly educated?"

Billy's commitment to love and mercy clashed prodigiously with obvious evil. "I would rather have a world filled with ignorant savages," he said, "than with civilized sophisticates without morality."

When we talked to John Akers about Billy's visits to Auschwitz and Treblinka, and his visiting refugees in India and elsewhere, we asked how that fit with his intense focus on his mission. "Simply this—he's a compassionate person," John said.

"In regard to the Holocaust, he was very aware of the history of Christians persecuting the Jews. He wanted to identify with their suffering, their moral outrage, and to agree that this must not be allowed to happen again. That's part of his moral leadership."

Gerald S. Strober, in his book *Graham: A Day in Billy's Life*, tells this story:

> Rivka Alexandrovich, a Soviet Jewish woman from the city of Riga, came to the United States to attempt to win public support for her daughter, Ruth, then a prisoner of conscience in Russia. I called Billy one afternoon and reached him in the barbershop of Washington's Madison Hotel. After hearing of Mrs. Alexandrovich's problem, Billy invited me to bring her to Chicago in two days' time so he could meet and talk with her. The Chicago session was packed with emotion. There was definite positive chemistry alive in the room, and Billy expressed great sympathy for young Ruth Alexandrovich. At one point in the conversation, he walked to the telephone, took out an address book, and dialed a long-distance number.
>
> "Is Henry there?" he asked. "Well, tell him to call me the minute he comes in."
>
> No one in the room had to ask who "Henry" was, and there was little doubt in our minds that the call had been placed to Key Biscayne, Florida, where Henry was staying with his boss, the President of the United States.
>
> Five minutes later the telephone rang, and it was Henry [Kissinger]. Graham gave him a briefing on Mrs. Alexandrovich (he had carefully jotted down the pertinent facts as she talked), and he then asked the caller to try to do something for the distraught émigré. Later that night, Graham issued a statement from his Minneapolis headquarters calling attention to the plight of the Soviet Jews. Two months after the Chicago meeting, Ruth Alexandrovich landed at Lod Airport in Tel Aviv.

■ ■ ■

Yet for all Billy's kindness and compassion, he felt the normal human emotions. At times, he was confronted with situations requiring more than compassion. C. S. Lewis observed, "Love is something more stern and splendid than mere kindness."

Billy has been portrayed as a nice do-gooder with little awareness or starch in the spine. But *agape* love can be tough love. For instance, John Akers told us that although Billy could usually disarm hostile situations, sometimes he was forced to be stern. "He was in Communist East Germany to speak to a Lutheran synod," John told us. "The reception was so cold, the conveners so arrogant, that when he got up he said, 'When I came in, I had seldom met such a hostile group, and it shouldn't be that way. We are brothers in Christ, and I love you. But this atmosphere does not reflect that.'"

John remembers that Billy's forthright statements "just wiped them out." They got the message—sometimes "tough love" requires redemptive correction.

We asked Cliff Barrows what he thought about John Corts's statement that the ultimate distinctive of Billy's leadership was his leading in love. "I think it's so true," he responded. Cliff went on to describe how Graham "was always inquiring about my children. He showed genuine interest in them, in my first wife, Billie, and in myself. He displayed that love in many different ways."

After his wife died of cancer, Cliff met Ann, whose husband had also died of cancer. "I told Bill I wanted him to meet her," Cliff told us. "We were engaged but not married yet. So I drove her up to his house, and he was already out the door, coming toward the car. He saw Ann, and he opened up his arms and said, 'Ann, welcome to our home, welcome to our hearts, welcome to the BGEA.' He just immediately accepted her with total ease and a gracious spirit. And his wife, Ruth, did the same. That meant so much to us."

Frank Thielman told us stories of Billy's generosity, including handing over their house keys. Frank's father was the Grahams' pastor. "When my dad was sick and in need of rest," Frank explained, "the Grahams sensed his need. They were going away for three weeks, and they told my mom and dad to just come up there and stay at their house. So our family did that for three weeks. That's amazing—it's a real example to me."

Frank also told of their helping the destitute. "Montreat is in the rural southern Appalachian mountains. They would unhesitatingly give and help the poor. They are very generous people."

Billy described his own awakening to the needs of the Appalachian poor. "One Christmas Eve a friend came to my house and said, 'Would you like to go out with me distributing Christmas packages up in the mountains?' I was glad to go. And I was in for one of the greatest surprises of my life! I thought everybody in our community had all the necessities of life. But I was taken back into some little mountain valleys where people did not have enough to wear, enough to eat, and could not even afford soap to wash their bodies. Appalled and humbled, I asked God to forgive me for neglecting the people in my own community."

Disgraced televangelist Jim Bakker also testifies to the love of Billy Graham and his family. Despite the fact that Bakker's public scandal, which involved sex, hush money, and defrauded investors in a real estate scheme, had brought suspicion and scorn on all evangelists, the Grahams maintained a friendship with Bakker throughout his imprisonment and afterward.

Bakker recalls with appreciation the time that Ruth Graham "took all of Billy's Bibles in his library that he wasn't using and gave them to me to give to other inmates." When he got out of prison, the Grahams paid for a house for him to live in and provided him a car. And something more—confidence.

"The first Sunday out," Bakker said, "Ruth Graham called the halfway house I was living in at the Salvation Army and asked permission for me to go to the Montreat Presbyterian Church with her that Sunday morning. When I got there, the pastor welcomed me and sat me with the Graham family. There were like two whole rows of them—I think every Graham aunt and uncle and cousin was there. The organ began playing and the place was full, except for a seat next to me. Then the doors opened and in walked Ruth Graham. She walked down that aisle and sat next to inmate 07407–059. I had only been out of prison forty-eight hours, but she told the world that morning that Jim Bakker was her friend.

"Afterward, she had me up to their cabin for dinner. When she asked me for some addresses, I pulled this envelope out of my pocket to look for them—in prison you're not allowed to have a wallet, so you just carry an envelope. She asked, 'Don't you have a wallet?' And I said, 'Well, yeah, this is my wallet.' After five years of brainwashing in prison you think an envelope *is* a wallet. She walked into the other room and came back and said, 'Here's one of Billy's wallets. He doesn't need it. You can have it.'"

■ ■ ■

Sometimes love is shown by a thoughtful word, by willingness to help an employee in trouble or by refusal to retaliate when attacked; other times love is shown by simply showing up.

At the time Billy was in his mid-eighties and struggling physically, Leighton and Jean Ford's daughter, Debbie—Billy's niece— had successfully endured cancer treatments but then learned the cancer had recurred. Debbie was apprehensive as she entered the Mayo Clinic in Jacksonville, Florida, for a bone scan.

"I was very fearful of cancer being found somewhere else in my body," Debbie told us. As she walked back to her room, she glanced down the empty hallway. There at the end, sitting in a wheelchair and facing her direction, was a frail, older man. She realized it was Billy, who happened to be at Mayo for some tests.

"Knowing I was there, he had asked the Mayo staff to locate where I was in the clinic. I ran and threw my arms around him and sobbed with all my heart. He held me tenderly, saying over and over, 'I love you.'

"When I looked up to tell him how frightened I was about my recurrence, I saw that he was also crying. In his own weakened state, he met me at my weakness."

Debbie was deeply touched by this evidence of Billy's love for her. "Certainly he's a great evangelist and confidant of leaders," said Debbie. "He's also a tender and frail older man.

Despite the fact that he hurts like I do and has concerns for his body like I do, he's thoughtful and caring and willing to take time for me, just as I am."

LEADERSHIP LESSONS | **Love**

Applying the Principles

So what more can be said about applying this principle? Not much. When we consider Billy's love toward Debbie, Cliff, Jim, and the poor of Appalachia—and his colleagues' frequent assertions that it was Billy's spirit of love that bonded them to him and radiated out to others—we understand how essential love was to his leadership.

Yet what about us? Can we—should we—apply this to our own leadership? The implications may feel overwhelming. Leaders must get things done. Communities and organizations are massively needy, and unless we're chaplains, we can't spend all our time lifting the broken and encouraging the stricken. Besides, some employees need to be fired, competition must be faced head-on, deadlines met. Stretching ourselves beyond our limits benefits no one.

Those realities will always be with us, and a wealth of leadership and biographical resources can help us meet our obligations. Yet this dynamic of love in leadership intrigues. Wherever we might be on the spiritual spectrum, we may well profit by considering this compelling phenomenon shown in the Graham team.

With all the pressures and urgencies thrust upon him, Billy knew that leading with love was beyond his human capacities. But that was the point. He could in weakness become a conduit for a greater force.

How did he become a conduit? By regularly opening himself to that greater force of love. "Every day the Psalms give me strength for the day and a realization of the power of God's love," Billy has said. "His love has seen me through sickness, discouragement, and frustration. His love has sustained me during times of disappointment and bewilderment."

"God is love," says the Bible. "And I have come that you might have joy." The fruit of the Spirit, say the Scriptures, are "love, joy, peace . . ." The Graham team often expressed great wonder that they were included in those promises. Instead of dutiful drudgery, they saw giving everything to the cause as a source of high privilege.

George Beverly Shea, Billy's featured soloist for more than fifty-five years, perhaps captured this best of all with his signature song, "The Wonder of It All."

> There's the wonder of sunset at evening;
>> The wonder as sunrise I see.
> But the wonder of wonders that thrills my soul
>> Is the wonder that God loves me.

That spirit among the Graham team lifted them to want to share that love as the driving purpose to which all else was secondary.

So where does that leave the rest of us who have not experienced the spiritual chemistry of the Graham team? Most of us, looking deep within, recognize that love for others does not come nearly as naturally as love for ourselves. If we want to pursue this phenomenon, this receiving wonder, joy, and love and integral forces of our leadership, we must look beyond the pragmatic. The transcendent sources— writings of the mystics and saints, Shakespeare and *Pilgrim's Progress* and the Bible—the vast wealth of spiritual challenge and empowerment can be studied through a leadership lens.

It is not how much we do, but how much love we put into the doing.

MOTHER TERESA

Among the greatest expressions of all literature is the soaring pinnacle of the apostle Paul's writing, the love chapter of 1 Corinthians 13. It calls for the *agape* love Martin Luther King Jr. spoke about. To apply it to our own challenges, we might apply a leadership lens on a few portions of it this way:

> If I lead others like an angel from God,
>> but have not love,
> I am a clanging cymbal.

Love is patient; love is kind.

Love doesn't envy.

Love does not boast, is not proud.

Love is not self-seeking.

Love is not easily angered; it keeps no record of wrongs.

So there remain many essential elements of leadership,
among them, courage, humility,
faith, hope, and love.

But the greatest of these is love.

POINTS TO PONDER

BILLY GRAHAM:

In an age that is given over to cynicism, coldness, and doubt
and in which the fire and warmth of God is conspicuous for
its absence in the world, my heart cry is, Let the fire fall. . . .

O, God, let the fire of your love fall on us.

THE BIBLE:

There is no fear in love. But perfect love drives out fear.

1 JOHN 4:18

ACKNOWLEDGMENTS

This book was written as part of the fiftieth anniversary celebration of Christianity Today International to help recognize and pass on the legacy of its founder, Billy Graham. Billy originally perceived a need, processed a wide range of thinking about it, created a vision paper, communicated it to influential people who could make it happen, and raised the necessary capital. He recruited the highest caliber leaders to CTI's board, slogging with them through the inevitable difficulties of launching a magazine. He then continued to give board leadership to the organization for more than five decades, and it grew from one magazine to a multimagazine and Internet communications ministry. All proceeds from this book go to the nonprofit ministry of CTI (and for a sample copy and risk-free trial subscription to the magazine Billy launched, *Christianity Today*, go to *www.christianitytoday.com/go/graham*).

Clearly, we owe much to Billy for his foresight and commitment to CTI, as well as his blessing on the writing of this book.

Many others also made vital contributions. We are grateful to the scores of those we interviewed, many of them Billy's close associates. We were able to quote directly only a fraction of what they so generously gave us. Others provided valuable background information, and even though their names do not appear in the text itself, their contributions shaped in a significant way the content of this book.

Collin Hansen offered outstanding service as a researcher and interviewer. A recent graduate of Northwestern University, Collin quickly became fluent in the Graham literature and the many records of his ministry.

In addition, Laurie Powell made major contributions as project coordinator and chief transcriber. We also received valuable help from CTI's Harold Smith and Harry Genet and the staff at the Billy Graham Center archives. The team at Zondervan, especially

Paul Engle and Bob Hudson, made significant suggestions. We also want to mention the generosity of our families, who for several months understood that long days and weekends were being claimed by "the Billy book." So, many thanks, Jeanette, Rick, Josh, and Lindsey, and Susan, Stacey, Kelsey, and Bayly. We're back.

Harold Myra and Marshall Shelley
Wheaton, Illinois, March 2005

FOR FURTHER READING

Allison, Lon, and Mark Anderson. *Going Public with the Gospel: Reviving Evangelistic Proclamation*. InterVarsity Press, 2004.

Ambrose, Stephen E. *Eisenhower: Soldier and President*. Touchstone/Simon and Schuster, Inc., 1990.

———. *The Victors—Eisenhower and His Boys: The Men of World War II*. Touchstone/Simon and Schuster, 1998.

Armerding, Hudson T. *The Heart of Godly Leadership*. Crossway Books/Good News Publishers, 1992.

Bennis, Warren G., and Burt Nanus. *Leaders: Strategies for Taking Charge*. HarperCollins Publishers, 2003.

———. *On Becoming a Leader*. Perseus Publishing, 2003.

Brother Lawrence and Frank Laubach. *Practicing His Presence*. The SeedSowers, 1973.

Brown, Mary Ann. *Hand of Providence: The Strong and Quiet Faith of Ronald Reagan*. WND Books/Thomas Nelson Publishers, 2004.

Bruns, Roger. *Billy Graham: A Biography*. Greenwood Press, 2004.

Collection of HBR articles. *Harvard Business Review on Leadership*. Harvard Business School Press, 1998.

Collins, James C. *Good to Great: Why Some Companies Make the Leap . . . and Others Don't*. HarperCollins Publishers, 2001.

Collins, James C., and Jerry I. Porras. *Built to Last: Successful Habits of Visionary Companies*. HarperCollins Publishers, 1994.

Crocker, H. W. *Robert E. Lee on Leadership*. Prima Publishing, 2000.

DePree, Max. *Leadership Jazz*. Dell Publishing/Bantam Doubleday Dell Publishing Group, 1993.

Drucker, Peter E. *The Effective Executive*. HarperCollins Publishers, 1967.

Eiseley, Loren. *The Star Thrower*. Harvest/HBJ, 1978.

Ford, Leighton. *Transforming Leadership: Jesus' Way of Creating Vision, Shaping Values and Empowering Change*. InterVarsity Press, 1991.

Gardner, Howard. *Leading Minds*. HarperCollins Publishers UK, 1996.

Gergen, David. *Eyewitness to Power—The Essence of Leadership: Nixon to Clinton*. Simon and Schuster, 2002.

Graham, Billy. *A Biblical Standard for Evangelists*. WorldWide Publishing, 1984.

———. *Footprints of Conscience*. WorldWide Publishing, 1991.

———. *Hope for the Troubled Heart*. Word Publishing, 1991.

———. *Just As I Am*. HarperSanFrancisco/Zondervan, 1977.

———. *Peace with God*. Word Books and Worldwide Publications, 1984.

———. *The Secret of Happiness*. Word Publishing, 1985.

Graves, Stephen R., and Thomas G. Addington. *Life @ Work on Leadership: Enduring Insights for Men and Women of Faith*. Jossey-Bass/a Wiley Imprint, 2002.

Griffin, William, and Ruth Graham Dienert, compilers. *The Faithful Christian: An Anthology of Billy Graham*. McCracken Press, 1994.

Guiness, Os. *The Call*. W Publishing Group/Thomas Nelson, Inc., 2003.

———. *Character Counts: Leadership Qualities in Washington, Wilberforce, Lincoln and Solzhenitsyn*. Baker Books, 2000.

Hybels, Bill. *Courageous Leadership*. Zondervan, 2002.

Jones, Howard O., with Edward Gilbreath. *Gospel Trailblazer: An Autobiography*. Moody Publishers, 2003.

Katzenbach, Jon R., and Douglas K. Smith. *The Wisdom of Teams*. Harvard Business School/HarperCollins Publishers, 1994.

Lewis, C. S. *The Silver Chair—Book 4 in the Chronicles of Narnia*. Scholastic, Inc./Macmillan Publishing, 1987.

Loehr, James E. *Stress for Success*. Three Rivers Press/Random House, 1997.

———. *Toughness Training for Life*. Plume/Penguin Putnam, Inc., 1994.

Lowney, Chris. *Heroic Leadership: Best Practices from a 450-year-old Company That Changed the World*. Loyola Press, 2003.

MacDonald, Gordon. *The Life God Blesses*. Thomas Nelson Publishers, 1994.

————. *Mid-Course Correction: Re-Ordering Your Private World for the Next Part of Your Journey.* Thomas Nelson, Inc., 2000.

Maney, Kevin. *The Maverick and His Machine: Thomas Watson, Sr., and the Making of IBM.* John Wiley and Sons, Inc., 2003.

Martin, William. *A Prophet with Honor.* William Morrow and Company, 1991.

Maxwell, John C. *The 17 Indisputable Laws of Teamwork.* Thomas Nelson, 2001.

————. *The 21 Indispensable Qualities of a Leader.* Thomas Nelson, 1999.

————. *Failing Forward: Turning Mistakes into Stepping Stones for Success.* Thomas Nelson, 2000.

McCullough, David. *Mornings on Horseback.* Touchstone/Simon and Schuster, 1981.

McLellan, Vernon K., compiler. *Billy Graham: A Tribute from Friends.* Warner Faith, 2002.

Nadler, David A., and Janet L. Spencer. *Executive Teams.* Jossey-Bass Publishers, 1998.

Noonan, Peggy. *When Character Was King: A Story of Ronald Reagan.* Pergum Books/Penguin Putnam, Inc., 2002.

Pamplin, Robert B., Jr., with Gary K. Eisler. *American Heroes.* MasterMedia Limited, 1995.

Paulson, Terry L. *They Shoot Managers; Don't They? Managing Yourself and Leading Others in a Changing World.* Paulson, Ten Speed Press, 1991.

Phillips, Donald T. *Lincoln on Leadership: Executive Strategies for Tough Times.* Warner Books/a Time Warner Company, 1993.

Pollard, C. William. *The Soul of the Firm.* Zondervan/HarperCollins, 1996.

Pollock, John. *The Billy Graham Story.* Zondervan, 2003.

Reynolds, Joe. *Out Front Leadership: Discovering, Developing, and Delivering Your Potential.* Mott and Carlisle/Bard Productions, 1994.

Safire, William, and Leonard Safir. compilers and editors. *Leadership: A Treasury of Great Quotations for Those Who Aspire to Lead.* Galahad Books/BBS Publishing Corporation, 2000.

Senge, Peter. *The Dance of Change: The Challenges to Sustaining Momentum in Learning Organizations.* A Currency Book/Doubleday/Random House, Inc., 1999.

Sheehy, Gail. *Pathfinders.* Bantam Books/William Morrow and Company, 1982.

Smith, Fred, Sr. *Leading with Integrity: Competence with Christian Character.* The Pastor's Soul Series, Bethany House Publishers, 1999.

———. *Learning to Lead: Bringing Out the Best in People.* The Leadership Library, Leadership/Word Books, 1986.

———. *You and Your Network.* Word Books, 1984.

Strober, Gerald S. *Graham: A Day in Billy's Life.* Spire Books/Fleming H. Revell/Doubleday and Company, 1977.

Strock, James M. *Reagan on Leadership: Executive Lessons from the Great Communicator.* Forum/Prima Publishing, 1998.

———. *Theodore Roosevelt on Leadership.* Forum/Prima Publishing, 2001.

Tada, Joni Eareckson. *The God I Love.* Zondervan, 2003.

Thielicke, Helmut. *Our Heavenly Father: Sermons on the Lord's Prayer.* Baker Book House, 1974.

Watson, Thomas J., Jr., and Peter Petre. *Father, Son and Co.: My Life at IBM and Beyond.* Bantam Books, 1991.

Wilson, Grady. *Count It All Joy.* Grason/Broadman Press, 1984.

Wirt, Sherwood Eliot. *Billy: A Personal Look at Billy Graham, the World's Best-Loved Evangelist.* Crossway Books/Good News Publishers, 1997.

WHO'S WHO

The following people were interviewed by the authors and graciously provided information and insight into the leadership of Billy Graham.

David Aikman, former reporter, *Time* magazine; author, *Great Souls: Six Who Changed a Century*

John N. Akers, special assistant to Billy Graham; CTI board member

Lon Allison, director, Billy Graham Center, Wheaton College

Leith Anderson, pastor, Wooddale Church, Eden Prairie, Minnesota; former president, National Association of Evangelicals

Cliff Barrows, program director, Billy Graham Evangelistic Association (BGEA)

Gerald Beavan, early BGEA board member; charter board member, Christianity Today International (CTI)

George Bennett, former treasurer, Harvard University; board member and treasurer BGEA

George K. Brushaber, president, Bethel University

Russ Busby, photographer, BGEA

Howard Butt, founder, Laity Lodge and the H. E. Butt Foundation; early BGEA board member; charter board member, CTI

Joel Carpenter, provost, Calvin College; former director, Institute for the Study of American Evangelicals

Robert E. Cooley, president emeritus, Gordon-Conwell Theological Seminary

John Corts, former president, BGEA

Mark Driscoll, pastor, Mars Hill Church, Seattle, Washington; author, *Radical Reformission*

Allan C. Emery Jr., board member, BGEA; CTI emeritus board member

Ted Engstrom, president emeritus, World Vision

Robert Evans, founder, Greater Europe Mission, CTI emeritus board member

Jean Ford, sister of Billy Graham

Leighton Ford, founder, Leighton Ford Ministries

Timothy George, dean, Beeson Divinity School at Samford University

Melvin Graham, businessman, brother of Billy Graham

Debbie Ford Gurley, niece of Billy Graham

Mark Hatfield, U.S. Senator (Oregon), retired

John A. Huffman Jr., pastor, St. Andrews Presbyterian Church, Newport Beach, California; board member and former chair, World Vision; board member, CTI

Sterling Huston, director of North American ministries, BGEA

Howard Jones, associate evangelist, BGEA

Graeme Keith, businessman; treasurer, BGEA

Jay Kesler, former president, Youth for Christ; president emeritus, Taylor University; board member, CTI

Gordon MacDonald, former pastor, Grace Chapel, Lexington, Massachusetts; editor at large, *Leadership;* chair of World Relief

Rick Marshall, former crusade director, BGEA

George Marsden, professor of history, Notre Dame University

William Martin, sociology professor, Rice University; author, *A Prophet With Honor,* the biography of Billy Graham

David McKenna, former president of Asbury Theological Seminary, Seattle Pacific University, and Spring Arbor College; director, National Association of Evangelicals

Bill Mead, businessman; early BGEA board member; former board member, CTI

Jack Modesett Jr., business executive; board chair, CTI

Richard Ostling, writer, *Time* magazine and Associated Press

James I. Packer, professor of theology, Regent College, Vancouver, B.C.; executive editor, *Christianity Today*

William C. Pollard, former CEO, ServiceMaster; board member, BGEA

Paul Robbins, president and publisher, CTI

Garth Rosell, professor, Gordon-Conwell Theological Seminary

A. Larry Ross, media/public relations consultant

Jeffrey Scheler, writer, *U.S. News & World Report*

David Schmidt, media consultant

Robert Shuster, director, Billy Graham Center Archives, Wheaton College

Fred Smith Sr., businessman; emeritus board member, CTI

Joni Eareckson Tada, author; speaker; founder of Joni And Friends Ministries

Frank Thielman, professor, Beeson Divinity School at Samford University; childhood friend of the Grahams

Grant Wacker, professor, Duke University

Rick Warren, pastor, Saddleback Church, Lake Forest, California; author, *The Purpose-Driven Life*

Warren Wiersbe, former pastor; former radio teacher, Back to the Bible

John Wilson, editor, *Books & Culture* magazine

Ron Wilson, former executive director, Evangelical Press Association

Ravi Zacharias, author; speaker; founder of Ravi Zacharias International Ministries

INDEX

vitality, economic, 111
voltage, 287–302
vulnerability, 48, 177

Warren, Rick, 242–44
Watergate, 26, 178–82
Watson, Tom Jr., 310–11
Waugh, Bill, 87
weakness, 48, 160, 273–86
WECEF (World Evangelism
    and Christian Education
    Fund), 115
Wesley, John, 301
Wheaton College, 13, 71, 138
Wiersbe, Warren, 290
Wilder, Ann, 297–99
Williams, John, 147
Wills, Garry, 145, 285–86
Wilson, George, 112, 243, 313
Wilson, Grady, 25, 41, 42, 43–
    44, 48, 49, 68, 152, 166–
    69, 243, 289–90

Wilson, Ron, 117
Wilson, T. W., 25, 41, 243,
    277, 289
Wirt, Sherwood, 12, 31, 124–
    27, 139
wisdom, 187
words, impact of, 267–68
World Evangelism and Chris-
    tian Education Fund
    (WECEF), 115
World Relief, 13, 249
World Vision, 13, 120, 207
Wylie, I. A. R., 159

Young, Andrew, 105–6, 288
youth, 74, 306–8
Youth for Christ, 13, 40–41,
    53–54, 119, 138, 239–40,
    306

Zacharias, Ravi, 67, 244–46
Zaleski, Carol, 99